McKEACHIE'S

TEACHING TIPS

MᴄKEACHIE'S

TEACHING TIPS

Strategies, Research, and Theory for College and University Teachers

■ ■ ■ ■ ■ ■ ■ ■ ■ ■ ■ ■ ■ ■ ■

ELEVENTH EDITION

Wilbert J. McKeachie
University of Michigan

with chapters by

Barbara Hofer, Middlebury College

Nancy Van Note Chism, Indiana University—Purdue University, Indianapolis

Erping Zhu and Matthew Kaplan, University of Michigan

Brian Coppola, University of Michigan

Andrew Northedge, The Open University

Claire Ellen Weinstein, University of Texas at Austin

Jane Halonen, James Madison University

Marilla Svinicki, University of Texas at Austin

HOUGHTON MIFFLIN COMPANY   Boston   New York

In memory of Bob Menges
good scholar
good human being
good friend

Editor-in-Chief: Patricia Coryell
Senior Sponsoring Editor: Sue Pulvermacher-Alt
Senior Development Editor: Lisa Mafrici
Editorial Assistant: Sara Hauschildt
Senior Project Editor: Aileen Mason
Editorial Assistant: Lindsay Frost
Associate Production/Design Coordinator: Christine Gervais
Senior Manufacturing Manager: Florence Cadran
Marketing Manager: Nicola Poser

Printed in the U.S.A.

Library of Congress Control Number: 2001131527

ISBN: 0-618-11649-4

2 3 4 5 6 7 8 9-QF-06 05 04 03 02

CONTENTS

PART 2

Basic Skills for Facilitating Student Learning   29

4 Facilitating Discussion: Posing Problems, Listening, Questioning   30

7 What to Do About Cheating   97

8 The ABC's of Assigning Grades   103

PART 3

Understanding Students   117

9 Motivation in the College Classroom   118

By Barbara Hofer, MIDDLEBURY COLLEGE

10 Valuing Student Differences   128

By Nancy Van Note Chism, INDIANA UNIVERSITY—PURDUE
UNIVERSITY, INDIANAPOLIS

11 Problem Students (There's Almost Always at Least One!)   148

12 Counseling, Advising, and Educating 161

PART 4

Adding to Your Repertoire of Skills and Strategies for Facilitating Active Learning 169

13 Teaching Students to Learn Through Writing: Journals, Papers, and Reports 170

17 Technology and Teaching

By Erping Zhu and Matthew Kaplan, UNIVERSITY OF MICHIGAN

PART 5

Skills for Use in Other Teaching Situations   225

18 Teaching Large Classes (You Can Still Get Active Learning!)   226

19 Laboratory Instruction: Ensuring an Active Learning Experience   235

By Brian Coppola, UNIVERSITY OF MICHIGAN

How Can You Get and Use Feedback to Continue to Improve Your Teaching?

In Conclusion

References

Index

PREFACE

TEACHING TIPS was originally written to answer the questions posed by new college teachers, to place them at ease in their jobs, and to get them started effectively in the classroom. It has proven useful as well to experienced instructors, to teachers in community colleges, to distance educators, adult educators, adjunct faculty, and faculty members in many other countries.

The organization of the book begins with the issues involved in getting started, then moves on to the basic skills needed by all teachers—getting student participation, lecturing, assessing learning, and assigning grades (Parts 1 and 2). Equally important are awareness of, respect for, and ability to adapt to differences among students (Part 3). Parts 4 and 5 deal with additional skills and strategies important for other aspects of teaching. In Part 6 we discuss goals of education going beyond simple memorization of facts, concepts, and theories, and in Part 7 we point toward your continued development as a teacher.

Effective teaching demands more than the acquisition of skills. To adapt to the educational needs of a particular class at a particular time, the teacher needs to understand the underlying theory of learning and teaching so that each teacher can develop his or her own methods. Thus the "teaching tips" are supported by discussion of relevant research and theory. Skill in teaching is not something to be learned and simply repeated; what makes it exciting is that there is always room to grow. As you reflect on your classes, you will get new insights and will continue to develop both your theory of teaching and learning and your repertoire of skills and strategies.

As with any revision, the Eleventh Edition reflects new developments in almost every chapter. Probably the fastest moving field is instructional technology. The chapter titled "Technology and Teaching," written by my colleagues Erping Zhu and Matthew Kaplan, will be helpful both to novices and more experienced teachers who want to use technology where and when it can help students learn. Because more faculty members are being asked to develop courses for distance education, a new chapter by Andrew Northedge has been added to this edition ("Teaching by Distance Education"). What I like about his chapter is that it is not just a description of new technology but rather based on principles of distance learning that are useful regardless of the media used. Chapters on diversity, motivation, learning, and thinking are also updated by specialists.

Teaching Tips has stressed learner-centered teaching since the very first edition, in which I emphasized the importance of active learning. In the second edition I introduced a longer section on learner-centered teaching and the role of the teacher as a facilitator of learning. It is gratifying that in the last few years authors have begun to write about the shift from teacher-centered to learner-centered education and the shift of the teacher's role from that of dispenser of information to facilitator of learning. Whether *Teaching Tips* has contributed to that shift, I do not know, but I hope that "learning-centered" does not become one of the buzz words that come and go—like the fifties' "master teachers" (who were to be televised and teach large numbers of students), or the sixties' "programmed learning" (which would teach more efficiently), or the seventies' "technological revolution." All were believed to be panaceas (and all contained worthwhile elements), but after a period of ascendancy, all faded before the next great enthusiasm. What counts in education is not so much what the teacher does as what goes on in the students' minds, and this will be true even if the term "learner-centered" falls into disuse. This does not mean, however, that "learner-centered" implies a particular method of teaching.

"Learner-centered" may appear to diminish the importance of the teacher. Not so! Your unique qualities as a person, your integrity, your commitment to your students' development—these are even more important than they were when the teacher's role was simply that of a talking textbook. Your role is now expanded to include that of mediator between your content specialization and your students' understanding of it, on multiple, and increasingly high, levels. *There is no one best way of teaching.* If you are to continue to develop as a teacher, you will need well-practiced skills, but you also need fresh thinking about why some things worked or didn't work in your last class. I do not offer a set of rules to follow. Rather I suggest strategies to consider and modify as needed by the ever-changing dynamics of your classes.

What is best for you may be quite different from what is best for me. By introducing research and theory relevant to the strategies suggested, I hope to encourage your reflection and continuing development as a thinking, observing, and caring teacher.

I am pleased that so many copies of previous editions of this guide have been used outside the United States. My increased interaction with colleagues in other countries who are concerned about improving teaching makes me aware of the cultural bias of much of my writing. I trust that *Teaching Tips* will nevertheless have value for everyone concerned with teaching and student learning.

The first edition of this book was prepared in collaboration with Gregory Kimble. His wit and wisdom are still evident at many points in the Eleventh Edition. My thanks go to Sara Hauschildt, my editor at Houghton Mifflin, who made many helpful suggestions, and to all the reviewers, who will see evidence of the impact of their comments:

Brian Fife, *Indiana University—Purdue University*
Kevin Kinser, *Louisiana State University*
Sharon Packer, *New School University*
Judy Reinhartz, *University of Texas, Arlington*
Lisa Weber, *University of Florence, Italy*
Barbara L. Whinery, *University of Northern Colorado*
Donald H. Wulff, *University of Washington*

WILBERT J. MCKEACHIE

TEACHING TIPS was originally written for my own teaching assistants. I am pleased that more experienced teachers have also found it to be helpful, but I still think of my primary audience as being beginning teachers. I began teaching as a teaching assistant (TA) and have worked with teaching assistants ever since. I try to involve my TAs in course planning both before and during the term. We grade tests in a group the evening after a test is given, bringing in sandwiches and brownies to maintain our energy and good spirits during sessions that may last until midnight. In short, I try to develop the spirit of a collaborative team.

However, I recognize that TAs are in the difficult position of being in the middle between the students and me. As TAs you want to be liked and respected by your students as well as by your professor; yet there are times when you don't agree with the professor's point of view or even with some of the course policies. You will be tempted to blame the professor or the system when students complain, but overusing this strategy only leads to students perceiving you as weak and powerless. On the other hand, this doesn't mean that you have to defend everything your professor says. Students, particularly first-year students, need to learn that absolute truth is hard to come by and that it is possible to have well-reasoned differences.

Yet one must be aware of student anxiety when TA and lecturer seem always to be at odds with one another. Support your lecturer when you can, disagree when you must, but recognize that sometimes your students' learning will be best served by your silence. Often your role is that of a coach helping students develop skills in learning and thinking, using the knowledge provided by the lecturer and textbook.

Many of you will find it hard to believe that the students will accept your authority and expertise, and you will be ambivalent about whether to dazzle them with your brilliance or to play the role of being just one of the group. Relax! The power of role expectations always amazes me. If you are the teacher, students will accept your authority and expertise. You don't need to be dictatorial, but you do need to be clear about your expectations of the students. Think of yourself as a more experienced scholar who can be a valuable coach. You may not know everything, but you have enough subject-matter expertise to be helpful. I hope this book will add to your helpfulness.

W. J. M.

McKEACHIE'S
TEACHING TIPS

■ ■

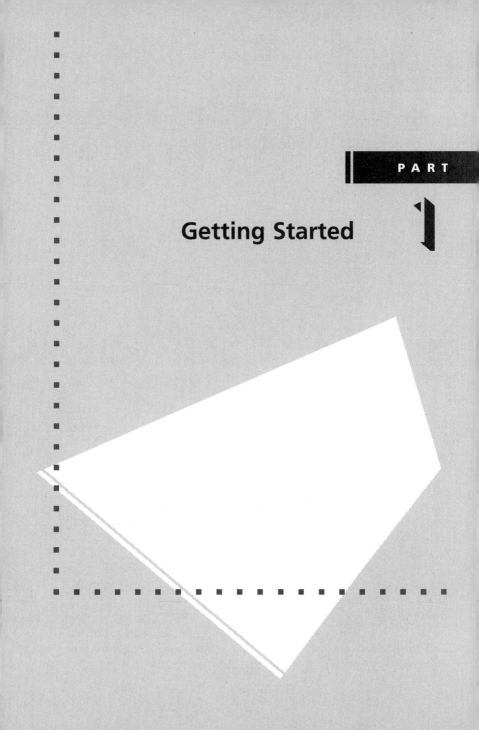

PART

1

Getting Started

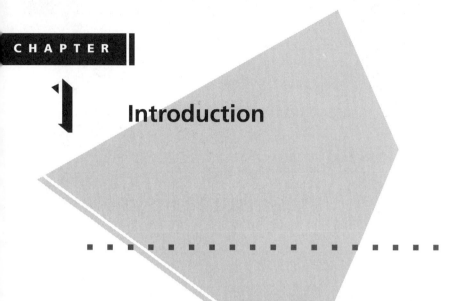

1 Introduction

The first few months and years of teaching are all-important. Experiences during this period can blight a promising teaching career or start one on a path of continued growth and development.

Most of us go into our first classes as teachers with a good deal of fear and trembling. We don't want to appear to be fools; so we have prepared well, but we dread the embarrassment of not being able to answer students' questions. We want to be liked and respected by our students; yet we know that we have to achieve liking and respect in a new role which carries expectations, such as evaluation, that make our relationship with students edgy and uneasy. We want to get through the first class with éclat, but we don't know how much material we can cover in a class period.

In most cases anxiety passes as one finds that students do respond positively, that one does have some expertise in the subject, and that class periods can be exciting. But for some teachers the first days are not happy experiences. Classes get off on the wrong foot. Sullen hostility sets in. The teacher asserts authority and the students resist. The teacher knows that things are not going well but doesn't know what to do about it.

One likely response of the teacher is retreat—retreat to reading lectures with as little eye contact with students as possible, retreat to threats of low grades as a motivating device, retreat to research and other aspects of the professional role. What makes the difference in these first few days? It's probably not the subject matter. More often than not, the key to a good start is not the choice of interesting content (important as that may be) but rather the ability to manage the activities of the class effectively. Simple teaching techniques get the students involved so that they can get to work and learn.

The new teacher who has techniques for breaking the ice, for encouraging class participation, and for getting the course organized is more likely to get off to a good start. Once you find that teaching can be fun, you enjoy devoting time to it, you will think about it, and you will develop into a competent teacher.

When you are just starting, discussions of philosophy of education and theories of learning and teaching can be helpful, but they are probably not as important as learning enough techniques and simple skills to get through the first few weeks without great stress and with some satisfaction. Once some comfort has been achieved, you can think more deeply about the larger issues discussed in later chapters.

THE COLLEGE OR UNIVERSITY CULTURE

A course cannot be divorced from the total college or university culture.

First of all, the institution makes certain requirements of instructors. In most you must submit grades for the students' work. You probably must give a final course examination. A classroom is assigned for the class, and the class meets in this assigned place. The class meets at certain regularly scheduled periods.

There are, in addition, areas not covered by the formal rules or routine practices of the college, in which instructors must tread lightly. For example, in most college cultures instructors who become intimately involved with their students are overstepping the bounds of propriety. Certain limits on class discussion of religion, sex, or politics may exist. Instructors must learn not only to operate within the fences of college regulations but also to skirt the pitfalls of the college mores. And it is not just the culture of the institution that matters. Each department or discipline has its own culture with customs related to teaching methods, testing, and styles of communication and instruction.

But instructors who consider only local folkways in plans for their courses are ignoring a far more important limitation on teaching, for the college or university culture has not only placed limitations on instructors but also pretty much hobbled the students. To stay in college, students must show evidence of achievement. Admission to good careers depends on evidence of outstanding achievement.

Each reader will need to adapt my suggestions to the college culture of which he or she is a part. When you begin a new teaching position, talk to other faculty members about their perceptions of the students, about how these instructors teach and perceive others as teaching. Ask for examples of syllabi, tests, and other course materials.

In many institutions, students have had experience in previous classes with instructors who, in a more or less parental way, gave information and rewarded those students who could best give it back. The sort of tests, frequency of tests, and methods of grading also have conformed closely to certain norms. As a result, instructors who attempt to revolutionize teaching with new methods or techniques may find that they are only frustrating the needs and expectations their students have developed in the culture of the college. So, if you are trying something new, be sure that students understand why the new method is likely to be valuable.

Although there are many norms and folkways that characterize an entire campus, you need to recognize that there are many subcultures. Some of them are subcultures of faculty in different disciplines, but it is important to recognize that there are student subcultures that have their own norms and expectations. And within the student cultures there are important individual differences among students. Taking account of the diversity of students is so important in teaching that "Understanding Students" is a separate part (Part 3) of this book.

RESEARCH VERSUS TEACHING?

One aspect of the local culture critical for new teachers is the definition of the proper role of a faculty member. In many universities, for example, formal definitions of the criteria for promotion give research and teaching equal weight, but it is not uncommon to find that research is "more equal."

Studies have demonstrated that research and teaching are not necessarily in conflict. Many faculty members are excellent researchers and excellent teachers as well. Some excellent researchers are poor teachers; some excellent teachers do not publish research. Most faculty members enjoy both teaching and scholarship. Most also provide service to their institutions, and many provide service to their community and nation.

Teaching as Scholarship

In 1990, Ernest Boyer's book *Scholarship Reconsidered* stimulated discussion throughout higher education about the nature of scholarship. In most American universities scholarship has been evaluated in terms of published research. Boyer suggested that teachers who keep up with current developments, who devise better ways to help students learn, or who do research on methods of teaching are also scholars. As a result of the debates about Boyer's proposal, there is increasing acceptance of the idea that good teaching involves much scholarly activity.

Find out what the local norms are, and if you feel a conflict, choose the balance that suits your own talents and interests with an informed awareness of the likelihood of support for that self-definition. Although time is not infinitely elastic, most faculty members find that a 50- to 60-hour work week is satisfying because they enjoy both teaching and research.

Whatever your choice, it is likely that teaching will be a part of your role. *Teaching skillfully may be less time consuming than teaching badly.* Teaching well is more fun than teaching poorly. Moreover, you will be better able to focus on your research if you are not worrying about teaching. Thus some investment of time and attention to developing skill in teaching is likely to have substantial payoff in self-satisfaction and effectiveness in your career.

IN CONCLUSION

Because the suggestions I make are based on my own philosophy of teaching, you should be forewarned of six of my biases or hypotheses.

1. What is important is learning, not teaching. Teaching effectiveness depends not just on what the teacher does, but rather on what the student does. Teaching involves listening as much as talking. It's important that both teacher and students are actively thinking, but most important is what goes on in the students' minds. Those minds are not blank slates. They hold expectations, experiences, and conceptions that will shape their interpretation of the knowledge you present. Your task is to help them develop mental representations of your subject matter that will provide a basis for further learning, thinking, and use.

2. Teachers can occasionally be wrong. If they are wrong too often, they should not be teaching. If they are never wrong, they belong in heaven, not a college classroom.

3. Classes are unpredictable. This can be frustrating, but it also makes teaching continually fascinating. Don't be discouraged if some students don't appreciate your teaching. You can interest all of your students some of the time; you can interest some of your students all of the time; but you can't interest all of your students all of the time.

4. There are many important goals of college and university teaching. Not the least of these is that of increasing the student's motivation and ability to *continue* learning after leaving college.

5. Most student learning occurs outside the classroom. This is a both humbling and reassuring thought for the beginning teacher. It means that the students' education will neither succeed nor fail simply because of what you do or don't do in the classroom. At the same time it reminds one to direct attention to stimulating and guiding student learning outside class even more than to preparing to give a dazzling classroom performance.

6. One key to improvement is reflection—thinking about what you want to accomplish, and what you and the students need to

do to achieve these goals. What is contained in this book will not make you a Great Teacher. It may be that Great Teachers are born and not made, but anyone with ability enough to get a job as a college teacher can be a *good* teacher. This book will give you some tips for avoiding common problems and some concepts to think with, but eventually it comes down to you, your personality, and your values. My hope is that this book will help you feel enough at ease that you can reveal the best that is in you.

Supplementary Reading

When the first edition of *Teaching Tips* was published, it was almost the only book offering guidance to college teachers. Now there are a great many, as well as journals and newsletters published in the United States and other countries. Almost every discipline has a journal concerned with teaching that discipline. Check out the holdings of your institution's library. If your institution has a faculty/instructional developmental center, it will have lots of material and a helpful staff.

I am reluctant to list only a few of the many good books on college teaching because I see them all as meeting a need and complementing one another as well as *Teaching Tips*. I will limit myself to seven.

R. Boice, *Advice for New Faculty: Nihil Nimus* (Boston: Allyn & Bacon, 2000).

B. G. Davis, *Tools for Teaching*, 2nd ed. (San Francisco: Jossey-Bass, 1993).

K. Eble, *The Craft of Teaching*, 2nd ed. (San Francisco: Jossey-Bass, 1988).

Don't think that a 1988 book must be out of date by now. This is a good book to read when you've lost your initial anxiety and want to think about teaching as a craft and a calling.

T. Grasha, *Teaching with Style* (Pittsburgh: Alliance Publishers, 1996).

K. W. Prichard and R. McLaren Sawyer, *Handbook of College Teaching* (Westford, CT: Greenwood Press, 1994).

The following two books come from authors writing from the perspective of experience in Great Britain and Australia. Their contents are relevant to university teachers in all countries.

J. Biggs, *Teaching for Quality Learning at University* (Buckingham and Philadelphia: Society for Research into Higher Education and Open University Press, 1999).

P. Ramsden, *Learning to Teach in Higher Education* (London and New York: Routledge, 1992).

Many university faculty development centers publish newsletters for their own faculties. In addition there are two national publications on college teaching: *The National Teaching and Learning Forum* and *The Teaching Professor*. Both have helpful articles.

Countdown for Course Preparation

For teachers, courses do not start on the first day of classes. Rather, a course begins well before you meet your students. I shall present a series of steps, but planning does not usually follow a perfectly orderly, linear pattern. Experts typically say that you should start with your objectives, but don't get stuck on this. In all your planning, you'll do at least one thing that will remind you to modify earlier steps. So, you move back and forth as you progress. The main thing is to get started!

TIME: THREE MONTHS BEFORE THE FIRST CLASS*

Write Objectives, Goals, or Outcomes

The first step in preparing for a course is working out course objectives, because the choice of text, the selection of the type and

---

This chapter incorporates material from Graham Gibbs's chapter in the tenth edition, "Planning Your Students' Learning Activities."

* I have borrowed the idea of three months, two months, and so on from P. G. Zimbardo and J. W. Newton, *Instructor's Resource Book to Accompany Psychology and Life* (Glenview, IL: Scott, Foresman, 1975).

order of assignments, the choice of teaching techniques, and all the decisions involved in course planning should derive from your objectives. What are your students like? What do they expect? What outcomes do you expect them to achieve? At this point your list of goals or objectives should be taken only as a rough reminder to be revised as you develop other aspects of the course plan and to be further revised in interaction with students. Writing out your goals helps clarify your thinking.

Some of you have heard of behavioral or performance objectives and may wish to phrase your objectives in behavioral terms. If so, do so. The advantage of stating what you expect students to be able to do is that it guides both you and the students toward outcome assessment. One of the most common weaknesses in teaching is that our evaluation methods are often pale reflections of the goals we proclaimed (and may or may not have achieved!). But don't omit important objectives simply because you can't think of good ways to convert them to behavioral language. The purpose of phrasing objectives behaviorally is to encourage you to be specific, but usually the performance specified in a behavioral objective is an indicator of a more general objective you want to achieve.* Your objectives have the great advantage of pointing clearly to what you can look for as evidence that the objective has been achieved. Your students see your methods of assessing or testing achievement of the objectives as the most important operational definition of your goals; hence goals and testing are inseparable teaching tasks. This does not mean that all of your goals should be assessed and count toward a grade. Some of your goals will involve motivational, attitudinal, and value outcomes, as discussed in the chapters "Motivation in the College Classroom," "Learning Strategies and Self-Regulation," and "Teaching Values." Course grades are typically based only on cognitive and skill outcomes.

---

* Duchastel and Merrill (1973) reviewed empirical studies of the effects of behavioral objectives. Amid the plethora of nonsignificant results are some studies indicating that sharing objectives with students may help focus their attention or assist them in organizing material. So, if you've worked out objectives, let your students know what they are, and if possible give them a chance to help revise them. (This study and others mentioned in the text are found in the References at the back of the book.)

What Goals?

The answer obviously depends on the course and discipline, but it is important to note that the overall course objectives involve *educating students*; the objective of a course is not to cover a certain set of topics, but rather *to facilitate student learning and thinking*. Ordinarily we are not concerned simply with the learning of a set of facts, but rather with learning that can be applied and used in situations outside course examinations. In fact, *in most courses we are concerned about helping our students in a lifelong learning process; that is, we want to develop interest in further learning and provide a base of concepts and skills that will facilitate further learning and thinking*. Thus, in framing your goals, think about what will be meaningful to your students. Will these goals really be relevant to them now and in the future?

Your personal values inevitably enter into your choice of goals. Although many of us were taught to be strictly objective, I have come to believe that this is impossible. Our teaching is always influenced by our values, and students have a fairer chance to evaluate our biases or to accept our model if we are explicit about them. Hiding behind the cloak of objectivity simply prevents honest discussion of vital issues.

In thinking about your goals, remember that each course contributes to other general goals of a university education that transcend specific subject matter, such as critical thinking, being willing to explore ideas contrary to one's own beliefs, and knowing when information or data are relevant to an issue and how to find that information.

In addition to this general perspective, you need to keep in mind characteristics of the setting in which you teach. What is the role of this course in the curriculum? Are other instructors depending on this course to provide specific kinds of background knowledge or skill? What are your students like? How do they differ? (See the part on "Understanding Students.") What are their current concerns? Self-discovery? Social action? Getting a job? How can their goals be integrated with other goals of the course? Talk to some of your colleagues.

A committee of college and university examiners developed two books, which are now classics, to assist faculty members in thinking about their objectives: *Taxonomy of Educational Objectives*,

Handbook I: Cognitive Domain (Bloom, 1956) and *Handbook II: Affective Domain* (Krathwohl et al., 1964). Krathwohl and others have completed a revision (Anderson et al., 2001). Another good framework is the SOLO (*S*tructure of the *O*bserved *L*earning *O*utcome) taxonomy (see Biggs, 1999).

Having said all this about the importance of starting with clear goals, I would nonetheless not want to make you feel guilty if you started on your syllabus with only vague notions about goals. Although it seems logical to start with goals, content, teaching methods, and the nature of the students, all of these interact in dynamic ways. So, if you find it easier to start by outlining the content of the course, do so. Ideally you would then tie the content to goals, but many effective teachers never state their goals very explicitly, yet their students achieve the kinds of motivational and cognitive outcomes that we all desire. College teachers are individualists. There are lots of different ways to do a good job. Goals emerge as you teach.

Order Textbooks or Other Resources Students May Need

Should You Use a Text?   With paperback books, reprint series, photocopiers,* and the World Wide Web, young instructors are immediately beguiled by the thought that they can do a much better job of compiling a set of required readings than any previous author or editor. "Coursepacks"—compilations of relevant articles and book chapters—may be used in place of a textbook or as supplementary reading.

There is much to be said for such a procedure. It provides flexibility, a variety of points of view, and an opportunity to maintain maximum interest. Moreover, since no single text covers every topic equally well, the use of a variety of sources enables the teacher to provide more uniformly excellent materials, ranging from theoretical papers and research reports to applications.

The disadvantages of not using a textbook are apparent. Without a text the task of integration may be so overwhelming

---

* Check the copyright laws before making multiple copies.

that great pressure is placed on instructors to provide integration. This may limit your freedom to use the class period for problem solving, applications, or other purposes. With a well-chosen textbook, you may rely on the students to obtain the basic content and structure of the subject matter through reading and thus be freer to vary procedures in the classroom. Moreover, the managerial task of determining appropriate readings and arranging to have them available for students is not to be taken lightly. If students are expected to use certain print sources in the library, consult a librarian to be sure enough copies are available. Access to course resources is particularly important in distance learning.

A final consideration is the extent to which you want to use required versus free reading, as in my use of a journal (see the chapter "Teaching Students to Learn Through Writing: Journals, Papers, and Reports"). I use a text as a base to provide structure and then require students to write journal entries on readings they choose. To assign diverse required readings and additional free reading seems to me to require too much integration even for well-prepared, bright students.

Choosing a Text or Reading Materials*

In choosing reading materials the most important thing is that they fit your objectives. One of the most annoying and confusing practices for students is instructor disagreement with the textbook. It is doubtful that any book will satisfy you completely, but if you use a text, choose one that is as much in line with your view as possible.

Students prefer going through a book as it was written. If the author also wrote the book in a systematic way, building one concept on another, there may be good pedagogical reasons for following the author's order. Since I know of no text that completely suits many teachers, however, I can only recommend that you keep skipping around to a minimum and make sure that students understand why.

---

* Some of these ideas were stimulated by Russell Dewey's article, "Finding the right introductory psychology textbook," *APS Observer*, March 1995, 32–35.

There is no substitute for detailed review of the competing texts for the course you are teaching. As texts multiply, it becomes increasingly tempting to throw up your hands in frustration over the time required for a conscientious review and to choose the book primarily on the basis of appearance, the personality of the sales representative, or the inclusion of your name as author of one of the studies cited. Yet research on teaching suggests that the major influence on what students learn is not the teaching method but the textbook. What should you do?

1. Winnow the possibilities down to two to five.* You may be able to do some winnowing on the basis of the table of contents and preface, by checking with colleagues who have taught the course, or by reading reviews.

2. Read a couple of chapters. It is tempting to simply leaf through each book, reading snatches here and there. But reading a couple of complete chapters will give you a better idea of the difficulty and interest level of each book. Try picking one chapter on a topic you know well and one that is not in your area of expertise.

3. Pick three or four key concepts. See how each text explains them. Will the explanations be clear to students? Interesting?

Letting the Students Choose Their Textbook   Having given you advice about how to choose your text, it may seem heretical to let students choose a text, but in my own introductory psychology section, I do that. All of the introductory psychology textbooks have been reviewed and polished by so many reviewers and editors that they all cover the major topics usually included in an introductory psychology course. Thus I do use the procedures described above to review possible texts, but I then select two or three from which students may choose. I ask the bookstores to

---

* In my introductory psychology course, my teaching assistants and I choose two or three textbooks and then allow each student to choose the book he or she prefers. All the texts cover the essential material, but having a choice helps student motivation. Before students make their choice, they discuss in small groups what characteristics of textbooks help their learning. Each student compares at least two books, reporting back to the class for further discussion and the final decision.

have these in stock, and I make sure that copies are in the library on reserve. The first day of class I divide students into groups of six and ask them to spend five minutes discussing what characteristics of a textbook help them learn most effectively. We list these on the board. I then tell them that they can use these and other criteria to choose their textbook. Within each group of six, each student is to choose two books to compare and report on to the group at the next class meeting. The group must ensure that each book is reviewed by at least two people who do not compare that book with the same alternative.

At the next meeting the groups reassemble, discuss their findings, and then report their evaluations to the class. I list the relative strengths and weaknesses of each book on the board and then ask whether they want to agree on a single book for the entire class, agree on a particular book for their own subgroup, or allow each student to choose what he or she wishes to use.

TIME: TWO MONTHS BEFORE THE FIRST CLASS

Begin Drafting a Syllabus for the Course

When we think about teaching, we usually think about what goes on in the classroom, but most student learning occurs outside the classroom. Planning assignments and out-of-class activities is even more important than planning for class meetings. A syllabus typically contains such a plan, with assignments correlated with topics to be discussed in class. If you are teaching a distance learning course, a syllabus is indispensable. Like a contract, a syllabus should help students understand both their responsibilities and yours.

Constructing your syllabus will force you to begin thinking about the practicalities of what you must give up in order to achieve the most important objectives within the limitations of time, place, students, and resources. If you have taught the course before, what worked? What didn't?

How Much Student Time Does Your Course Involve?   It is easy to imagine that your course is the only one your students are taking. After all, it is the only one you see. However, your students may be taking three, four, or five other courses in parallel. Given a realistic studying week of about 40 hours, you therefore have between about 6 and 10 hours a week of your students' time available to allocate to learning on your course, including in-class time. If your students spend 3 hours a week in class with you, then you have between 3 and 6 hours a week of out-of-class learning activity to plan. You should expect to use all of this time, and you should be quite explicit with your students about what you expect them to do with it. Exactly how many hours you have and are taking up is rather important. Students experience wide variations in demands among courses because teachers often do not estimate or plan this time carefully. The most common problems are caused by, at one extreme, specifying nothing, and leaving students to their own devices. At the other extreme, teachers overload students with inappropriate and unproductive activities which actually limit their learning. For example, science teachers often fill their students' time with writing up lab reports, leaving them no time to read. It can be helpful to calculate the total number of study hours available to your course and to plan what all of those hours would ideally be used for, estimating the time demands of each activity. In reality students will vary. Some will work harder or slower than others, and some will spend more of their time on some learning activities, and on some of their courses, than on others. But being explicit will help you to make realistic demands and will help students to see what is expected of them.

What Should Be in the Syllabus?   There is no one model. Take the following as suggestions, not rules. If you have followed my recommendations up to this point, you now have a list of goals, have chosen a textbook, and have a general schedule of when you will cover each topic. The core of your syllabus will be that schedule. In introducing the schedule, explain the purpose for the organization you have chosen.

Under the topic headings, you can schedule assignments and the dates when they are due. This relieves you of the task of making assignments every few days and of repeating the assignments for students who have been absent when each assignment was announced. State your expectations and policies about class attendance.

As you lay out your schedule, consider alternate ways students might achieve the goals of a particular day or week of class. You will seldom have perfect attendance at every class. Why not build in periodic alternatives to your lecture or class discussion? Be sure also to consider the diversity of your students. Alternative assignments can help. Students who have options and a sense of personal control are likely to be more highly motivated for learning.

Be clear about when and how learning will be assessed. What students do is strongly influenced by their anticipation of the ways learning will be evaluated. You may also include other items that will be helpful for student learning, such as sites on the World Wide Web, interesting readings to supplement textbook assignments, strategies for maximizing learning, and what to do when having difficulty.

Finally, you may include any special rules you want to emphasize, such as a statement to the effect that assignments for the course are to be completed by the dates indicated in the course outline.

But isn't a syllabus that is printed or on a web site a cue that the course is really instructor centered and that student needs are not going to be considered? Not necessarily so. Research by Mann et al. (1970) suggests that students may see a less organized approach as an indication that the teacher is not interested in their learning. The syllabus helps students discover at the outset what is expected of them and gives them the security of knowing where they are going. At the same time, your wording of assignment topics can convey excitement and stimulate curiosity.

TIME: ONE MONTH BEFORE THE FIRST CLASS

Begin Preparing Lesson Plans

If you are planning to lecture, outline the content of the first few lectures and the ways you will get student involvement. If you are planning to teach by discussion, cooperative learning, or other methods, don't assume that they will take less preparation. Work out your plans. (See also the chapters "Meeting a Class for the First Time" and "Facilitating Discussion.")

Plan for Out-of-Class Learning

It is easy for teachers to imagine that what happens in class is overwhelmingly important to students' learning and that they and their classes are at the center of students' learning universe. It is the component of student learning that teachers see—the rest is often invisible. When they do their planning, most teachers give their attention to covering content in class rather than to what happens out of class (Stark & Lattuca, 1997). However, in studies of what students believe most influenced change during the college years, and of what students believe were their most important experiences at college, ideas presented by instructors in courses, and instructors themselves, rank far behind a range of other influences (Feldman & Newcomb, 1969). In most courses students spend at least as much time studying out of class as they do in class. Thus you need to focus as much on what you expect students to do outside class as on what goes on in class. Look at your ojectives. If you want students to become better problem solvers or critical thinkers, they need to practice these skills.

Reading an assignment passively will produce poorer learning than reading with an activity in mind, such as preparing a question for class discussion, drawing a concept map, or writing examples or possible applications.

Choose Appropriate Teaching Methods

A final point at which your preparation for a course is determined by your objectives is in the type of instruction you will use. For some goals and for some materials, an orthodox lecture presentation is as good as or better than any other. For others, discussion may be preferable. For the accomplishment of still other ends, cooperative learning or role-playing techniques described later in the book may be useful. Probably most successful teachers vary their methods to suit their objectives. Thus you may wish one day to present some new material in a lecture. You may then follow this with a class discussion on implications of this material or with a laboratory or field exercise. Since your choice in the matter is determined as much by your own personality as by your course objectives, I shall not dwell on it here. From the description of these techniques in later sections of the book, you may be able to decide which techniques are suited to your philosophy of teaching, your abilities, the class you are teaching, and the particular goals you are emphasizing at a particular time.

Select Appropriate Technology

It is quite possible to teach an effective course without technology. Nonetheless there is much that can be helpful. The chapter "Technology and Teaching" gives you a good overview of some of the possibilities. When used appropriately, technology can provide opportunities for students to interact with the content and with one another. It is an important instructional resource. But just as in considering other resources, ask yourself, "Will this help my students learn more effectively?"

TIME: TWO WEEKS BEFORE THE FIRST CLASS

Preparation and planning are not done when you've firmed up the syllabus. Now look back over the syllabus to see what resources are required. Presumably your check, as suggested in the chapter "Getting Started," with a colleague has turned up any gross problems—such as assuming an unlimited budget for films. This is a good time for another check. What are the library policies relevant to putting on reserve any books you may want? What computer resources are available? Can you assume unlimited photocopying of exams and course materials to give to students? What do you do if you want to show a film? Go on a field trip?

Visit the classroom you've been assigned. Will the seating be conducive to discussion? Can it be darkened for films? If the room is unsuitable, ask for another.

TIME: ONE WEEK BEFORE THE FIRST CLASS

At this point you're ready to prepare for the first class. For ideas about what to do and how to handle this meeting, read the following chapter.

Supplementary Reading

Chapter 7 of Robert Diamond's *Designing and Improving Courses and Curricula in Higher Education* (San Francisco: Jossey-Bass, 1989) is a practical guide for linking objectives to assessment.

Barbara Davis's good book *Tools for Teaching*, 2nd ed. (San Francisco: Jossey-Bass, 1993) has a fine chapter on the syllabus (pp. 14–28).

Chapter 6, "The Natural History of the Classroom," in *The College Classroom* by Richard Mann, S. M. Arnold, J. Bender, S. Cytrynbaum, B. M. Newman, B. Ringwald, J. Ringwald, and R. Rosenwein (New York: Wiley, 1970), is still the best material on the changing needs of classes over the course of a semester.

Teaching Within the Rhythms of the Semester by Donna K. Duffy and Janet W. Jones (San Francisco: Jossey-Bass, 1995) is also a perceptive and readable guide to thinking about the flow of the course over the term.

An excellent aid for preparing your syllabus is M. A. Lowther, J. S. Stark, and G. G. Martens, *Preparing Course Syllabi for Improved Communication* (Ann Arbor: NCRIPTAL, University of Michigan, 1989).

If you are teaching first-year students, the book *Teaching College Freshmen* by Bette Erickson and D. W. Strommer (San Francisco: Jossey-Bass, 1991) will be helpful to you.

Meeting a Class for the First Time

3

The first class meeting, like any other situation in which you are meeting a group of strangers who will affect your well-being, is at the same time exciting and anxiety-producing for both students and teacher. Some teachers handle their anxiety by postponing it, simply handing out the syllabus and leaving. This does not convey the idea that class time is valuable, nor does it capitalize on the fact that first-day excitement can be constructive. If you have prepared as suggested in the previous chapter, you're in good shape; the students will be pleased that the instruction is under control, and focusing on meeting the students' concerns can not only help you quell your own anxiety but also make the first class interesting and challenging.

Other things being equal, anxiety is less disruptive in situations where stimulus events are clear and unambiguous. When the students know what to expect, they can direct their energy more productively. An important function of the first day's meeting in any class is to provide this structure; that is, to present the classroom situation clearly, so that the students will know from the date of this meeting what you are like and what you expect. They come to the first class wanting to know what the course is all about and what kind of person the teacher is. You need to know what the students expect. To these ends, the following concrete suggestions are offered.

One point to keep in mind both the first day and throughout the term is that yours is not the students' only class. They come to you from classes in chemistry, music, English, or physical education, or rushing from their dormitory beds or from parking lots. The first few minutes need to help this varied group shift their thoughts and feelings to you and your subject.

You can ease them into the course gradually, or you can grab their attention with something dramatically different, but in either case you need to think consciously about how you set the stage to facilitate achieving the course objectives. Even before the class period begins you can communicate nonverbally with such actions as arranging the seats in a circle, putting your name on the board, and chatting with early arrivals about what class they have come from or anything else that would indicate your interest in them. While students are coming in, suggest that they spend the time before class starts by getting acquainted with the students sitting near them.

BREAKING THE ICE

You will probably want to use the first period for getting acquainted and establishing goals. You might begin by informally asking first-year students to raise their hands, then sophomores, juniors, seniors, or out-of-staters. This gives you some idea of the composition of the class and gets students started participating.

In my relatively large lecture classes I have then asked the students to take a minute or two to write down words and phrases that describe their feelings on the first day of class. I then ask them, "What have you written?" and list their responses on the board.

Next I ask them, "How do you think your teacher feels on the first day of class?" This takes them aback, but they begin writing. We now list these responses in a second column, and they see some parallels. I comment briefly on my own feelings. (I remember with special affection the senior who came up to me after class and said, "I've been at this university almost four years, and this is the first time it ever occurred to me that professors have feelings.")

I admit that I'm anxious—that I'm concerned about how the students will relate to me and the material, but I'm not sure that everyone should do this. Students need to feel that you're secure enough to admit your own feelings. If they see you as being uncertain about your ability to fill the roles of authority and expert when needed, students may become more anxious.

In a small class you might then ask all class members (including yourself) to introduce themselves, tell where they're from, mention their field of concentration, and answer any questions the group has. Or you can ask each student to get acquainted with the persons sitting on each side and then go around the class with each student introducing the next or each repeating the names of all those who have been introduced—a good device for developing rapport and for helping you learn the names, too. A more demanding but surprisingly effective device is to have each person introduce everyone who was introduced before, ending with the teacher repeating everyone's names. (Try it! You'll be surprised at how well you do.)

Learning names is a start, but students are probably even more interested in you than in their classmates; so give them a chance to ask questions of you. Sometimes I have asked for one or two students to act as interviewers for the class, asking questions they think the other students would like to ask.

Even if you remembered all of the students' names in the "Name Game," you may not recall them later; so it is helpful to supplement the memory in your head with an external memory. I pass out file cards and ask students to write their names, phone numbers, e-mail addresses, and other information on the card. The "other information" might include previous experience relevant to the course, interests, distinctive characteristics that will help me remember them, possible major field, and so on.

Having established some freedom of communication, you can then go on to assess students' expectations and goals, and let them know what yours are. One technique for doing this is problem posting.

PROBLEM POSTING

Problem posting is a method of getting students involved and active which can be used in classes of all sizes. For this first class meeting you might say, "Let's see what problems you'd like to tackle during the course. What sorts of concerns do you think we might deal with?" or "What are your expectations for this course?" or "What goals do you have for this course?" or "What have you heard about this course?"

You might ask students to write for a minute their response to the question and then ask them what they have written. Your task then becomes that of recorder, listing responses on the board, overhead, or electronic smartboard. To make sure you understand, you may restate the response in your own words. If you feel that some response is ambiguous or too general, you might ask for an example, but you must be ready to accept all contributions, whether or not you feel they are important. It is crucial that the atmosphere be accepting and nonevaluative. Students should feel that you are genuinely interested in what they have to contribute.

By the end of the problem posting the class normally has become better acquainted, has become used to active participation, has taken the first step toward developing an attitude of attempting to understand rather than competing with one another, has reduced the attitude that everything must come from the teacher, has learned that the teacher can listen as well as talk (and is not going to reject ideas different from his or her own), and, I hope, has begun to feel some responsibility for solving its own problems rather than waiting for them to be answered by the instructor.

INTRODUCING THE SYLLABUS

Your syllabus will provide some of the answers to the concerns raised in the problem posting. In presenting the syllabus you give the students some notion of the kind of person you are. The syllabus is a contract between you and your students. But a contract cannot be one-sided. Thus it is important to give students time to read and discuss it. Give them a chance to make inputs and to be sure that they understand what you expect. Help the students understand the reasons for the plan you have presented, but if they have good reasons for changes, accept them. The students are, of course, interested in course requirements, but they are at least as much interested in what kind of person you are. One important issue is fairness.

Testing, Grading, and Fairness

Promoting the notion that you are objective or fair can best be handled in connection with marks and the assignment of grades (see the chapters "Assessing, Testing, and Evaluating" and "The ABC's of Assigning Grades"). A large part of the students' motivation in the classroom situation is (perhaps unfortunately) directed toward the grades they hope to get from the course. The very least that students can expect of you is that their marks will be arrived at on some impartial basis. Thus give some time to discussing this section of your syllabus. Try to help the students understand how grading and testing are tied to course goals.

The simplest way to show students that you are objective and fair is to let them know that you are willing to meet and advise them. Indicate your office hours. In addition, students appreciate it if you are willing (and have the time) to spend a few minutes in the classroom after each class, answering specific questions. Such queries most often concern questions of fact which can be answered briefly and would hardly warrant a trip to your office at a later time. If time permits, adjournment to a convenient snack bar or lounge may give students with special interests a chance to pursue them and get to know you better. If you teach an evening class, schedule some evening time to see students.

The first class is not the time to make sure students understand your inadequacies and limitations. Frankly admitting that you don't know something is fine after the course is under way, but apologies in advance for lack of experience or expertise simply increase student insecurity. They need to feel that you are competent and in charge even if you are shaking in your boots.

INTRODUCING THE TEXTBOOK

To continue with the discussion of the first meeting of the class, we turn now to the presentation of the textbook. Explain the features that led you to choose it.* Describe how students can learn from it most effectively. In case disagreement between the teacher and the text is inevitable, the students have a right to know what they are supposed to do about such discrepancies on examinations. By facing the situation squarely, you can not only escape from the horns of this dilemma but also turn it to your advantage. Explain that rival interpretations stand or fall on the basis of pertinent evidence and plan to give your reasons for disagreeing with the textbook. This procedure will accomplish two things: (1) it will give the student the notion that your opinions are based on evidence, and (2) it will frequently point out current problems in theory which often have great appeal for the serious student.

ASSESSING PRIOR KNOWLEDGE

The most important characteristic determining student learning is prior knowledge. Thus you need to get some sense of the diversity of your class's background. You might simply ask questions like, "How many have had more than X previous courses in this subject?" or you might give a short, noncredit test of relevant knowledge sometime during the first few class sessions. For students who lack sufficient background, you might advise that they transfer to the needed courses, or if this isn't feasible, you can at least suggest materials for their own self-study which would help them keep up with the other students. For those with very high scores, you might suggest that they skip your course and go on to a more advanced course, or at least suggest supplementary materials that would be enriching and challenging.

In a diverse class, adult students or students from other cultures may feel at a disadvantage relative to students who have

---

* In the chapter "Countdown for Course Preparation" I described my first-day procedures for giving students the choice of textbook.

had previous courses that are relevant. Reassure them by pointing out that a diversity of experiences not directly related to the course can enrich class discussion and contribute to learning.

QUESTIONS

Even in a large lecture it seems wise to interrupt these first descriptions of the course for student questions. Some of the questions will be designed as much to test you as to get information. Often the underlying questions are such:

- "Are you rigid?"
- "Will you really try to help students?"
- "Are you easily rattled?"
- "Are you a person as well as a teacher?"
- "Can you handle criticism?"

Ask students to take two minutes at the end of class to write their reactions to the first day (anonymously). This accomplishes two things: (1) it indicates your interest in learning from them and starts building a learning climate in which they are responsible for thinking about their learning and influencing your teaching; and (2) it gives you feedback, often revealing doubts or questions students were afraid to verbalize orally.

WHAT ABOUT SUBJECT MATTER?

Many instructors dismiss class early on the first day. As the preceding sections indicate, I think the first day is important even though the students have had no prepared assignment. I like to give at least some time to subject matter. Typically I give at least a brief overview of the course, indicate some of the questions we'll try to answer, and perhaps introduce a few key concepts. Either on the first day or during the second class period, I ask students to fill in concepts on a concept map (a diagram of key concepts and their relationships).

But there is a limit to what you can do. The balance between content and other activities is one that different teachers will decide in different ways. My only admonition is to use the time. The first day is important, and by using it fully you communicate that you take class periods seriously. By the end of the class period, students should feel, "This is going to be an exciting course."

IN CONCLUSION

By the end of the first day, students will have

1. A sense of where they're going and how they'll get there.
2. A feeling that the other members of the class are not strangers, that you and they are forming a group in which it's safe to participate.
3. An awareness that you care about their learning.
4. An expectation that the class will be both valuable and fun.

Supplementary Reading

B. G. Davis, *Tools for Teaching*, 2nd ed. (San Francisco: Jossey-Bass, 1993), Chapter 3.

"The First Day of Class: Advice and Ideas," *The Teaching Professor*, August/September 1989, 3(7), 1–2.

Basic Skills for Facilitating Student Learning

4

Facilitating Discussion: Posing Problems, Listening, Questioning

Active learning is the buzz word (or phrase) in contemporary higher education. The prototypic teaching method for active learning is discussion. Discussion methods are among the most valuable tools in the teacher's repertoire. Often teachers in large classes feel that they must lecture because discussion is impossible. In fact, discussion techniques can be used in classes of all sizes. Generally, smaller classes *are* more effective, but large classes should not be allowed to inhibit the teacher's ability to stimulate active learning—learning experiences in which the students are *thinking* about the subject matter.

Discussion techniques seem particularly appropriate when the instructor wants to do the following:

1. Help students learn to think in terms of the subject matter by giving them practice in thinking.
2. Help students learn to evaluate the logic of and evidence for their own and others' positions.
3. Give students opportunities to formulate applications of principles.
4. Develop motivation for further learning.
5. Help students articulate what they've learned.

6. Get prompt feedback on student understanding or misunderstanding.

Why should discussion be the method of choice for achieving
such objectives? The first justification is a very simple extrapola-
tion of the old adage "Practice makes perfect." If instructors
expect students to learn how to integrate, apply, and think, it
seems reasonable that students should have an opportunity to
practice these skills. To help students learn and think, you need to
find out what is in their heads. Discussion can help.

A LITTLE BIT OF THEORY

Research in cognitive psychology has found that memory is
affected by how deeply we process new knowledge (see the chapter "Teaching Students How to Learn"). Simply listening to or
repeating something is likely to store it in such a way that we
have difficulty finding it when we want to remember it. If we
elaborate our learning by thinking about its relationship to other
things we know or by talking about it—explaining, summarizing,
or questioning—we are more likely to remember it when we need
to use it later. This may help relieve your anxiety about covering
the material. In lectures teachers cover more material, but
research shows that most of the material covered does not get into
the students' notes or memory (Hartley & Davies, 1978). Classic
studies over the last five decades have repeatedly shown that, in
discussion, students pay attention and think more actively.

Because many students are accustomed to listening passively
to lectures, in introducing discussion you need to explain why
and how discussion will help them construct knowledge they can
find and apply when needed.

PROBLEMS IN TEACHING BY DISCUSSION

In discussion groups the instructor is faced with several
problems:

1. Getting participation in the discussion.

2. Making progress (or making the student aware of the progress) toward course objectives.
3. Handling emotional reactions of students.

This chapter should help you cope with each of these problems.

STARTING DISCUSSION

After a class has been meeting and discussing problems successfully, there is little problem in initiating discussion, for it will develop almost spontaneously from problems encountered in reading, from experiences, or from unresolved problems from the previous meeting. But during the first meetings of new groups, you need to create an expectation that something interesting and valuable will occur.

Starting Discussion with a Common Experience

One of the best ways of starting a discussion is to refer to a concrete, common experience through presentation of a demonstration, film, role play, short skit, or brief reading. It could be a common experience of all students or an issue on campus or in the media, or you can provide the experience. Following such a presentation it's easy to ask, "Why did ——————?"

Such an opening has a number of advantages. Because everyone in the group has seen it, everyone knows something about the topic under discussion. In addition, by focusing the discussion on the presentation, the instructor takes some of the pressure off anxious or threatened students who are afraid to reveal their own opinions or feelings.

However, you will not always be able to find the presentation you need to introduce each discussion, and you may be forced to turn to other techniques of initiating discussion. One such technique is problem posting, which was discussed in the previous chapter.

Starting Discussion with a Controversy

A second technique of stimulating discussion is through disagreement. Experimental evidence is accumulating to indicate that a certain degree of surprise or uncertainty arouses curiosity, a basic motive for learning (Berlyne, 1960). Some teachers effectively play the role of devil's advocate; others are effective in pointing out differences in point of view. I have some concerns about the devil's advocate role. I believe that it can be an effective device in getting students to think actively rather than accept passively the instructor's every sentence as "Truth." Yet it has its risks, the most important of which is that it may create lack of trust in the instructor. Of course, instructors want students to challenge their ideas, but few want their students to feel they are untrustworthy, lying about their own beliefs.

Two other dangers lurk in the devil's advocate role. One is that it will be perceived as manipulative. Students may feel (with justification) that the instructor "is just playing games with us—trying to show how smart he is and how easily he can fool us." It can also be seen as a screen to prevent students from ever successfully challenging the instructor.

Not only are all of these possible problems infuriating for the student, but they maintain a superior-subordinate relationship antithetical to the sort of learning environment that this book is plugging for.

Yet the devil's advocate role can be effective. Its success depends a good deal on the spirit with which it is played. My own compromise solution is to make it clear when I'm taking such a role by saying, "Suppose I take the position that ———" or "Let me play the role of devil's advocate for a bit."

In any case the instructor should realize that disagreement is not a sign of failure but may be used constructively. When rigid dogmatism interferes with constructive problem solving following a disagreement, the instructor may ask the disagreeing students to switch sides and argue the opposing point of view. Such a technique seems to be effective in developing awareness of the strengths of other positions.

As Maier (1963) has shown in his studies of group leadership, one barrier to effective problem solving is presenting an issue in such a way that participants take sides arguing the apparent solution rather than attempting to solve the problem by considering data and devising alternative solutions. Maier suggests the following principles for group problem solving:

1. Success in problem solving requires that effort be directed toward overcoming surmountable obstacles.
2. Available facts should be used even when they are inadequate.
3. The starting point of the problem is richest in solution possibilities.
4. Problem-mindedness should be increased while solution-mindedness should be delayed.
5. The "idea-getting" process should be separated from the "idea evaluation" process because the latter inhibits the former.

Starting Discussion with Questions

The most common discussion opener is the question, and the most common error in questioning is not allowing students time enough to think. You should not expect an immediate response to every question. If your question is intended to stimulate thinking, give the students time to think. Five seconds of silence may seem an eternity, but a pause for 5 to 30 seconds will result in better discussion. In some cases you may plan for such a thoughtful silence by asking the students to think about the question for a few seconds and then write down one element that might help answer the question. Such a technique increases the chance that the shyer or slower students will participate, since they now know what they want to say when the discussion begins. In fact, you may even draw one in by saying, "You were writing vigorously, Ronnie. What's your suggestion?"

Factual Questions   There are times when it is appropriate to check student background knowledge with a series of brief factual questions, but more frequently you want to stimulate problem solving. One common error in phrasing questions for this purpose is to ask a question in a form conveying to students the message, "I know something you don't know and you'll look stupid if you don't guess right."

Application and Interpretation Questions   Rather than dealing with factual questions, discussions need to be formulated so as to get at relationships, applications, or analyses of facts and materials. Solomon, Rosenberg, and Bezdek (1964) found that teachers who used interpretation questions produced gains in student comprehension. A question of the type: How does the idea that————apply to————? is much more likely to stimulate discussion than the question: What is the definition of ————? The secret is not to avoid questions or to lecture in statements, but rather to listen and to reflect on what is heard. Dillon (1982), a leading researcher on questioning, advises that once you have defined the issue for discussion, keep quiet unless you are perplexed or didn't hear a comment. Questions are tools for teaching, but as Dillon demonstrated, they sometimes interfere with, as well as facilitate, achievement of teaching goals. What happens depends on the question and its use.

Problem Questions   A question may arise from a case, or it may be a hypothetical problem. It may be a problem whose solution the instructor knows; it may be a problem which the instructor has not solved. In any case it should be a problem that is meaningful to the students, and for the sake of morale, it should be a problem they can make some progress on. And even if the teacher knows an answer or has a preferred solution, the students should have a chance to come up with new solutions. The teacher's job is not to sell students on a particular solution, but rather to listen and to teach them how to solve problems themselves. Don't be afraid to express your own curiosity, question, or "what if . . ." wonder about a topic. Ask the students what they think. It is better to be an open-minded, curious questioner than the font of all knowledge.

A common error in question phrasing is to frame the question at a level of abstraction inappropriate for the class. Students are most likely to participate in discussion when they feel that they have an experience or idea that will contribute to the discussion. This means that discussion questions need to be phrased as problems that are meaningful to the students as well as to the instructor. Such questions can be devised more easily if you know something of the students' background. An experiment by Sturgis (1959) showed that a teacher's knowledge of student background makes a significant difference in students' learning.

Suppose you ask a question and no one answers, or the student simply says, "I don't know." Discouraging as this may be, it should not necessarily be the end of the interaction. Usually the student can respond if the question is rephrased. Perhaps you need to give an example of the problem first; perhaps you need to suggest some alternative answer and ask the student what evidence might or might not support it; perhaps you need to reformulate a prior question. More often than not, you can help the students discover that they are more competent than they thought.

Other Types of Questions   *Connective and causal effect questions* involve attempts to link material or concepts that otherwise might not seem related. One might, for example, cut across disciplines to link literature, music, and historical events or one might ask, "What are the possible causes of this phenomenon?"

Comparative questions, as the name suggests, ask for comparisons between one theory and another, one author and another, one research study and another. Such questions help students determine important dimensions of comparison.

Evaluative questions ask not only for comparisons but for a judgment of the relative value of the points being compared; for example, "Which of two theories better accounts for the data? Which of two essays better contributes to an understanding of the issue?"

Critical questions examine the validity of an author's arguments or discussion. Television, magazines, and other media provide opportunities for using critical or evaluative questioning. For example, "— states '—.' Under what conditions might that not be true?" Being so critical that students feel that their reading has been a waste of time is not helpful, but presenting an alternative argument or conclusion may start students analyzing their reading more carefully, and eventually you want students to become critical readers who themselves challenge assumptions and conclusions.

Starting Discussion with a Problem or Case Using Developmental Discussion

The chapter "Problem-based Learning" discusses problem-based learning and the case method. Developmental discussion is a problem-solving discussion method that can be used with cases or other kinds of problems.

The term *developmental discussion* was coined by Professor Norman R. F. Maier (1952) to describe a problem-solving discussion technique in which the teacher breaks problems into parts so that all group members are working on the same part of the problem at the same time. One of the reasons discussion often seems ineffective and disorganized is that different members of the group are working on different aspects of the problem and are thus often frustrated by what they perceive as irrelevant comments by other students.

Stages of Developmental Discussion

In developmental discussion the teacher tries to keep the students aware of the stage of discussion that is the current focus. Typical stages might be

1. Formulating the problem.
2. Suggesting hypotheses.
3. Getting relevant data.
4. Evaluating alternative solutions.

Often an appropriate problem for discussion is the application or implications of principles or findings presented in the assignment or lecture. When starting a discussion with a question or problem, take time after stating the problem to write it on the chalkboard or overhead. This gives students time to think, and it decreases the possibility that the discussion will wander away from the topic. You might ask the students to use the time in listing concepts that seem relevant.

Breaking a Problem into Subproblems

One of Maier's important contributions to effective group problem solving, as well as to teaching, is to point out that groups are likely to be more effective if they tackle one aspect of a problem at a time rather than skipping from formulation of the problem, to solutions, to evidence, to "what-have-you," as different members of the group toss in their own ideas. In developmental discussion the group tackles one thing at a time.

One of the first tasks is likely to be a *clarification of the problem.* Often groups are ineffective because different participants have different ideas of what the problem is, and group members may feel frustrated at the end of the discussion because "the group never got to the real problem."

A second task is likely to be: What do we know? or *What data are relevant?*

A third task may be: *What are the characteristics of an acceptable solution?*—for example: What is needed?

A fourth step could be: *What are possible solutions?* and a fifth step may be to *evaluate these solutions* against the criteria for a solution determined in the previous step.

The developmental discussion technique can be used even in large groups, since there are a limited number of points to be made at each step regardless of the number of participants. Maier and Maier (1957) have shown that developmental discussion techniques improve the quality of decisions compared with freer, more nondirective discussion methods.

Socratic Discussion

The "classic" (and I do mean *classic*) discussion technique is the Socratic method. In television, novels, and anecdotes about the first year of law school it is usually portrayed as a sadistic, anxiety-producing method of eliciting student stupidity, and even when I place myself in the role of slave boy taught by Socrates in the *Meno,* I feel more like a pawn than an active learner.

Perhaps this is why I've never been very good at Socratic teaching; nonetheless I believe that it can be used as an effective method of stimulating student thinking, and it can have the quality of an interesting game rather than of an inquisition. The leading modern student of Socratic teaching is Allen Collins, who has observed a variety of Socratic dialogues and analyzed the strategies used (1977; Collins & Stevens, 1982).

Basically, most Socratic teachers attempt to teach students to reason to general principles from specific cases. Collins (1977) gives 23 rules, such as the following:

1. Ask about a known case. For example, if I were trying to teach a group of teaching assistants about student cheating,

I might say, "Can you describe a situation in which cheating occurred?"

2. Ask for any factors. "Why did the cheating occur?"

3. Ask for intermediate factors. If the student suggests a factor that is not an immediate cause, ask for intermediate steps. For example, if a teaching assistant says, "Students feel a lot of pressure to get good grades," I might say, "Why did the pressure for grades result in cheating in this situation?"

4. Ask for prior factors. If the student gives a factor that has prior factors, ask for the prior factors. For example, "Why do students feel pressure to get good grades?"

5. Form a general rule for an insufficient factor. For example, "Do all students who feel pressure cheat?"

6. Pick a counterexample for an insufficient factor. For example, "Do you think these students cheat on every test?"

7. Form a general rule for an unnecessary factor. For example, if a teaching fellow suggests that cheating occurs when tests are difficult, I might say, "Probably the pressure to cheat is greater when tests are difficult, but does cheating occur only on difficult tests?"

8. Pick a counterexample for an unnecessary factor. For example, "Is cheating likely to occur on college admissions tests, such as the SAT?"

9. Pick a case with an extreme value. For example, "Why is cheating minimized on SAT tests?"

10. Probe for necessary or sufficient factors.

11. Pose two cases and probe for differences. For example, "Why is there more cheating in large classes than in small ones?"

12. Ask for a prediction about an unknown case.

13. Trace the consequences of a general rule. For example, if the teaching assistants conclude that cheating will occur when tests are difficult and are not well proctored, I might say, "Engineering classes are considered difficult, and I understand that there is little cheating even though tests are unproctored." (The school has an honor code.)

In general, the rules involve formulating general principles from known cases and then applying the principles to new cases. Even if one does not use the Socratic method to its fullest, the questioning strategies described in Collins's rules may be generally useful in leading discussions.

BARRIERS TO DISCUSSION

One of the important skills of discussion leaders is the ability to appraise the group's progress and to be aware of barriers or resistances that are blocking learning. This skill depends on attention to such clues as inattention, hostility, or diversionary questions.

Barriers to Discussion: Why Students Don't Participate

- Student habits of passivity
- Failure to see the value of discussion
- Fear of criticism or of looking stupid
- Push toward agreement or solution before alternative points of view have been considered
- Feeling that the task is to find the answer the instructor wants rather than to explore and evaluate possibilities

A primary barrier to discussion is the students' feeling that they are not learning. Occasional summaries during the hour not only help students chart their progress but also help smooth out communication problems. A summary need not be a statement of conclusions. In many cases the most effective summary is a restatement of the problem in terms of the issues resolved and those remaining. Keeping a visible record on the chalkboard of ideas, questions, data, or points to explore helps maintain focus and give a sense of progress. Asking students to summarize progress and what now needs to be done helps them develop as learners.

Another common barrier to good discussion is the instructor's tendency to tell students the answer before the students have developed an answer or meaning for themselves. Of course, teachers can sometimes save time by tying things together or stating a generalization that is emerging. But all too often they do this before the class is ready for it.

Agreement can be a barrier to discussion. Usually instructors are so eager to reach agreement in groups that they are likely to be happy when the students are agreeing. But agreement is not the objective of most educational discussions. Students come to class with certain common naive attitudes and values. Although the attitudes they hold may be "good" ones, they may be so stereotyped that the students fail to develop an understanding of the complex phenomena to which their attitudes apply. The teacher's task is often directed not so much toward attitude change as toward increased sensitivity to other points of view and increased understanding of the phenomena to which the attitude applies. As I suggested earlier, the instructor may sometimes need to assume a role of opposition.

When you oppose a student's opinions, you should be careful not to overwhelm the student with the force of the criticism. Your objective is to start discussion, not smother it. Give students an opportunity to respond to criticisms, examining the point of view that was opposed. Above all, avoid personal criticism of students.

WHAT CAN I DO ABOUT NONPARTICIPANTS?*

In most classes some students talk too much, and others never volunteer a sentence. What can the teacher do?

Unfortunately, most students are used to being passive recipients in class. Some of your students may come from cultures whose norms discourage speaking in class. To help students become participants I try to create an expectation of participation

---

* Some students who are reluctant to participate orally will participate in a computer conference or by e-mail.

in the discussion section. You can start to do this in the first meeting of the course by defining the functions of various aspects of the course and explaining why discussion is valuable. In addition to this initial structuring, however, you must continually work to increase the students' awareness of the values of participation. Participation is not an end in itself. For many purposes widespread participation may be vital; for others it may be detrimental. But you want to create a climate in which an important contribution is not lost because the person with the necessary idea did not feel free to express it.

What keeps a student from talking? There are a variety of reasons—boredom, lack of knowledge, general habits of passivity, cultural norms—but most compelling is a fear of being embarrassed. When one is surrounded by strangers, when one does not know how critical these strangers may be, when one is afraid of the teacher's response, when one is not sure how sound one's idea may be, when one is afraid of stammering or forgetting one's point under the stress of speaking—the safest thing to do is keep quiet.

What can reduce this fear? Getting acquainted is one aid. Once students know that they are among friends, they can risk expressing themselves. If they know that at least one classmate supports an idea, the risk is reduced. For both these reasons the technique of subgrouping helps; for example, you can ask students to discuss a question in pairs or small groups before asking for general discussion.

Asking students to take a couple of minutes to write out their initial answers to a question can help. If a student has already written an answer, the step to speaking is much less than answering when asked to respond immediately. Even the shy person will respond when asked, "What did you write?"

Rewarding infrequent contributors at least with a smile helps encourage participation even if the contribution has to be developed or corrected. Calling students by name seems to encourage freer communication. Seating is important too. Rooms with seats in a circle help tremendously.

Getting to know the nonparticipant is also helpful. For example, I have found that it is helpful to ask students to write a brief life history indicating their interests and experiences relevant to the course. These autobiographies help me to gain a better knowledge of each student as an individual, to know what problems or illustrations will be of particular interest to a number of students, and to know on whom I can call for special information. One of the best ways of getting nonparticipants into the discussion is to ask them to contribute in a problem area in which they have special knowledge.

The technique of asking for a student's special knowledge deals directly with one of the major barriers to class discussion—fear of being wrong. No one likes to look foolish, especially in a situation where mistakes may be pounced upon by a teacher or other students. One of the major reasons for the deadliness of a question in which the teacher asks a student to fill in the one right word—such as, "This is an example of what?"—is that it puts the student on the spot. There is an infinity of wrong answers, and obviously the teacher knows the one right answer; so why should the student risk making a mistake when the odds are so much against the student? And even if the answer is obvious: Why look like a pawn for the teacher?

One way of putting the student in a more favorable position is to ask general questions that have no wrong answers. For example, you can ask, "How do you feel about this?" or "How does this look to you?" as a first step in analysis of a problem. Students' feelings or perceptions may not be the same as yours, but as reporters of their own feelings, they can't be challenged as being inaccurate. While such an approach by no means eliminates anxiety about participation (for an answer involves revealing oneself as a person), it will more often open up discussion that involves the student than will questions of fact. Problem posting, the technique discussed in the previous chapter as a method for establishing objectives during the first day of class, is an example of a discussion technique minimizing risk for students. It can be useful in introducing a new topic at the conclusion of a topic, or for analysis of an experiment or a literary work. An added advantage is that it can be used in large as well as small groups.

Another technique for reducing the risk of participation for students is to ask a question a class period before the discussion and ask students to write out answers involving an example from their own experience. Similarly, one can ask students to bring one question to class for discussion. This helps participation, helps students learn to formulate questions, and also provides feedback for you.

Finally remember that out-of-class learning is often more important than that in class. E-mail, computer conferencing, and other interactive technologies can support active learning, discussion, and debate.

All of these techniques will still not make every student into an active, verbal participant. Two group techniques can help. One is buzz groups; the other is the inner circle technique.

Buzz Groups—Peer Learning

One of the popular techniques for achieving student participation in groups is the buzz session. In this procedure, classes are split into small subgroups for a brief discussion of a problem. Groups can be asked to come up with one hypothesis that they see as relevant, with one application of a principle, with an example of a concept, or with a solution to a problem. In large classes I march up the aisles saying, "Odd," "Even," "Odd," "Even" for each row and ask the "odd" row to turn around to talk to the "even" row behind, forming themselves into groups of four to six. I tell them to first introduce themselves to one another and then to choose a person to report for the group. Next they are to get from each member of the group one idea about the problem or question posed. Finally they are to come up with one idea to report to the total class. I give the group a limited time to work, sometimes five minutes or less, occasionally ten minutes or more, depending on the tasks. Peer-led discussions need not be limited to five or ten minutes or even to the classroom (see the chapter on active learning).

The Inner Circle or Fishbowl

In using the inner circle technique I announce that at the next class meeting we are going to have a class within a class, with several of the students (6 to 15) acting as the discussion group and the others as observers. If the classroom has movable chairs, I then arrange the seating in the form of concentric circles. I am impressed that students who are normally silent will talk when they feel the increased sense of responsibility as members of the inner circle.

THE DISCUSSION MONOPOLIZER*

If you have worked on nonparticipation effectively, the discussion monopolizer is less likely to be a problem, but there will still be classes in which one or two students talk so much that you and the other students become annoyed. As with nonparticipation, one solution is to raise with the class the question of participation in discussion—"Would the class be more effective if participation were more evenly distributed?"

A second technique is to have one or more members of the class act as observers for one or more class periods, reporting back to the class their observations. Perhaps assigning the dominant member to the observer role would help sensitivity.

A third possibility is to audiotape a discussion, and after playing back a portion, ask the class to discuss what might be done to improve the discussion.

A fourth technique is to use buzz groups with one member chosen to be reporter.

Finally, a direct approach should not be ruled out. Talking to the student individually outside class may be the simplest and most effective solution.

HOW CAN WE HAVE A DISCUSSION IF THE STUDENTS HAVEN'T READ THE ASSIGNMENT?

It's hard to have a discussion if students haven't studied the material to be discussed. What to do?

One strategy is to give students questions at the end of one class, asking them to get information on the questions before the next class. You might even give different assignments to teams of students. Another strategy is to ask students to bring one or more questions on the assignment to be turned in at the beginning of the next class.

---

* Be sensitive to the fact that the most common monopolizer is the teacher. In our research, our observers reported that in a typical discussion class the teacher talked 70 to 80 percent of the time.

If there are extenuating circumstances, you (or a student who is prepared) can summarize the needed points. Alternatively, you can give students a few minutes to scan the material before beginning the discussion. If used often, however, such strategies may discourage out-of-class preparation.

If the problem persists, present it to the students. What do they suggest? One likely proposal is a short quiz at the beginning of class—which usually works. However, you'd like to have students motivated to study without the threat of a quiz. Usually the quiz can be phased out once students find that discussion really requires preparation and that the assignments are more interesting as they develop competence.

HANDLING ARGUMENTS AND EMOTIONAL REACTIONS

In any good discussion conflicts will arise. If such conflicts are left ambiguous and uncertain, they, like repressed conflicts in the individual, may cause continuing trouble. You can focus these conflicts so that they may contribute to learning.

- Reference to the text or other authority may be one method of resolution, if the solution depends on certain facts.

- Using the conflict as the basis for a library assignment for the class or a delegated group is another solution.

- If there is an experimentally verified answer, this is a good opportunity to review the method by which the answer could be determined.

- If the question is one of values, your goal may be to help students become aware of the values involved.

- Sometimes students will dispute your statements or decisions. Such disagreements may often be resolved by a comparison of the evidence for both points of view, but since teachers are human, they are all too likely to become drawn into an argument in which they finally rest on their own authority. To give yourself time to think, as well as to indicate understanding and acceptance of the students' point, I suggest listing the objections on the board. (Incidentally, listing evidence or arguments is also a good technique when the conflict is between two members of the class.) Such listing tends to prevent repetition of the same arguments.

■ In any case it should be clear that conflict may be an aid to learning, and the instructor need not frantically seek to smother it.

■ If you're having problems with a particular student, check the chapters "Problem Students" and "Counseling, Advising, and Educating."

The Two-Column Method

Another of Maier's techniques, the two-column method, is a particularly effective use of the board in a situation in which there is a conflict or where a strong bias prevents full consideration of alternative points of view. Experimental studies (Hovland, 1957) suggest that, when people hear arguments against their point of view, they become involved in attempting to refute the arguments rather than listening and understanding. Disagreement thus often tends to push the debaters into opposite corners, in which every idea is right or wrong, good or bad, black or white. The truth is often more complex and not in either extreme.

The two-column method is designed to permit consideration of complications and alternatives. As in problem posting, before the issues are debated, all the arguments on each side are listed on the board. The leader heads two columns "Favorable to A" and "Favorable to B" or "For" and "Against" and then asks for the facts or arguments that group members wish to present. The instructor's task is to understand and record in brief the arguments presented. If someone wishes to debate an argument presented for the other side, the instructor simply tries to reformulate the point so that it can be listed as a positive point in the debater's own column. But even though an argument is countered or protested it should not be erased, for the rules of the game are that the two columns are to include all ideas that members consider relevant. Evaluation can come later.

When the arguments have been exhausted, discussion can turn to the next step in problem solving. At this point the group can usually identify areas of agreement and disagreement, and in many cases it is already clear that the situation is neither black nor white. Now the issue becomes one of *relative* values rather than good versus bad. When discussion is directed toward agreements, some of the personal animosity is avoided, and some underlying feelings may be brought to light. The next stages of the discussion are thus more likely to be directed toward constructive problem solving.

Challenges and disagreements may be an indication of an alert, involved class. But the instructor should also be aware of the possibility that they may be symptoms of frustration arising because the students are uncertain of what the problem is or how to go about solving it.

Emotional Reactions

Although conflicts may arouse emotions, emotions may also arise because a topic touches a particular student in a vulnerable spot. You may notice during a discussion that one student is near tears or that a student is visibly flushed and angry. This poses a dilemma for you. You want to be helpful, but you also must have respect for the student's feelings. What should you do?

A lot depends on your knowledge of the student. If you say, "Joe (Jo), you seem to have some feelings about this," will the student be embarrassed?

If you don't wish to call attention to the student at the moment, you might say before the end of the class period, "Joe (Jo), would you stop by for a moment after class?" You could then say, "You seemed to be upset when we discussed —. Would you like to come to my office to talk about it?"

Sometimes the best thing to do is simply wait to see if the student brings the feelings out in the discussion. If the student seems angry, I wouldn't ordinarily say, "Why are you so angry?" but if you know the student well and the class is a small one in which there is a good deal of acceptance of one another, that might be appropriate. So what will work depends on the student, the class, and your relationship with the student. Whatever the case, try to be understanding and nonconfrontational. Keep cool. This, too, will pass.

TEACHING STUDENTS HOW TO LEARN THROUGH DISCUSSION

I have already implied that classes don't automatically carry on effective discussions. To a large extent students have to learn how to learn from discussions just as they have to learn how to learn from reading. How can this occur?

First, they need to understand the importance of discussion for learning. Expressing one's understanding or ideas and getting reactions from other students and the teacher makes a big difference in learning, retention, and use of knowledge.

What skills need to be learned? One skill is clarification of what the group is trying to do—becoming sensitive to confusion about what the group is working on and asking for clarification.

A second attribute is the students' development of a willingness to talk about their own ideas openly and to listen and respond to others' ideas. It is important for students to realize that it is easy to deceive themselves about their own insights or understandings and that verbalizing an idea is one way of getting checks on and extensions of it. Teachers can encourage development of listening skills by asking one group member to repeat or paraphrase what another said before responding to it, and repeatedly pointing out the purpose and values students gain from discussion.

A third skill is planning. Discussions are sometimes frustrating because they are only getting under way when the end of the class period comes. If this results in continuation of the discussion outside the class, so much the better, but often learning is facilitated if students learn to formulate the issues and determine what out-of-class study or followup is necessary before the group breaks up.

A fourth skill is building on others' ideas in such a way as to increase their motivation rather than make them feel punished or forgotten. Often students see discussion as a competitive situation in which they win by tearing down other students' ideas. As Haines and McKeachie (1967) have shown, cooperative discussion methods encourage more effective work and better morale than competitive methods.

A fifth attribute is skill in evaluation. If classes are to learn how to discuss issues effectively, they need to review periodically what aspects of their discussion are proving to be worthwhile and what barriers, gaps, or difficulties have arisen. Some classes reserve the last five minutes of the period for a review of the discussion's effectiveness.

A sixth attribute is sensitivity to feelings of other group members. Students need to become aware of the possibility that feelings of rejection, frustration, dependence, and so on may influence group members' participation in discussion. Sometimes it is more productive to recognize the underlying feeling than to focus on the content of an individual's statement. One way of helping students develop these skills is to use student-led discussions preceded by a training meeting with the student leader.

Peer learning techniques, such as those discussed in the chapter on active learning, help in building the sense of community that enables students to confront one another openly and helpfully. Such community does not come overnight, but building a sense of community may be even more important for student learning than covering every chapter in the textbook.

TAKING MINUTES OR NOTES, SUMMARIZING

One of the problems with discussion is students' feeling that they have learned less than in lectures where they have taken voluminous notes. Thus I like to summarize our progress at the end of the period or ask students to contribute to a summary. Better yet, use the last 5 to 10 minutes for getting feedback. For example, ask students to write a summary of the issues discussed, the pros and cons, and their conclusions.

ONLINE DISCUSSIONS

E-mail, list serves, computer conferences, and other online experiences extend the opportunities for discussion. They also provide practice in writing. They can facilitate cooperative learning. The impersonality of e-mail may reduce the inhibitions of those who are shy in the classroom, but research suggests that it may also reduce inhibitions against rudeness. Thus, in initiating an online discussion, remind your students that respect for others and rational support for arguments are just as important online as in the classroom.

You also need to be clear about your expectations for participation. I have used online discussions off and on since it first became possible to do so, but my success has been variable. If I simply recommend use of the opportunity, a few students who love computers participate, but their discussions often have little to do with the course. I tried posting questions, topics, or problems, and that helped some, but many students still did not participate. One of my teaching assistants, Richard Velayo, tackled this problem for his dissertation. He found that what worked best was to require discussion of a question each week.

IN CONCLUSION

Teaching by discussion differs from lecturing because you never know what is going to happen. At times this is anxiety-producing, at times frustrating, but more often exhilarating. It provides constant challenges and opportunities for both you and the students to learn. When you can listen for several minutes without intervening, you will have succeeded.

Supplementary Reading

S. D. Brookfield and S. Preskill, *Discussion as a Way of Teaching: Tools and Techniques for Democratic Classrooms* (San Francisco: Jossey-Bass, 1999).

J. H. Clarke, "Designing Discussions as Group Inquiry," *College Teaching,* 1988, *36*(4), 140–146.

A. Collins, "Different Goals of Inquiry Teaching," *Questioning Exchange,* 1988, *2*(1), 39–45.

J. T. Dillon, *Teaching and the Art of Questioning* (Bloomington, IN: Phi Delta Kappa Educational Foundation, 1983).

B. S. Fuhrmann and A. F. Grasha, *A Practical Handbook for College Teachers* (Boston: Little, Brown, 1983), Chapter 6.

S. L. Yelon and C. R. Cooper, "Discussion: A Naturalistic Study of a Teaching Method," *Instructional Science,* 1984, *13*, 213–224.

5 How to Make Lectures More Effective

■ ■ ■ ■ ■ ■ ■ ■ ■ ■ ■ ■ ■ ■ ■ ■ ■ ■

The lecture is probably the oldest teaching method and still the method most widely used in universities throughout the world. Through the ages a great deal of practical wisdom about techniques of lecturing has accumulated. Effective lecturers combine the talents of scholar, writer, producer, comedian, entertainer, and teacher in ways that contribute to student learning. Nevertheless, it is also true that few college professors combine these talents in optimal ways and that even the best lecturers are not always in top form. Lectures have survived despite the invention of printing, television, and computers.

Is the lecture an effective method of teaching? If it is, under what conditions is it most effective? These questions will be answered not only in light of research on the lecture as a teaching method but also in terms of analyses of the cognitive processes used by students in lecture classes.

RESEARCH ON THE EFFECTIVENESS OF LECTURES

A large number of studies have compared the effectiveness of lectures with other teaching methods. The results are discouraging for those who lecture. Discussion methods are superior to lectures in student retention of information after the end of a course;

transfer of knowledge to new situations; development of problem solving, thinking, or attitude change; and motivation for further learning (McKeachie et al., 1990).

Similarly, print offers advantages over lecture. Students can read faster than lecturers can lecture, and they can go back when they don't understand, skip material that is irrelevant, and review immediately or later. Lectures go at the lecturer's pace, and students who fall behind are out of luck. But don't despair; lectures can still be useful.

WHAT ARE LECTURES GOOD FOR?

- Presenting up-to-date information (There is typically a gap between the latest scholarship and its appearance in a textbook.)
- Summarizing material scattered over a variety of sources
- Adapting material to the background and interests of a particular group of students at a particular time and place
- Helping students read more effectively by providing an orientation and conceptual framework
- Focusing on key concepts, principles, or ideas

Lectures also have motivational values apart from their cognitive content. By helping students become aware of a problem, of conflicing points of view, or of challenges to ideas they have previously taken for granted, the lecturer can stimulate interest in further learning in an area. Moreover, the lecturer's own attitudes and enthusiasm have an important effect on student motivation. Research on student ratings of teaching as well as on student learning indicates that the enthusiasm of the lecturer is an important factor in effecting student learning and motivation. You may feel that enthusiasm is not learnable. Clearly some people are more enthusiastic and expressive than others, but you can develop in this area just as in others. Try to put into each lecture something that you are really excited about. Notice how your voice and gestures show more energy and expressiveness. Now try carrying some of that intensity and animation over into other topics. Like other learned behaviors, this takes practice, but you can do it. Murray (1997) showed that enthusiastic teachers move around, make eye contact with students, and use more gestures and vocal variation, and that teachers could learn these behaviors. Both research and theory support the usefulness of enthusiastic behaviors in maintaining student attention.*

The lecturer also models ways of approaching problems, portraying a scholar in action in ways that are difficult for other media or methods of instruction to achieve. You can say, "Here is how I go about solving this kind of problem (analyzing this phenomenon, etc). Now you try it." This can be either an in-class or an out-of-class assignment. In fact, there is some evidence suggesting that one of the advantages of live professors is the tendency of people to model themselves after other individuals whom they perceive as living, breathing human beings with characteristics that can be admired and emulated. So lectures can be effective—but sometimes more effective in stimulating our own learning and thinking than in stimulating that of the students!

A LITTLE BIT OF THEORY

The preceding section has included a good bit of theory of learning and motivation, but I want to be more explicit about one aspect of the cognitive theory of learning and memory. As I noted in the preceding chapter, memory depends heavily on the learner's activity—thinking about and elaborating on new knowledge. A key difference between modern theories of memory and earlier theory is that earlier theory thought of knowledge as single associations, in some ways like tucking each bit of knowledge into a pigeonhole. Now we think of knowledge as being stored in structures such as networks with linked concepts, facts, and principles. The lecture thus needs to build a bridge between what is in the students' minds and the structures in the subject matter. Metaphors, examples, and demonstrations are the elements of the bridge. Providing a meaningful organization is

---

* Don't feel that you have to show high energy every minute. There will be times when calm, quiet, slow speech may be needed—times when you may need to wait and reflect before responding.

thus a key function of the lecture. Our research (Naveh-Benjamin et al., 1989) showed that students begin a course with little organization, but develop conceptual structures during a course that more and more closely resemble that of the instructor.

PLANNING LECTURES

A typical lecture strives to present a systematic, concise summary of the knowledge to be covered in the day's assignment. Chang, Crombag, van der Drift, and Moonen (1983, p. 21) call this approach "conclusion oriented." *Don't do it!* The lecturer's task in university teaching is not to be an abstractor of encyclopedias, but to *teach students to learn and think.*

I was a conclusion-oriented lecturer for 30 years. Now more of my lectures involve analyzing materials, formulating problems, developing hypotheses, bringing evidence to bear, criticizing and evaluating alternative solutions—revealing methods of learning and thinking.

One of the implications of the theoretical approach I have taken is that what is an ideal approach to lecturing early in a course is likely to be inappropriate later in the course. As noted earlier, the way students process verbal material depends on the structures that not only enable them to process bigger and bigger chunks of subject matter but also give them tacit knowledge of the methods, procedures, and conventions used in the field and by you as a lecturer. Intentionally or not, you are teaching students how to become more skilled in learning from your lectures.

Because this is so, one should in the first weeks of a course go more slowly, pause to allow students with poor backgrounds time to take notes, and give more everyday types of examples. Pausing to write a phrase or sketch a relationship on the chalkboard will not only give students a chance to catch up but also provide visual cues that can serve as points of reference later. Later in the term, students should be able to process bigger blocks of material more quickly.

Adapting to the differences in students' knowledge from the beginning to the later stages of a course is but one example of the principle that one key to good lecturing is an awareness of the audience, not only in lecturing but in preparing the lecture. In every class there is student diversity—not only in background knowledge but also in motivation, skills for learning, beliefs about what learning involves, and preferences for different ways of learning (learning styles).

PREPARING YOUR LECTURE NOTES

One of the security-inducing features of lectures is that one can prepare a lecture with some sense of control over the content and organization of the class period. In lectures the instructor is usually in control, and this sense of controlled structure helps the anxious teacher avoid pure panic.

But no matter how thoroughly one has prepared the subject matter of the lecture, one must still face the problem of how to retrieve and deliver one's insights during the class period. If one has plenty of time and is compulsive, one is tempted to write out the lecture verbatim. Don't! Or if you must (and writing it out may be useful in clarifying your thoughts), don't take a verbatim version into the classroom. Few lecturers can read a lecture so well that students stay awake and interested.

At the same time, few teachers can deliver a lecture with no cues at all. Hence you will ordinarily lecture from notes. Most lecturers use an outline or a sequence of cue words and phrases. Try forming your notes as a series of questions.

Day (1980) studied lecture notes used by professors at over 75 colleges and universities. She notes that extensive notes take the instructor out of eye contact with students so that students fall into a passive, nonquestioning role. Day suggests the use of graphic representations to increase teaching flexibility and spontaneity. Tree diagrams, computer flowcharts, or network models enable a teacher to have at hand a representation of the structure that permits one to answer questions without losing track of the relationship of the question to the lecture organization. Pictorial representations using arrows, faces, Venn diagrams, or drawings that symbolize important concepts may not only provide cues for the instructor but can also be placed on PowerPoint or the board to provide additional cues for students.

Color coding your notes with procedural directions to yourself also helps. I have a tendency to run overtime, so I put time cues in the margin to remind me to check. I also put in directions to myself, such as

- "Put on board." (usually a key concept or relationship)
- "Check student understanding. Ask for examples."
- "Ask students for a show of hands."
- "Put students in pairs to discuss this."

Whatever your system, indicate *signposts* to tell students what is ahead, *transitions* that tell students when you are finishing one topic and moving to the next, *key points* or *concepts*, and *links* such as "consequently," "therefore," and "because."*

Finally, allow time for questions from students, for new examples or ideas that come to mind during the lecture and for your own misestimation of the time a topic will require. If perchance you finish early, let the students use the remaining time to write a summary.

ORGANIZATION OF LECTURES

In thinking about lecture organization, most teachers think first about the structure of the subject matter, then try to organize the content in some logical fashion, such as building from specifics to generalization or deriving specific implications from general principles. Too often we get so immersed in "covering" the subject that we forget to ask, "What do I really want students to remember from this lecture next week, next year?"

Some common organizing principles used by lecturers are cause to effect; time sequence (for example, stories); parallel organization such as phenomenon to theory to evidence; problem

---

* These four types of signposts are discussed in George Brown, *Lecturing and Explaining* (London: Methuen, 1978).

to solution; pro versus con to resolution; familiar to unfamiliar; and concept to application. Leith (1977) has suggested that different subjects are basically different in the ways in which progress is made in the field. Some subjects are organized in a linear or hierarchical fashion in which one concept builds on a preceding one. In such subjects one must follow a particular sequence of ideas in order to reach a sophisticated level. Other subjects are organized more nearly in the manner of a spiral or helix in which the path from one level to the next is not linear but rather depends on accumulating a number of related ideas before the next level can be achieved; and any of the related ideas at one level need not precede other ideas at that level.

The logical structure of one's subject should be one factor determining the lecture organization, but equally important is the cognitive structure in the students' minds. If we are to teach our students effectively, we need to bridge the gap between the structure in the subject matter and structures in the students' minds. As is indicated in all of the chapters in this book, you are not making impressions on a blank slate. Rather our task in teaching is to help students reorganize existing cognitive structures or to add new dimensions or new features to existing structures. Thus the organization of the lecture needs to take account of the student's existing knowledge and expectations as well as the structure of the subject matter. Analogies linking new ideas to similar ones that students already know can help.

Remember that what you are trying to do is get an organization into your students' heads that will help them fit in relevant facts and form a base for further learning and thinking. Handing out a skeletal outline with main headings and space for students to fill in their own notes will help (Kiewra, 1989).

The Introduction

One suggestion for organization is that the *introduction* of the lecture should point to a gap in the student's existing cognitive structure or should challenge or raise a question about something in the student's existing method of organizing material in order to arouse curiosity (Berlyne, 1954a, 1954b). There is a good deal of research on the role of prequestions in directing attention to features of written texts. Prequestions in the introduction of a lecture may help students to discriminate between more and less important features of lectures. For example, before a lecture on cognitive changes in aging, I ask, "Do you get more or less intelligent as you get older?" and "What is a fair test of intelligence for older people?" Such questions may help create expectations that enable students to allocate their cognitive capacity more effectively. If students know what they are expected to learn from a lecture, they learn more of that material (sometimes at the expense of other material; Royer, 1977).

Another approach is to begin with a demonstration, example, case, or application that captures attention. In many fields it is possible to begin some lectures with presentation of a problem or case from a current newspaper or television show, then ask students how they would think about it in the light of this course, or alternatively illustrate in the lecture how experts in this field would think about it.

The Body of the Lecture

In organizing the *body* of the lecture, the most common error is probably that of trying to include too much. The enemy of learning is the teacher's need to cover the content at all costs. When I began lecturing, my mentor told me, "If you get across three or four points in a lecture so that students understand and remember them, you've done well." Lecturers very often overload the students' information processing capacity so that they become less able to understand the material than if fewer points had been presented. David Katz (1950), a pioneer Gestalt psychologist, called this phenomenon "mental dazzle." He suggested that, just as too much light causes our eyes to be dazzled so that we cannot see anything, so too can too many new ideas overload processing capacity so that we cannot understand anything.

Use the board, an overhead projector, or PowerPoint to give the students cues to the organization of the lecture. Going to the board to construct an outline or to write key words is useful in three ways:

1. It gives a *visual* representation to supplement your oral presentation. Using a diagram or other graphic representation will help visualization.
2. Movement (change) helps retain (or regain) attention.
3. It gives students a chance to catch up with what you've said (perchance to think!).

Using Examples   Move from the concrete to the abstract. To link what is in your head with what is in the students' heads, you need to use examples that relate the subject to the students' experience and knowledge. I am not as effective a teacher today as I was decades ago because I do not know the students' culture and am thus limited in finding vivid examples of a concept in students' daily lives. Since no single example can represent a concept fully, you usually need to give more than one example. Concept formation research suggests that examples differing from one another are likely to be most effective if you point out the essential features of the concept exemplified in each example. And, most important, give students a chance to give examples.

Explaining   George Brown (1978) describes three types of explanations: explaining *what* something is or means, explaining *how* to do something, and explaining *why*. In preparing an explanation, think about what your students already know that is relevant, what they need to know, and what is likely to be interesting. Write down the question your explanation will answer and the analogies, metaphors, examples, or key points you will use. Plan to summarize your explanation.

Periodic Summaries Within the Lecture   From our knowledge of students' note-taking behavior we know that students would be better able to learn from lectures if there were periodic summaries of preceding material. These give students a chance to catch up on material covered when they were not tuned in and also give them a check on possible misperceptions based on inadequate or misleading expectations. Repeat main points once, twice, thrice, during the lecture. Such summaries can help make clear to students transitions from one theme to another, so that they are aided in organizing the material not only in their notes but in their minds. In fact, you might try thinking of your lecture as two or more minilectures separated by short periods for questions, discussion, or writing.

Checking Student Understanding   Although it may seem irrational to cover material when students are not learning from it, one should not underestimate the compulsion one feels to get through one's lecture notes. A remedy for this compulsion is to put into the lecture notes reminders to oneself to check the students' understanding—both by looking for nonverbal cues of bewilderment or of lack of attention and by raising specific questions that will test the students' understanding.

Most lecturers recognize that they need to check student understanding periodically; so they ask, "Any questions?" and after three to five seconds without response assume that everyone understands. Not so! If you really want to know, give students a minute to write down a question, then have them compare notes with students sitting near them before asking for questions. You'll get some.

Once you have used this procedure a few times, so that students have found that questioning is not dangerous, you can simply say, "What questions do you have?"

The Conclusion   In the conclusion of the lecture, one has the opportunity to make up for lapses in the body of the lecture. Encouraging students to formulate questions or asking questions oneself can facilitate understanding and memory. By making the oral headings visible once again, by recapitulating major points, by proposing unanswered questions to be treated in the reading assignments or the future lectures, and by creating an anticipation of the future, the lecturer can help students learn. One good (and humbling) technique is to announce that you will ask a student to summarize the lecture at the end of the period. Another— less threatening—is to have students spend three minutes writing a summary of main points. Either method helps the process of elaboration which is critical for memory.

Having suggested all this, I must admit that my own greatest problem as a lecturer is that I never seem to be ready for the conclusion until it is already past time to dismiss the class.

HOW CAN LECTURES BE IMPROVED?

The message of this chapter is that one way of improving lectures is to think about how students process lectures. What are students trying to do during a lecture?

As one looks at students at a lecture and observes their behavior, the most impressive thing one notices is the passive role students have in most classrooms. Some students are having difficulty in staying awake; others are attempting to pass the time as easily as possible by reading other materials, counting lecturer mannerisms, or simply doodling and listening in a relatively effortless manner. Most students are taking notes. Ideally, many students are attempting to construct knowledge by linking what the lecturer says with what they already know.

Attention

One of the factors determining students' success in information processing is their ability to attend to the lecture. Attention basically involves focusing one's cognitions on those things that are changing, novel, or motivating. Individuals have a limited capacity for attending to the varied features of their environment. The individual's total capacity for attention may vary with the degree of activation or motivation. At any one time, part of the capacity may be devoted to the task at hand (in this case listening to the lecturer), part may be involved in taking notes, and part may be left over to shift primary attention to distractions or daydreams when boredom occurs.

Hartley and Davies' (1978) review of the research on attention of students during lectures reports that attention typically increases from the beginning of the lecture to ten minutes into the lecture and decreases after that point.

One of the characteristics of a passive lecture situation in which a lecturer is using few devices to get students to think actively about the content of the lecture is that attention tends to drift. Probably all of us have had the experience of listening to a speaker and finding with a start that we have not heard the speaker for some time because our attention has drifted on to thoughts that are tangential to the lecturer's theme.

What Can Be Done to Get Attention?

In determining how to allocate attention, students use various strategies. Any lecturer knows that one way of getting attention is to precede the statement by the phrase, "This will be on the test." In addition, students listen for particular words or phrases that indicate to them that something is worth noting and remembering. Statements that enumerate or list are likely to be on tests and thus are likely to be attended to.

Changes in the environment recruit attention. The ability of changes to capture attention can work to the advantage of the lecturer. Variation in pitch, intensity, and pace of the lecture; visual cues such as gestures, facial expression, movement to the board; the use of demonstrations or audiovisual aids—all of these recruit and maintain attention to the lecture.

Auditory attention is directed to some extent by visual attention. Distracting movements in the classroom are thus likely to cause students to fail to recall what the lecturer has said. On the positive side, students' comprehension is greater when the students can see the speaker's face and lips (Campbell, 1999). Look at your audience; eye contact helps communication.

Motivation is important in holding student attention. Linking lectures to student interests, giving examples that are vivid and intriguing, building suspense toward resolution of a conflict— these are all techniques of gaining and holding attention.

All of these devices will help, but recall the Hartley and Davies finding that students' attention tends to wane after ten minutes. The best device for maintaining attention is to break up the lecture rather than trying to hold attention for an hour or more. Student activities such as problem posting, the minute paper,* pairing, or small-group activities can reactivate students' attention.** If you spot signs of drowsiness or fidgeting, ask students to stand up and stretch. Bligh's research summary indicated that

---

* The minute paper (Wilson, 1986) is described later in this chapter in the section "How to Get Students Actively Thinking in a Lecture Situation." The name of the University of California physics professor who invented the minute paper was revealed to me just as this edition was going to press. It is Charles Schwartz.

** Brown and Atkins (1988, p. 29) list these and other student activities to get students' attention and thinking during lectures.

the gain in learning after such a break more than compensates for any learning that might have occurred in the time taken for the break (Bligh, 2000).

TEACHING STUDENTS HOW TO BE BETTER LISTENERS

We assume that listening is an innate skill, but you can train your students to be better listeners. For example, you might begin by asking students to write for one minute on "What do I hope to get out of this lecture?" or "What was the most important point in the reading assignment for the day?" Then explain how this strategy will help them to be more effective listeners in any lecture. Both of these strategies act as a "warm-up," focusing attention and activating relevant prior knowledge.

Another useful strategy is to ask students to listen to you (for 5 to 15 minutes) without taking notes and then to write a summary. You might then ask them to compare their summaries with those of one or two classmates sitting near them.

A related strategy is to tell students that you will give them five minutes at the end of the lecture to summarize the main points of the lecture for someone sitting near them. At the end of the class period, ask them what effect this had on their listening to the lecture, and point out that they can use this approach to lectures even if they summarize them only in their own notes.

HOW DO STUDENTS PROCESS THE CONTENT OF A LECTURE?

Let's assume that students are allocating attention appropriately to the lecture. This alone, however, does not ensure that the content of the lecture will be understood, remembered, and applied appropriately. Even though students are trying to meet the demands of the situation, they may differ in the ways they go about processing the words that they have heard.

Marton and Säljö (1976a, 1976b) and other researchers at the University of Göteborg have described differences in the way students go about trying to learn educational materials. Some students process the material as little as possible, simply taking as many verbatim notes as they can. This would be described by Marton as a "surface approach." Other students try to see implications of what the lecturer is saying, relate what is currently being said to other information either in the lecture or in their own experience and reading, and try to understand what the author intended. They elaborate and translate the instructor's words into their own. They may question. This more thoughtful and more active kind of listening is what Marton and Säljö refer to as "deep processing."

Experienced students can probably vary their strategies from verbatim memory to memory of concepts, depending on the demands of the situation. Generally, deep processing better enables students to remember and use knowledge for thinking and further learning. Pointing out relationships, asking rhetorical questions, or asking questions to be answered by class members are ways of encouraging deeper processing. You can also ask for examples of how students apply concepts to their own experiences, thus encouraging all students to realize that it is important to try to think about how concepts relate to oneself.

SHOULD STUDENTS TAKE NOTES?

Note taking is one of the activities by which students attempt to stay attentive, but note taking is also an aid to memory. *Working memory,* or *short-term memory,* is a term used to describe the fact that one can hold only a given amount of material in mind at one time. When the lecturer presents a succession of new concepts, students' faces begin to show signs of anguish and frustration; some write furiously in their notebooks, while others stop writing in complete discouragement. Note taking thus is dependent on one's ability to maintain attention, understand what is being said, and hold it in working memory long enough to write it down. Studies of student notes show, not surprisingly, that students fail to get most of the lecture content into their notes, and some of the notes are wrong. However, research supports two values of note taking. One is that the notes provide an external memory which can be reviewed later; the other is that note taking involves elaboration and transformation of ideas, which aids memory (Hartley & Davies, 1978; Peper & Mayer, 1978). But note taking has costs as well as benefits. Student note-taking strategies differ. Some students take copious notes; others take none. We know that cognitive capacity is limited; that is, people can take in, understand, and store only so much information in any brief period of time. Information will be processed more effectively if the student is actively engaged in note taking—analyzing and processing the information rather than passively soaking it up, but taking notes takes capacity that may be needed for comprehension if material is difficult. Thus, encourage students to take *fewer* notes and to listen carefully when you are introducing new, difficult material. They can then fill in their notes after class.

Students' ability to process information depends on the degree to which the information can be integrated or "chunked." No one has great ability at handling large numbers of unrelated items in active memory. Thus when students are in an area of new concepts or when the instructor is using language that is not entirely familiar to the students, students may be processing the lecture word by word or phrase by phrase and lose the sense of a sentence or of a paragraph before the end of the thought is reached. This means that lecturers need to be aware of instances in which new words or concepts are being introduced and to build in greater redundancy, as well as pauses during which students can catch up and get appropriate notes.

Snow and Peterson (1980) point out that brighter students benefit more from taking notes than less able students. For students with less background knowledge, note taking takes capacity needed for listening and comprehending, so they simply miss much of what is being said. This is not simply a matter of intelligence; rather, a student's ability to maintain materials in memory while taking notes and even to process and think about relationships between one idea and other ideas depends on the knowledge or cognitive structures the student has available for organizing and relating the material.

Some faculty members hand out prepared notes or encourage the preparation of notes for students to purchase. Hartley's research, as well as that of Annis (1981) and Kiewra (1989), suggests that a skeletal outline is helpful to students, but that with detailed notes students relax into passivity. It is better simply to provide an overall framework which they can fill in by selecting important points and interpreting them in their own words. Because student capacity for information processing is limited and because students stop and go over a confusing part of a lecture again, you need to build more redundancy into your lectures than into writing, and you need to build in pauses where students can catch up and think rather than simply struggle to keep up.

One can train students to write better notes by collecting student notes, evaluating the degree to which they summarize, translate, and show relationships as opposed to simply representing more or less verbatim accounts.

HOW TO GET STUDENTS ACTIVELY THINKING IN A LECTURE SITUATION

As we have seen, a major problem with the lecture is that students assume a passive, nonthinking, information receiving role. Yet, if they are to remember and use the information, they need to be actively engaged in thinking about the content presented. One easy and effective device is the "minute paper." The minute paper is, as its title indicates, a paper literally written in a minute (or it can be a two-minute or three-minute paper). Announce at the beginning of the class period that you will interrupt your lecture midway through the period so that the students may write a one-minute paper on a topic derived from the lecture or that you will ask them at the end of the lecture to write the most important thing they have learned. Even better, you can ask them also to write the most important thing they learned from the previous week's lecture.

In the chapter "Teaching Large Classes" I describe other activities to stimulate thinking. The chapters "Facilitating Discussion" and "Active Learning" also describe methods for getting discussion in large classes.

Since many students feel that the best way to learn is to listen to an expert, you will need here (as in other departures from lecturing) to explain why active thinking is vital for effective learning.

DISTRIBUTION OF LECTURE AND DISCUSSION TIME

What research adds up to is the use of lecture for communicating information and modeling problem solving, and discussion for practicing problem-solving skills. One way of doing this is to schedule separate lecture and discussion periods. This administrative arrangement is supported by a study in the teaching of psychology in which discussion meetings were substituted for one-third of the lectures (Lifson et al., 1956). There were no significant differences in achievement. However, the partial discussion method, as compared with the all-lecture method, resulted in more favorable student attitudes, which persisted in a followup study two years later.

Warren (1954) compared the effectiveness of one lecture and four recitations to two lectures and three demonstrations per week. The four-recitations plan was superior.

In a course in which the instructors must not only give information but also develop concepts, the use of both lectures and discussions would thus seem to be a logical and popular choice. In the chapter "Teaching Large Classes" I will discuss how to handle discussion sections as well as methods for carrying out discussions in large lecture classes.

IN CONCLUSION

What is the role of the lecturer in higher education? The lecture is sometimes an effective way of communicating information, particularly in classes where variations in student background, ability, or interest make feedback to the lecturer important. We have also shown that the organization and presentation of lectures may influence their effectiveness in achieving application of knowledge or in influencing attitudes. Discussion, however, is likely to be more effective than lecturing in achieving higher-level cognitive and attitudinal objectives.

Becoming conscious of what is going on in the students' heads as we talk; being alert to feedback from students through their facial expressions, nonverbal behavior, and oral comments; adjusting your strategies in reference to these cues—these will help you learn and help students to learn more effectively.

Supplementary Reading

The most comprehensive book on lecturing is Donald Bligh's *What's the Use of Lectures?* (San Francisco: Jossey-Bass, 2000).

A very practical guide for lecturers is George Brown's classic paperback, *Lecturing and Explaining* (London: Methuen, 1978).

Barbara Davis's *Tools for Teaching*, 2nd ed. (San Francisco: Jossey-Bass, 1993) gives practical tips on preparing, delivering, and personalizing lecture classes.

Jerry Evensky's chapter "The Lecture," in L. Lambert, S. L. Tice, and P. Featherstone (eds.), *University Teaching* (Syracuse, NY: Syracuse University Press, 1996) is excellent. I like his statement "You should not think of the lecture as the passive period to be relieved by 'Now we're going to do active learning.'"

6 Assessing, Testing, and Evaluating: Grading Is Not the Most Important Function

When we think about evaluating learning, most of us think about examinations—multiple-choice tests, essay tests, oral examinations, perhaps performance tests. Currently there is much interest in other methods of assessment. In this chapter I will begin with suggestions for conventional testing and then suggest other methods of assessing student learning.

Let me start with nine assertions:

1. What students learn depends as much on your tests and methods of assessment as on your teaching.

2. Don't think of tests simply as a means for assigning grades. Tests should facilitate learning for you as well as for your students.

3. Use some nongraded tests and assessments that provide feedback to the students and you.

4. Check your assessment methods against your goals. Are you really assessing what you hoped to achieve: for example, higher-order thinking?

5. Some goals (values, motivation, attitudes, some skills) may not be measurable by conventional tests. Look for other evidence of their development.

6. Assessment is not synonymous with testing. You can assess students' learning with classroom and out-of-class activities.

7. After the course is over, students will not be able to depend on you to assess the quality of their learning. If one of our goals is continued learning, students need practice in self-assessment.*

8. Don't rely on one or two tests to determine grades. Varied assessments will give you better evidence to determine an appropriate grade.

9. To summarize: assessment is *not* simply an end-of-course exercise to determine student grades. Assessments can be learning experiences for students. Assessment throughout a course communicates your goals to students so that they can learn more effectively; it will identify misunderstandings that will help you teach better; it will help you pace the development of the course; and, yes, it will also help you do a better job of assigning grades.

Since grades in many courses are determined to a great degree by test scores, tests are among the most frustrating aspects of the course to many students and arouse a great deal of overt and covert aggression. If teachers attempt to go beyond the usual practice of asking simply for memory of information from the textbook or lectures, they are immediately deluged with the complaint, "These are the most ambiguous tests I have ever taken!"

REDUCING STUDENT FRUSTRATION AND AGGRESSION

To most beginning teachers the aggression that students direct against them after a test is very disturbing. It is likely to impair the rapport of the instructor with the class and may actually be a block to learning. Hence devices for reducing the aggression seem to be worthwhile.

---

* Peckham and Sutherland (2000) showed that developing accurate student self-assessment requires training and practice. Peer assessment of one another's papers helps develop assessment skill and improves performance (Gibbs, 1999).

The most obvious solution to the problem is to reduce the frustration involved in taking tests. An aid in this area is to emphasize the contribution the course can make to the students' long-range goals, so that the need of a good grade is not the only one involved in the situation. Explaining how and why you test as you do will help. A nongraded practice test will provide guidance. Using periodic assessments of learning (not necessarily graded) to help students assess their own progress and to help you identify problems, with frequent explanations of why and how you test and assess learning, should reduce student anxiety and frustration about testing.

Yet, no matter how much you emphasize long-range goals, the tests will in large measure determine what students do. Do you want the students to memorize details? Then give the usual memory-of-details test.

But if you want more, make your objectives clear, and make sure that your tests measure their attainment. If you used the Bloom Taxonomy of Educational Objectives or Biggs's SOLO Taxonomy as suggested in the chapter "Countdown for Course Preparation," remind the students of these levels before each test. McNett, Harvey, Athanassiou, and Allard (2000) use the Bloom taxonomy as a framework throughout their courses. The levels of thinking described in the taxonomy are discussed early in the course and referred to when research papers or other assignments are made and evaluated.

PLANNING METHODS OF TESTING AND ASSESSMENT

The first step in assessment of learning is to list your goals for the course. Once you have specified objectives you can determine which kind of assessment is appropriate for each. You'll probably be surprised to find out how many of your test items pile up in certain categories. The major error in teacher-made tests is to ask questions about the things that are easiest to measure.

One way of maintaining a balance is to construct a grid, listing objectives along the side of the page and content areas along the top. If you then tally items as you write them, you can monitor the degree to which your test adequately samples the objectives and content desired.

Because some course examinations emphasize recall of facts, many students demand *teaching* that emphasizes memorization of facts. One student wrote on a slip evaluating me, "The instructor is very interesting and worthwhile, but I have rated him low because he doesn't give us enough facts. The sort of job I get will depend on my grades, and I have little chance of beating other students out for an A unless I can get a couple of pages of notes each period."

Students may object at first to tests requiring them to think, but if you emphasize that the tests will measure the students' abilities to use their knowledge, you can greatly influence their goals in the course. This is indicated by a student comment we received: "More of the course should be like the tests. They make us apply what we've learned." Marton and Säljö (1976b) showed that questions demanding understanding rather than memory of detailed facts resulted in differing styles of studying for later tests and better retention. Foos and Fisher (1988) showed that tests requiring inferences enhanced learning more than those requiring memorized knowledge.

Admittedly it is more difficult to devise measures of the more complex, higher-level objectives. Yet the very effort to do so will, I believe, have an influence on student motivation and learning. Moreover, consideration of these objectives may help you break out of the conventional forms of testing. For example, in my classes in introductory psychology, the desired goals include developing greater curiosity about behavior, awareness of dimensions of behavior that might ordinarily be ignored, and increased ability to describe and analyze behavior objectively. To get at this I have sometimes used a film or videotape as a stimulus, with the test questions having to do with the students' reactions to the film; or I have asked students to leave the classroom for 15 minutes and then return and report on some interesting behavior they have observed. I have brought in scientific journals and asked students to find an article of interest and to write their reactions to it. I have asked for analyses of newspaper items to get at the degree to which students can read critically. Using materials with somewhat greater apparent relevance to course objectives than typical test items is more fun for the students taking the test—and more fun to grade.

WHEN TO TEST

Because tests are so important in operationalizing goals and influencing student methods of learning, I give an ungraded quiz during the first week and a graded test after the third or fourth week of a 14-week semester. To reduce the stress I weight early tests very little in determining the final grade. But an early test gets students started, in that they don't delay their studying until the conventional midterm examination, and it will help you to identify problems early, while they are still remediable. Thus early tests should demand the style of learning you expect and need to be constructed carefully, even though their purpose is more motivational and diagnostic than evaluative.

I usually also give midterm and final examinations, but the amount and frequency of tests should depend on the background of your students. In a first-year course in an area new to students, frequent short tests early in the term facilitate learning, as demonstrated in the Personalized System of Instruction (Keller, 1968). Generally, however, I want to wean students from studying for tests, so that they become lifelong learners who will be able to evaluate their own learning. This implies less frequent testing as learners become more experienced. It probably also implies questions requiring broader integration and more detailed analysis as the learners advance. For this reason my tests are all cumulative; that is, they cover material previously tested as well as material learned since the last test. Give the students a chance to comment on the dates of tests or other assessments. They may know of potential conflicting events that could influence due dates.

TEST CONSTRUCTION

In planning your tests you may want to use a mix of different types of questions in order to balance measurements of the varied goals of education. The following sections describe the strengths and weaknesses of each type of question, as well as tips on constructing items.

Choosing the Type of Question

The instructor who is about to give an examination is in a conflict situation. There are two time-consuming procedures involved in the administration of an examination: the first is the construction of the examination; the second is the grading. Unfortunately, it appears to be generally true that the examinations that are easiest to construct are the most difficult to grade and vice versa.

Teachers often choose questions solely in terms of class size, using multiple-choice tests for large classes, short-answer questions for medium-sized classes, and essay questions for small classes. Class size is obviously an important factor, but your educational goals should take precedence. This almost always implies use of some essay questions, problems, or other items requiring analysis, integration, or application.

Problems   In mathematics, science, and some other disciplines, a test typically consists of problems. The value of problems depends on the degree to which they elicit the sort of problem-solving skills that are your goals. Some problems are too trite and stereotypic to have much value as indicators of whether or not students understand the steps they are following. In other cases the answer depends to such a large extent on tedious calculations that only a small sample of problems can be tested. In such cases you might provide calculations leading up to a certain point and ask the student to complete the problem, or you might use a multiple-choice question about the proper procedure; for example, "Which of the following problems can be solved by procedure x?" Many teachers now use problems that may be solved in more than one way or that have more than one satisfactory answer.

Short-Answer Items   An example of a short-answer item might be this: "Give one example from your own experience of the concept of elaboration." In responding, a student might describe an experience in explaining a concept to another student or in thinking of the relationship of a fact to a general principle.

Such a question is restricted enough that it is not often difficult to judge whether the expected answer is there. Furthermore, such questions can be presented in a format that allows only a small amount of space for the answer. The student's tendency to employ the "shotgun" approach to the examination is thus inhibited. Short-answer questions permit coverage of assigned materials without asking for petty details. Unfortunately, many short-answer questions test only recall of specific facts.

Short-answer questions can do better than testing facts. If you are trying to develop skill in analysis or diagnosis, for example, you may present case material or description of an experiment and ask the students what questions they would ask. You can then provide additional information that the students can use in an analysis. Or a short-answer question can ask students to solve a problem or propose a hypothesis relevant to information learned earlier. An example is the following question from a course on the psychology of aging:

1. Given the *differences* in ways in which men and women experience middle age, and the fact that depression rises as a psychiatric symptom in middle age, how might the *causes* of the depression differ for men and women at this time in life?

Essay Items   Although the short-answer examination is very useful in certain situations, I would recommend that, if possible, you include at least one essay question on examinations in most college courses. Experiments indicate that students study more efficiently for essay-type examinations than for objective tests (d'Ydewalle et al., 1983; McClusky, 1934; Monaco, 1977). Thus in addition to the values of essay tests as evaluation devices, you should take into consideration their potential educational value as stimuli to student reflection about conceptual relationships, possible applications, or aspects of thinking. One strategy is to pass out several questions the week before the test and tell students that these are the sorts of questions you will use; that, in fact, you may even use one of these very questions.

Where the tests can be returned with comments, essay examinations may give students practice in organized, creative thinking about a subject and an opportunity to check their thinking against the standards of someone with more experience and ability in the field. Johnson (1975) demonstrated that, when marginal comments on earlier tests emphasized creativity, creativity on the final exam was improved.

Finally, if you read the examinations yourself (or at least some of them), you get some excellent information on what students are learning. While the teacher can also learn from students' responses to objective tests, the impact on the teacher of what students are learning seems to be greater and more vivid in reading essay tests.

True-False Items   Although true-false examinations are rather easy to make up, I don't ordinarily advocate their use. Toppino & Brochin (1989) showed that students tend after the test to remember the false items as being true—not conducive to achieving your objectives. If you do use true-false items, ask students to explain their answers. This will encourage reflection and help you understand why there were some common misunderstandings.

Multiple-Choice and Matching Items   It is improbable that most teachers can adequately measure all their objectives with a test made up entirely of multiple-choice questions. Matching questions are similar to multiple-choice, in that the student must discriminate between the correct answer and other choices. Nonetheless, for some purposes multiple-choice items are useful. They can measure both simple knowledge and precise discrimination. They can measure ability to apply concepts or principles; they can assess elements of problem solving. But they are not likely to assess organization of ideas, conceptual relationships, or many of the skills involved in higher-order thinking.

Good multiple-choice questions are difficult to construct. (As a matter of fact, the greater your experience in their construction, the more you realize how long it takes per item to construct a reasonably fair, accurate, and inclusive question.) Because of this difficulty, the construction of such items is probably not worthwhile unless they will be administered to several hundred students, either in a single year or in successive years. The box that follows contains hints for their construction.

Constructing Multiple-Choice Items

1. Teachers' manuals that are provided for many textbooks contain multiple-choice items. You will not be able to rely on a manual as the source of all your questions, because it often will not contain many good questions and may cover only textbook material. You need to assess what students have learned in class as well as what they have read.

2. A second source of such items is the students themselves. This is not a particularly satisfactory source of test questions, because only about 10 percent of the items thus received will be usable. However, this technique is a useful pedagogical device because it gets the students to read their assignments more analytically. It also gives the instructor a good index of what the students are getting out of the various sections of their reading and gives you a chance to remind them of the goals of the course going beyond memory of details.

3. There are statistical methods for evaluating questions, but the best suggestions for improvement come from students themselves in their discussion of the test. It seems almost criminal to waste this experience with items; therefore I recommend a permanent file.

4. If you have a problem, but no good distractor (incorrect alternative), give the item in short-answer or essay form and use the students' own responses for alternatives for a later use of the item in multiple-choice form.

5. Multiple-choice questions typically have four or five alternatives. Rather than wasting your and your students' time with extra alternatives that don't test a discrimination that is important, use only as many alternatives as make meaningful discriminations. Costin (1972) showed that three-choice items are about as effective as four-choice.

6. For measuring understanding, I like questions that require the student to predict the outcome of a situation rather than those that simply ask the student to label the phenomenon.

7. Multiple-choice items need not stand alone. You can use a sequence of related items to measure more complex thinking.

8. Rules for stating the problem.

(cont.)

a. The problem should be stated briefly but completely; the problem should not test the student's ability to understand complex sentence structure except when the teacher is deliberately measuring that ability.

b. The problem should be stated in a positive, not a negative, form. Somehow, even intelligent adults often fail to see a "not" in reading a sentence. If you must use "not," underline it.

c. It should be possible to understand the problem without reading the alternatives.

d. The test is more interesting if the questions are worded in concrete rather than abstract terms. Such items are particularly worthwhile if you wish to measure the student's ability to apply concepts to concrete situations. In math and science, problems arising in the application of the math or theory are not only more interesting but also more likely to encourage students to generalize the concepts or algorithms to situations in which they will use them.

9. Grouping items under headings will improve student performance (Marcinkiewicz & Clariana, 1997).

10. Rules for developing the suggested solutions.

a. The suggested wrong answers should represent errors commonly made by the students being tested.

b. The correct answer should be unquestionably the best, checked by one or more colleagues.

c. The suggested answers should be as brief as possible.

d. The position of the right answers should be scattered.

e. Numerical answers should be placed in numerical order.

f. Even wrong alternatives should not contain words unfamiliar to students.

g. Use "all of the above" and "none of the above" rarely. Usually they are tossed in when you can't think of another good distractor.

h. The right answer should not be given away by irrelevant clues. A few examples of commonly occurring irrelevant clues are:

1. Alternatives that include absolute terms such as "always" and "never" are rarely right answers.

2. Alternatives that are longer and more elaborate than the others are frequently right answers.

(cont.)

3. If the lead of the item is an incomplete statement, then alternatives that do not complete it grammatically are obviously wrong.*

*Many of the foregoing rules are derived directly or indirectly from notes taken in the "Test Construction" class of Dr. R. M. W. Travers. For a more detailed exposition, see his book, *How to Make Achievement Tests* (New York: Odyssey Press, 1950), which is still an excellent source.

Even if you don't pretest the items on students, it is worthwhile to have someone take the test before it is in its final form. If you can persuade a skilled test taker who doesn't know the subject matter to take the test, you will probably be surprised at how many he or she gets right simply from cues you've provided in the questions.

How Many Questions Should I Use?

Obviously the number of questions depends on the type and difficulty of each question. I prefer to give tests without a time limit, but the constraints of class scheduling usually require that you clear the classroom so that the next class can begin. Thus you must plan the length of the exam so that even the slower students have time to finish before the end of the period. As a rule of thumb I allow about 1 minute per item for multiple-choice or fill-in-the-blank items, 2 minutes per short-answer question requiring more than a sentence answer, 10 or 15 minutes for a limited essay question, and a half-hour to an hour for a broader question requiring more than a page or two to answer.

Instructions to the Students

The test instructions should indicate whether or not students are to guess, what the time limit is, and any other directions that define the nature of the expected responses. Emphasizing in the multiple-choice test introduction that the students should choose the *best* answer may help prevent lengthy discussion with the student who can dream up a remote instance in which the correct alternative might be wrong.

In taking a multiple-choice examination, the student has a right to know whether there is a penalty for guessing. For the typical classroom examination, there is no point in a correction for guessing.

Research by McKeachie, Pollie, and Speisman (1955) and by Smith and Rockett (1958) demonstrated that on multiple-choice tests the instruction "Feel free to write comments," with blank space by each question for the comments, results in higher scores, especially for anxious students.

HELPING STUDENTS BECOME TEST-WISE

Particularly in the case of multiple-choice examinations, I have found that a good morale builder is spending 15 minutes or so the day before the first test telling students how to take a test of this sort.

Some of the points that I make in such a lecture follow.

Taking Multiple-Choice Tests

The student taking a multiple-choice examination is essentially in the same position as a poker player. The object is to get into a position where you are betting on a sure thing. If this is impossible, at least make your bet on the choice where the odds are in your favor. In poker, you are obviously in the strongest position if you know exactly what the opponent has; and in the examination situation, you are also in the strongest position if you know the material. There is no substitute for study. At the same time, it is unlikely that you will be absolutely certain of all the right answers. In these cases certain techniques may help.

What I recommend (to the student) is this: go through the examination a first time and answer all of the items you know. In addition to getting a certain amount of the examination done without wasting too much time on single, difficult items, it is frequently true that going through the complete test once in this way will suggest the answers to questions that might have been difficult had they been answered in serial order. When you have gone through the test once in this fashion, go through it again and answer any questions that are now obvious. There will still usually remain a few questions that have been left unanswered. It is in connection with these that certain tricks may be useful.

If the item is multiple choice, don't simply guess at this stage of the game. See whether or not it is possible to eliminate some of the choices as incorrect. In a four-choice multiple-choice item, the probability of getting the answer right by pure guesswork is one in four; if you can eliminate two of them, your chances are 50-50. So take advantage of the mathematics of the situation.

Once the examination has been answered completely, it is a good idea to go through the whole thing again to check your choices on the various items to make sure that they are the ones you still regard as correct and to make sure that you have made no clerical errors in recording them. In this connection, it is worthwhile to point out the common misconception that, when you change your answers, you usually change from right answers to wrong ones. As a matter of fact, Mueller and Wasser (1977) reviewed 18 studies demonstrating that most students gain more than they lose on changed answers.

Taking Essay Tests

My instructions for essay exams are simpler.

1. Outline your answer before writing it. This provides a check against the common error of omitting completely one part of the answer.

2. If a question completely baffles you, start writing on the back of your paper anything you know that could possibly be relevant. This starts your memory functioning, and usually you'll soon find that you have some relevant ideas.

3. If you are still at a loss, admit it and write a question you can answer, and answer it. Most instructors will give you at least a few points more than if you wrote nothing.

4. Write as well as you can. Even if I intended not to grade on writing ability, my judgment is negatively influenced when I have to struggle to read poor handwriting or surmount poor grammar and sentence structure. Moreover, since I believe that every course is responsible for teaching writing, writing will enter into my grading.

Why Teach Test Taking?

Some will question whether it is wise to give students these tips. The answer to this question depends on your purposes in giving the examination. If you want to test for "test-taking" ability, you will not want to give the students these hints. At any rate, this orientation seems to have the effect of giving students the notion that you are not out to "outsmart" them, but that you are interested in helping them get as high a grade as their learning warrants.

ADMINISTERING THE TEST

Handing out a test should be a simple matter. Usually it is, but in large classes, simple administrative matters can become disasters. It is hard to imagine how angry and upset students can become while waiting only ten minutes for the proctors to finish distributing the test forms. And if this doesn't move you, imagine your feelings when you find that you don't have enough tests for all of the students. (It has happened to me twice—deserving a place among my worst moments in teaching!)

How can you avoid such problems?

1. If you are having tests duplicated, ask for at least 10 percent extra—more if the test is administered in several rooms. (Some proctor always walks off with too many.) This gives you insurance against miscounting and against omitted or blank pages on some copies.

2. Unless there is some compelling reason to distribute the tests later, have your proctors pass out the tests as students come into

the room. This protects students from mounting waves of panic while they wait for the tests to be distributed.

3. Minimize interruptions. Tell students before the exam that you will write announcements, instructions, or corrections on the blackboard. Some exam periods are less a measure of achievement than a test of the students' ability to work despite the instructor's interruptions.

AFTER THE TEST

Grading Essay Questions

I recommend that you use essay questions because of their powerful effect on the way students study, but there is a drawback. Instructors don't grade essay tests very reliably.

One of the problems is that standards vary. First papers are graded differently than later papers; a paper graded immediately after several poor papers is graded differently than one graded after several good papers.

There are eight procedures you can initiate to improve your evaluation of essay examinations—but they entail work.

1. Establish a rubric or set of criteria—not just a list of facts to be included. Are you looking for integration, for analysis, for rational arguments for and against a conclusion? Be prepared to modify your criteria as you find student responses that you hadn't thought of.

2. Read exams without knowledge of the name of the writer.

3. Read all or several of the examinations in a preliminary fashion to establish some notion of the general level of performance.

4. Write (or choose after reading several papers) models of excellent, good, adequate, and poor papers to which you can refer to refresh your memory of the standards by which you are grading. This technique is particularly useful if an assistant is helping to grade or if grading is carried out over a period of time.

5. Having identified papers of differing levels of excellence, compare them to determine what the distinguishing features were. You will find some characteristics that were not in your original criteria. Now set up the criteria you will use, but don't be rigid. Give students credit when they come up with creative answers that don't fit the rubric.

6. Write specific comments on the papers. One of the problems in using essay exams and in assigning term papers is that students feel that the grading represents some mysterious, unfathomable bias. The more helpful comments you can write on the paper, the more students will learn. (I say more about this in the chapter "Teaching Students to Learn Through Writing.")

7. Develop a code for common comments. For example, you might want to use a vertical line alongside paragraphs that are particularly good or "NFD" for "needs further development."

8. Don't simply give points for each concept or fact mentioned. This simply converts the essay into a recall test rather than measuring higher-level goals of integration and evaluation. Developing rubrics (criteria of the standards you expect) can be helpful in increasing reliability of grading. However, don't use them mechanically. Your overall impression may be more valid.

9. If possible, do your grading in teams. My teaching assistants and I gather after administering a test. We bring in draft model answers for each question. We discuss what we expect as answers on each question. We then establish two- to three-person teams for each essay question. Each team then picks 8 to 12 test papers which are circulated among the team members, with each team member noting privately his or her grade for the question. The team then compares grades and discusses discrepancies until it has reached consensus. A second group of tests is then graded in the same way, with grades compared and discrepancies discussed. This procedure continues until the team is confident that it has arrived at common criteria. From this point on, each member grades independently. When a team member is not sure how to grade a paper, it is passed to another team member for an opinion.

We stay with the grading until all the papers are done, but we make a party of it to alleviate fatigue and boredom. Funny answers are read aloud. Sandwiches are brought in from a delicatessen. Teams help other teams for a change of pace or to balance the workload.

If you don't have a team, try to develop your own strategies for maintaining motivation. If you begin to be bored, irritated, or tired, take a break. Or before beginning, pull out the answers of some of your most interesting students and read those when you begin to feel dispirited. Take notes to use in discussing the papers in class. Also take separate notes for yourself on what seem to be common problems that you need to correct in your teaching in the future.

Grading papers is still time-consuming but does not become the sort of aversive task that makes for procrastination and long delays in providing feedback to students.

Helping Students Learn from the Test

The most important function of testing is *not* to provide a basis for grading. Rather, tests are an important educational tool. Not only do they direct students' studying, but they can provide important corrective feedback. The comments written on essay tests are far more important than the grade.

What kind of comments are helpful? First of all, rid yourself of the usual teacher's notion that most inadequacies are due to a lack of knowledge, so that improvement rests simply on supplying the missing knowledge. Rather, you need to look for cues that will help you identify the students' representations of knowledge. Usually the students' problems arise from a lack of ability to see relationships, implications, or applications of material. There is always some discrepancy between the structure of knowledge in the student's mind and that in the instructor's. Students construct their own knowledge based on their individual past experiences and their experiences in the course. Thus comments on essay items are more likely to be helpful if they help students find alternative ways of looking at the problem rather than simply noting that something is wrong.

Comments that provide correction and guidance may not achieve their purpose if students become so discouraged that they give up. Thus the motivational as well as the cognitive aspects of comments need to be considered. Misconceptions need to be identified, but not in overwhelming number. Encouragement and guidance for improvement should set the overall tone. Feedback that helps students see their progress helps build self-efficacy and motivation for further learning.

After you return the test, ask students to write a short account of what they learned from the test. What did they do well in preparing? What do they need to do to improve?

Helping Yourself Learn from the Test

Often we get so wrapped up in the pure mechanics of correcting and grading tests that we overlook the fact that measures of student performance not only can diagnose student weaknesses but also can reveal areas in which our teaching has failed to achieve its purposes. Once you've achieved some ease with the grading process, look back at the papers to see what they reveal about problems in student understanding. There may be some things about which the entire class seems a bit shaky; in addition there may be areas of difficulty experienced by certain subgroups of students—perhaps those with background knowledge or experience different from the rest of the class. In short, think about what *you* need to do as well as about what the *students* need to do.

Grading "on the Curve": Don't Do It!*

The papers have been corrected, errors noted, comments written, but now you have to worry about grading. I'll have more to say about grading in the chapter "The ABC's of Assigning Grades," but for the moment let's consider grades given on a test when you are expected to convert a number of points into a letter grade such as A, B, C, D, or F.

---

* Grading "on the curve" means to assign grades on the basis of how each student compares with other students who took the test rather than on the basis of the degree to which the student has achieved some standard of performance. For example, in grading on the curve one might give the top 10 percent of the scores A's, the next 25 percent B's, the next 35 percent C's, the next 20 percent D's, and the bottom 10 percent F's.

Grading based on *relative* achievement in a given group may encourage an undesirably high degree of competition. Grading on the curve stacks the cards against cooperative learning because helping classmates may lower one's own grade. It discourages the teacher from helping less able students because any student who moves up a grade moves another down. It increases student anxiety. Nonetheless, many teachers prefer to grade on a curve—some because they are not sure what standards are appropriate, some because they fear that if most students reach high standards of achievement they will be accused of contributing to grade inflation. This is bugaboo that persists despite evidence that grades have not gone up in the last two decades (Adelman, 1999).

I tell my students that I'll grade in terms of percentage of a possible score. Thus if a test has 150 possible points, I say:

If you make 140 or over (93%+), I'll guarantee an A

135 to 139 (90%+) A–

131 to 134 (87%+) B+

125 to 130 (83%+) B

120 to 124 (80%+) B–, etc.

If everyone gets over 140 points, everyone will get an A, and I'll be very pleased if you all do well.

I tell the students that I may grade more generously than the standards I have announced but will promise not to be tougher than announced. As it turns out, my distribution of grades has not turned out to be more generous than that of my colleagues—which may indicate that I'm not teaching as effectively as I'd like.

My "percentage of possible points" system is fairly easy to apply but lacks the educational value of criteria or standards tied more directly to course goals. Royce Sadler (1987) describes the use of exemplars and verbal descriptions of quality to set standards for grading.

Returning Test Papers

Remember that tests are important tools for learning and that discussion of the test is worthwhile use of class time. You might begin by asking students what they learned from the test. Were they accurate in their assessment of how well they had done? (Helping students learn to assess their own learning is a worthy objective.) You don't need to discuss every question, but where there are common errors, try to find out why the error occurred and suggest strategies for avoiding such problems in the future (see Schultz and Weinstein, 1990).

Students do learn from their corrected papers (McClusky, 1934). Although you may not wish to spend class time quibbling over some individual items, you should make known your willingness to discuss the test individually with students who have further questions.

On multiple-choice questions that many students missed, I recommend this sort of procedure:

Read the stem of the item and each of the choices. For each of the incorrect choices give your reasons for regarding it as incorrect.

This procedure gives you the jump on the chronic criticizer. It is more difficult to maintain that a given choice is right under these circumstances than it would be if you had said nothing about the various alternatives, and students could argue that the correct alternative was not completely correct.

There will still be cases in which a legitimate argument arises. If some ambiguities have gotten through the screening process, and an item is really capable of two equally correct interpretations, admit it and change scores. But remember that you can't escape aggression simply by changing scores, because every time you admit a new right answer, the students who originally had the question right are likely to feel injured.

For essay tests I try to describe what we expected in a good answer and the most common inadequacies. I may read an example of a good answer (without identifying the student), pointing out how it met the criteria, and I might construct a synthetic poor answer to contrast with the good one.

Dealing with an Aggrieved Student

What about the student who comes to your office in great anger or with a desperate appeal for sympathy but no educationally valid reason for changing the test grade? First of all, listen. Engaging in a debate will simply prolong the unpleasantness.

Ask the student to think aloud about what he or she was thinking when answering the questions that he or she is unhappy about.

Once you have heard the student out, if you have decided not to change the grade, try to convert the discussion from one of stonewall resistance to problem solving. Try to help the student find alternative modes of study that will produce better results. "What can we do to help you do better next time?" Encourage the student to shift from blaming you toward motivation to work more effectively. Ask the student to summarize what he or she plans to do before the next test.

My colleague Deborah Keller-Cohen asks students coming to see her with complaints about grades to write a paragraph describing their complaint or point of view. She declares her willingness to go over the test of anyone who brings in such a paragraph, noting that she may change the grade either positively or negatively. She reports that this technique has a calming effect, resulting in fewer unfounded complaints and more rational discussion with those who do come in.

While these suggestions may save the instructor some bitter moments, they cannot substitute for the time (and it takes lots) devoted to the construction of good tests.

What Do You Do About the Student Who Missed the Test?

In any large class some students are absent from the test. Their excuses vary from very legitimate to very suspicious, but making that discrimination is not always easy.

Makeup tests can involve a good deal of extra work for the instructor. If you devise a new test, you may have trouble assigning a norm with which to grade the makeup comparable to grades on the original test. If you use the same test that the student missed, you cannot tell how much the student has learned about the test from students who took it at the scheduled time. I simply average marks from the tests the student did take to determine the grade, counting the missed test neither for nor against the student.

OTHER METHODS OF ASSESSING LEARNING

Performance Assessment (Authentic Assessment)

Over two decades ago, Alverno College instituted a student-centered curriculum and performance assessment plan that has been a significant model for American colleges and universities. Faculty members construct learning situations in which they can observe student performance and judge the performance on the basis of specified criteria. The faculty has defined developmental levels in each of several abilities that students are expected to achieve. Since no one situation is sufficient for assessing a complex ability, the assessment plan stresses multiple modes of assessment related to real-life contexts. In addition, faculty actively train students in methods of self-assessment, an important outcome if students are to continue learning when there are no longer teachers around to evaluate their work (see Alverno College Faculty, 1994; Mentkowski & Loacker, 1985; Mentkowski & Associates, 2000).

Many other college teachers are now using methods of evaluating learning that are more authentically related to later uses of learning than are conventional tests. For example, in chemistry, mathematics, and engineering courses instructors now use fewer standard abstract problems that can be solved by algorithms and more problems describing situations in which more than one approach could be used and in which alternative solutions are possible.

Simulations (either on computers or role-played), hands-on field or laboratory exercises, research projects, and juried presentations (as are used in music, art, and architecture), are also examples of methods related more closely to later use of learning. Paper-and-pencil tasks may require similarity judgments, sorting, or successive choices or predictions following sequential presentation of information about a case, scenario, or situation.

Graphic Representations of Concepts

An organized framework of concepts is important for further learning and thinking. Graphic representations of conceptual relationships may be useful both for teaching and for assessing learning. Our research group (Naveh-Benjamin & Lin, 1991; Naveh-Benjamin et al., 1989; Naveh-Benjamin et al., 1986) has developed two methods (the "ordered tree" and "fill-in-the-structure," or FITS) that we have used to assess the development of conceptual relationships during college courses. In both of these methods the instructor chooses a number of concepts and arranges them in a hierarchical structure like that depicted in Figure 6.1 (which shows an example used in my Learning to Learn course). For the FITS task the instructor gives the students a copy of the basic structure with some concepts missing. The students are then asked to fill in the blanks.

Journals, Research Papers, and Annotated Bibliographies

Journals, research papers, and reports come closer to the goals of authentic assessment than most conventional tests. The chapter "Teaching Students to Learn Through Writing" deals with such writing in detail. Annotated bibliographies can be a useful preparation for writing as well as a tool for assessment. Moreover, annotated bibliographies can be a resource for the whole class (Miller, 1998).

Portfolios

Portfolios have traditionally been used in art or architecture classes, but they have become popular in a variety of subjects and at all levels of education. While there are many types of portfolios, they basically involve the student's presentation of work that has been accomplished over a period of time. They might include early as well as later examples in order to demonstrate the progress that has been made, or they may be simply a presentation of the student's best work, or, better yet, the student's descriptions of how the work helped his or her development. In mathematics or science the portfolio might consist of problems or lab reports representing various course topics written up to show the student's understanding. In other courses they might include entries from journals describing reactions to reading,

FIGURE 6.1 A Fill-in-the-Structure (FITS) Example

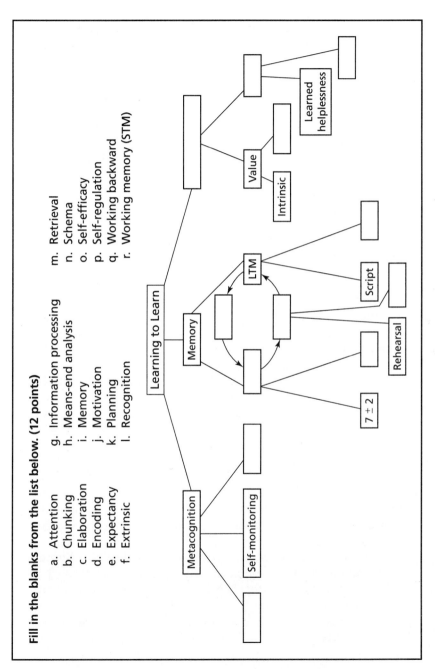

classroom experiences, or learning occurring outside the classroom. Papers, notes for presentations to the class, or other materials might be included.

Unless you provide instruction on how to construct a portfolio and describe the criteria you will use in evaluating it, assessing learning reliably will be difficult.

A portfolio helps both the students and me see how they have progressed. Students report increased self-awareness, and I frequently find evidence of learning that I would otherwise have missed.

Peer Assessment

Even with the best procedures some students will be frustrated. You can prevent some aggression if you help students develop skills in self-assessment. As mentioned earlier, this takes practice.

After collecting tests or papers, redistribute them randomly with a rubric for evaluation. Encourage the students to write helpful comments as well as an evaluation. After students have evaluated the papers they were given, ask them to exchange with a neighbor, evaluate the paper given to the neighbor, and then compare notes on their evaluations.

What you do next will probably depend on the size of your class. In a small class I collect the papers and evaluations and evaluate them before returning them to the evaluators and students evaluated. If the class is larger, I ask the class to discuss the process, what problems they encountered, and what they learned.

Assessing Group Work

As teachers use more and more team projects and cooperative learning, one of the frequent questions is, "How can I assess group work?"

I've sometimes asked group members to write individual reports. Students are told that purely descriptive parts, such as the research design, may be the same on all papers, but that parts representing thinking are to represent the students' own thinking—although students are encouraged to read and discuss each other's papers before submitting them.

I've sometimes included an exam question relevant to the group projects; currently I ask each group to submit a single report which I evaluate. I also ask each student to turn in a slip of paper listing the members of his or her group and dividing 100 points in proportion to each member's contribution. Almost all groups apportion the points equally because I monitor the group's progress and try to get problems solved before the final product. In addition, students understand that the grade will be lowered for any student whose contribution is perceived to be less than that of other group members. Thus on a 100-point project I might give only 50 points to a student whose contributions were 10 percent or less as judged by his or her teammates. In most such cases I would have been aware of the problem earlier and discussed it with the group and the student, but even then I try to talk with the student before assigning the lower grade.

Classroom Assessment

The primary purpose of assessment is to provide feedback to students and teacher so that learning can be facilitated. *Classroom assessment* is the term popularized by Pat Cross and Tom Angelo to describe a variety of nongraded methods of getting feedback on student learning. I have already described minute papers in the preceding chapter. Problem posting, discussed in the second chapter, and the two-column method mentioned in the "Facilitating Discussion" chapter are ways of getting feedback as well as of facilitating student learning. Angelo and Cross (1993) describe a variety of classroom assessment techniques.

IN CONCLUSION

1. Learning is more important than grading.
2. Tests and other assessments should be learning experiences as well as evaluation devices.
3. Providing feedback is more important than assigning a grade. You can use nongraded evaluation as well as evaluation for

assigning grades.

4. Try to assess attainment of all your objectives, even if some objectives (such as increased motivation for learning) are not appropriate criteria for grades.

5. Avoid evaluation devices that increase anxiety and competition.

Supplementary Reading

Paul Ramsden's chapter "Assessing for Understanding," in his book *Learning to Teach in Higher Education* (London: Routledge, 1992), presents a wise perspective on assessment and gives examples from chemistry, anatomy, materials technology, engineering, history of art, statistics, medicine, and physics.

500 Tips on Assessment by Sally Brown, Phil Race, and Brenda Smith (London: Kogan Page, 1996) is a marvelous compendium of useful suggestions on all types of assessment, ranging from self-assessment through group assessment, multiple-choice tests, and assessment of performance, lab work, and dissertations.

Modern methods of assessing learner-centered courses are described in Graham Gibbs's book, *Assessing Student-centered Courses* (Oxford: Oxford Centre for Staff Development, 1995). Chapters give case studies illustrating assessment of group work, projects, journals, skills, and portfolios.

Assessment Matters in Higher Education, edited by Sally Brown and Angela Glassner (1999), describes innovative approaches to assessment and current United Kingdom practices in a variety of disciplines. There is an entire section on peer assessment and self-assessment. (I suspect that the pun in the title was intentional.)

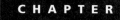

What to Do About Cheating

7

It may be hard for you to believe that your students would ever cheat—"Maybe other students cheat, but not mine!" Unfortunately, studies of cheating behavior over several decades invariably find that a majority of students report that they have cheated at some time (McCabe & Trevino, 1996). Most students would rather not cheat, but the pressures for good grades are so intense that many students feel that they, too, must cheat if they believe that other students are cheating. In my experience the most common excuse given by a student caught cheating is that other students were cheating and that the teacher didn't seem to care, at least not enough to do anything to prevent or stop cheating. Many students thus feel less stress when an examination is well managed and well proctored.

HOW DO STUDENTS CHEAT?

1. Students pass information to a neighbor; for example, they may loan a neighbor an eraser with the answer on the eraser.
2. Students use notes written on clothing, skin, or small note cards.

3. Students store answers in calculators or cassette recorders used during the exam.

4. Students peek at a knowledgeable neighbor's exam (sometimes seated in groups around the best student in the fraternity).

5. Students use tapping, hand code, or other communication.

6. Students accuse the teacher of losing an exam (which was not turned in).

7. Students pay someone else to take an exam or write a paper for them.

8. Students copy or paraphrase material for a paper without acknowledging the source.

PREVENTING CHEATING

"OK, so we want to prevent cheating. What can we do?"

An obvious first answer is to reduce the pressure. While you can't affect the general academic atmosphere that puts heavy emphasis on grades, you can influence the pressure in your own course, for example, by providing a number of opportunities for students to demonstrate achievement of course goals, rather than relying on a single examination. A second answer is to address the issue in your syllabus or have a discussion on the topic early in your course.

A third answer is to make reasonable demands and write a reasonable and interesting test. Some cheating is simply the result of frustration and desperation arising from assignments too long to be covered adequately or tests requiring memorization of trivial details. In some cases cheating is simply a way of getting back at an unreasonable, hostile teacher.

A fourth answer is to develop group norms supporting honesty. I frequently give my classes a chance to vote on whether or not we will conduct the tests on the honor system. I announce that we will not use the honor system unless the vote is unanimous, since it will not work unless everyone feels committed to it. If the vote is unanimous, I remind the students of it on the day of the exam and ask whether they still wish to have the test under the honor system. While I haven't collected data on the success of this approach, I've never had a complaint about it. Although only a minority of classes vote for the honor system, a discussion of academic dishonesty is itself useful in helping students recognize why cheating is bad.

Fifth, if some students are not doing well in the course, talk to them and find out what has gone wrong and what they can do to improve. Try to reduce the stress that leads to cheating. If there are stresses originating beyond your course, suggest counseling.

What else can be done?

One principle is to preserve each student's sense that he or she is an individual with a personal relationship both with the instructor and with other students. Students are not as likely to cheat in situations in which they are known as in situations in which they are anonymous members of a crowd. Thus, if a large course has regular meetings in small discussion or laboratory sections, there is likely to be less cheating if the test is administered in these groups than if the test is administered en masse. Moreover, if it is in their regular classroom, they may perform better because of the cues to their original learning (Metzger et al., 1979).

Even in small groups, cheating will occur if the instructor seems unconcerned. Graduate student teaching assistants often feel that any show of active proctoring will indicate that they do not trust the students. There is certainly a danger that the teacher will appear to be so poised to spring at a miscreant that the atmosphere becomes tense, but it is possible to convey a sense of alert helpfulness while strolling down the aisles or watching for questions.

The most common form of cheating is copying from another student's paper. To reduce this I usually ask to have a large enough exam room to enable students to sit in alternate seats. I write on the board before students arrive, "Take alternate seats." Some students fail to see the sign, so in large exams you not only need two proctors at each door passing out exams but at least one more to supervise seating.

In the event that you can't get rooms large enough to permit alternate seating, you probably should use two or more alternate forms of the test. Houston (1983) found that scrambling the order of items alone did not reduce cheating. Since I prefer to have items on a test follow the same order as the order in which the material has been discussed in the course, I scramble the order of items only within topics and also scramble the order of alternatives. I typically write separate sets of essay questions for the two tests. Since it is difficult to make two tests equally difficult, you probably will want to tabulate separate distributions of scores on each form of the test.

Whether you use one form or two, don't leave copies lying around your office or the typist's office. One of our students was nearly killed by a fall from a third-floor ledge outside the office where he hoped to steal the examination, and janitors have been bribed to turn over the contents of wastebaskets thought to contain discarded drafts of the test.

Plagiarism

Some plagiarism is simply the result of ignorance. Explaining what plagiarism is and indicating why it is a *serious* offense not only may prevent the naive student from plagiarizing but also may deter the intentional plagiarist. I discuss ways of preventing and handling plagiarism in the chapter "Teaching Students to Learn Through Writing."

To sum up: All this advice will not eliminate cheating. It is a sad commentary on our educational system that it occurs, but recognizing and preventing problems is likely to be less unpleasant than ignoring them.

HANDLING CHEATING

Despite preventive measures, almost every instructor must at some time or another face the problem of what to do about a student who is cheating. For example, as you are administering an examination you note that a student's eyes are on his neighbor's rather than his own paper. Typically you do nothing at this time, for you don't want to embarrass an innocent student. But when the eyes again stray, you are faced with a decision about what to do.

Most colleges have rules about the procedures to be followed in case of cheating. Yet instructors are often reluctant to begin the procedure. The reasons for instructor reluctance vary. Sometimes it is simply uncertainty about whether or not cheating really occurred. Students' eyes do wander without cheating. Answers may be similar simply because two students have studied together. "If the student denies the charge, what evidence do I have to support my accusation?"

Again, unwillingness to invoke the regulations concerning cheating may be based on distrust of the justice of the eventual disposition of the case. Cheating is common in colleges; many teachers have been guilty themselves at some stage in their academic careers. Thus most of us are understandably reluctant to subject the unfortunate one who gets caught to the drastic possible punishments that more skillful cheaters avoid. Such conflicts as these make the problem of handling a cheater one of the most disturbing of those a new teacher faces.

Unfortunately I've never been completely satisfied that I handle the problem adequately; so my "advice" should, like the rest of the advice in this book, be regarded simply as some ideas for your consideration rather than as dicta to be accepted verbatim.

First, let me support the value of following your college's procedures. Find out what they are and what legal precedents may affect what you should do. Even though it may not be long since you were taking examinations yourself, your role as a teacher requires that you represent established authority rather than the schoolboy code that rejects "tattlers." Moreover, your memories of student days may help you recall your own feelings when you saw someone cheating and the instructor took no action.

Further, student or faculty committees dealing with cheating are not as arbitrary and impersonal as you might expect. Typically, they attempt to get at the cause of the cheating and to help students solve their underlying problems. Being apprehended for cheating may, therefore, actually be of real long-term value to the students.

Finally, following college policies protects you in the rare case in which a student initiates legal action against you for an arbitrary punishment.

There still remain cases where the evidence is weak and you're not quite sure whether or not cheating actually occurred. Even here I advise against such individual action as reducing a grade. If you're wrong, the solution is unjust. If you're right, you've failed to give the student feedback which is likely to change ¹ behavior. In such cases I advise talking to the student and calling the chairman of the committee handling cheating cases or the student's counselor. It's surprising to find how often your suspicions fit in with other evidence about the student's behavior. Even when they don't, advice from someone who has additional information about the student will frequently be helpful.

Finally, let's return to the case of the straying eyes. Here you haven't time for a phone call to get advice; your decision has to be made now. Rather than arousing the whole class by snatching away the student's paper with a loud denunciation, I simply ask the student unobtrusively to move to a seat where he'll be less crowded. If he says he's not crowded, I simply whisper that I'd prefer that he move. So far no one's refused.

IN CONCLUSION

1. Prevention is preferable to punishment.
2. Dishonesty is less likely when students feel that the teacher and other students know them and trust them than in situations in which they feel alienated and anonymous.

Supplementary Reading

S. F. Davis, C. A. Grover, A. H. Becker, and L. N. McGregor, "Academic Dishonesty: Prevalence, Determinants, Techniques, and Punishments," *Teaching of Psychology,* 1992, *19*(1), 16–20.

J. McBurney, "Cheating: Preventing and Dealing with Academic Dishonesty," *APS Observer,* January 1996, 32–35.

One might assume that it would be un-British to cheat. But Stephen Newstead, Arlyne Franklyn-Stokes, and Penny Armstrong found that British students are not much different from Americans in this respect. Their article "Individual Differences in Student Cheating," *Journal of Educational Psychology,* 1996, *88,* 229–241, is consistent with American data.

The ABC's of Assigning Grades

8

Grading is currently in the news. Grade inflation, grading leniency, contract grading, mastery grading—all of these stimulate heated discussion and cries of dismay.* My own ideas of grading have become somewhat clearer as I have talked to my teaching assistants about grading policies, which may explain why I am less emotional about each of these issues.

First let's agree that grades are fundamentally a method of communication. The question then becomes: What does the professor intend to communicate to whom?

When one puts grading into this context, three things become apparent:

1. Evaluation is a great deal more than giving a grade. In teaching, the major part of evaluation should be in the form of comments on papers, responses to student statements, conversations, and other means of helping students understand where they are and how to do better. A professor giving a course grade is communicating to several groups—the student, professors teaching

---

* Some definitions: *Grade inflation* The fact that the average grades in American colleges are now higher than they were 40 years ago. *Grading leniency* Giving higher grades than are usually assigned for a given level of achievement.

advanced courses, graduate or professional school admissions committees, prospective employers, and so on.

2. What professors communicate by a grade depends on the meaning of the grade to the person reading it—the effect that it has on that person.

3. Professors cannot change the meaning of grades unilaterally. The users' interpretations will be colored by their previous experiences with grades, and they are likely to be disturbed, or to feel that they are being misled, when a professor uses grades in new ways. This explains the strong emotional reaction to so-called grade inflation, and to practices deviating from traditional meanings.

4. The meaning of A's, B's, and C's has changed over the 50 years I have taught. In 1946, C was the average grade. Today, B is more typical.* But this is not a problem as long as those who assign and interpret grades understand the current meaning.

What are grades used for? I suggest that the person reading a grade typically wants information with respect to some decision involving a judgment about the student's *future* performance. Mastery systems of grading, pass-fail grading, and other alternative systems are resisted because they may not be efficient conveyors of the information useful in predicting future performance. The box that begins below describes how three groups—students, professors, and employers—use grades.

What Do Students, Professors, and Employers Want from Grades?

Students
Students want to be able to use grades to assist them in decisions such as the following:

1. Will I do well if I take additional courses in this field?

(cont.)

---

* While average grades rose in the 1960s and 1970s, there has been no inflation in the past two decades (Adelman, 1999).

2. Should I major in this field? Does it represent a potential career in which I'm likely to be successful?
3. Do I have the skills and ability necessary to work independently in this field—learning more, solving problems, able to evaluate my own work?

Professors

Professors advising the student or determining admissions expect the grade to tell them:

1. Does this student have the motivation, skills, knowledge, and ability needed to do well in advanced courses (insofar as the type of problems dealt with in the earlier course are relevant to the demands of the advanced courses or program)?
2. What kind of person is this? What does the pattern of grades tell us about this student's ability and work habits?

Employers

Similarly, prospective *employers* want to use grades to assist in decisions about whether or not the student will do well on the job.

1. How well will the student be able to solve problems on jobs related to the area of his or her coursework?
2. Does the overall pattern of grades indicate that this is the sort of person who will do well in our organization?

From this analysis it seems evident that grades are used not just as a historical record of what has happened but rather as information about what the student can do in situations outside the class for which the grade was awarded. For users, the grade is not so much historical as potentially predictive.

DO GRADES PROVIDE INFORMATION USEFUL FOR DECISION MAKING?

One of the arguments against conventional grading is that grades do not provide useful information for the major purposes for which they are usually used.

Teachers assume that grades have some informational and motivational value for students. Critics, however, argue that the threat of low grades is often a crutch used by poor teachers. Moreover, a heavy emphasis on grades is likely to reduce motivation for further learning and may even result in poorer achievement for those students who are most motivated by grades. In fact, those who achieve the most tend to have moderate grade motivation and high intrinsic motivation (Lin, McKeachie, & Kim, in preparation).

What about information for employers? Probably most human resources psychologists would agree that the best predictor of success on a job is successful performance on a similar job. For a young person entering the job market, the only previous employment has been in low-level part-time jobs. The employer's decision must then depend largely on other information, such as interviews, letters of recommendation, biographical data, family background, and test scores. Each source is only partially adequate. Insofar as the new job involves at least some expenditure for training, it seems likely that grades, representing the result of skills applied in study, learning, and problem solving, will add some useful information, albeit incomplete.

Since grades are commonly used in combination with other variables, however, one should not expect them to correlate with success for those selected. This is not simply a problem that only the top students were selected; it is a simple mathematical truism that, when one uses several selection criteria, each of which has some validity, one should expect low positive, zero, or even negative correlations between any one selection variable and the ultimate criterion of performance. This occurs because one will balance criteria against one another, selecting some people low in other important attributes because they have high grades and vice versa. Thus the common criticism that grades don't predict later performances is largely invalid since most of the studies cited have been carried out in situations where grades and other predictors have already been used in selection.

CONTRACT GRADING

In contract grading, students and instructors develop a written contract about what the student will do to achieve given grade levels. Contracts typically specify papers to be written, books to be read, projects to be completed, and so forth. When linked to appropriate standards, contracts can be very useful. However, if students gain points not for achievement, but rather for carrying out activities that *should* be conducive to achievement, there may be wide differences in achievement among students who complete the contract. Some will do the minimum necessary, whereas others do excellent work. If contract grading is used, criteria for *quality* are needed. See Table 8.1.

Assigning grades on the basis of the quantity of work done rather than the degree of competence achieved is not a problem restricted to contract grading. Many instructors subtract points for absences, tardiness, or other things they dislike. In psychology classes, points are sometimes added for participation in research studies. This can be a very dubious grading practice unless it involves some assessment of what the students learned from research participation.

COMPETENCY-BASED GRADING

In competency-based, mastery, performance-based, or criterion-referenced systems, the students' grades are based on achievement of specified competencies. This focuses both teachers and students on course objectives and eliminates the negative effects of competition. In principle such systems should be an improvement over more conventional systems of assigning grades. However, there are two problems in implementing a competency-based system:

1. Developing appropriate and comprehensive definitions of the competencies desired

2. Developing adequate criteria for assessing achievement of each competency

	Pro	Con
Contract	Commitment to contract motivates students.	May reward quantity rather than quality.
	May be individualized.	
Competency	Ties grade to course goals.	May be difficult to operationalize.
	Encourages teacher and student to think about goals.	
Both	Reduce student anxiety about competition and grades.	
	Encourage student cooperation.	

TABLE 8.1   Contract Versus Competency Grading

Any assessment involves only a sample of the behaviors that define the competencies desired. But in competency-based or performance assessment systems, there is an attempt to use evidence from more authentic samples of the students' demonstration of the desired competencies in learning situations as well as in separate assessment sessions. The more limited the definition of those achievements that the students should "master," the less valid a test or grade is in terms of its ability to assess the students with respect to other problems, other concepts, or other generalizations in the total domain.

Letting students turn in papers or book reports over and over again until they do them correctly is a fine teaching technique. However, the student who writes an acceptable book report after ten trials is probably less able to write a new report acceptably than the student who does it right in the first place.

Nonetheless, mastery learning has positive features. It forces the teacher to think about goals, and it focuses students' learning. Such a focus results in better retention (Kulik, Kulik, & Bangert-Drowns, 1988).

ASSIGNING GRADES

Because grades represent to many students a fearsome, mysterious dragon, anxiety can sometimes be reduced by encouraging the students to participate in planning the methods by which grades will be assigned. Students usually can recognize the instructor's need to conform to college policy in grade distribution, but the dragon seems less threatening if they have helped determine the system by which they are devoured (or rewarded). Some instructors have gone so far as to let students determine their own grades or to have groups of students grade one another. I like the idea that students should develop the capacity for self-evaluation, but I recognize that many students resist this procedure, either through modesty or fear that they'll underrate themselves. If you use it, I'd suggest thorough discussion of the plan with students and an agreed-upon, well-defined set of criteria that all students should use.

Whether or not students participate, you need to be clear about your criteria. Examples of previously graded work may be helpful. Asking students to hand in their own estimates of their grades may help you to motivate them better and may also develop their abilities for self-evaluation.

In general, motivation is not helped simply by giving high grades; nor is it helped by setting very tough standards. Students are most motivated when they feel that they can achieve success with a reasonable effort (Harter, 1978).

In keeping students informed during the course about where they stand, you help them control much of the anxiety they feel when the grading system is indefinite and unstructured. Sometimes it may seem easier to fight off grade-conscious students by being very indefinite about grades, but student morale is better when the students know the situation with which they must cope.

Whatever your grading strategy, being more generous in assigning grades to tests and papers than in the final distribution of grades guarantees visits from aggrieved students. One way in which you get yourself into this position is by providing opportunities for students to omit questions on an exam, to throw out the lowest test grade, or to submit extra work for a higher grade.

Any of these procedures can have some educational justification, but you need to be able to convince administrators or colleagues that the pattern of grades you assign is appropriate for the achievement of your students.

GRADING ON THE CURVE: A MILD REPRISE

In the chapter "Assessing, Testing, and Evaluating," we talked about grading a test on the curve. Now we extend our discussion to final course grades. One of the persistent controversies in college teaching is whether to grade "on the curve" or in terms of an absolute standard. In fact, these two positions are probably not as far apart as the argument would indicate. Even teachers who grade on the curve are influenced in setting their cutoff points between grades in terms of their feelings about whether this was a good or a poor class. Similarly, teachers who do not grade on the curve set their standards in terms of what previous experience leads them to regard as reasonable accomplishment in the course. As I indicated earlier, I believe that grading on the curve is educationally dysfunctional. If possible, your grades should, both in the students' eyes and in actuality, be more nearly based on absolute standards than on relative standing in this particular class.

The use of an absolute standard is easier if you have formulated your major and minor objectives and tested their achievement. Travers (1950b) proposed one set of absolute standards:

- A: All major and minor goals achieved.
- B: All major goals achieved; some minor ones not.
- C: All major goals achieved; many minor ones not.
- D: A few major goals achieved, but student is not prepared for advanced work.
- E or F: None of the major goals achieved.

Ideally I should be able to list my goals for the course and at the end of the course have assessed each in such a way that I could use such a criterion-based system. In fact, however, my tests, papers, journals, research studies, and other elements of the assessment of learning are seldom pure measures of a single goal. For example, my tests assess knowledge and understanding of the major concepts and facts as well as ability to apply and think with these concepts. To separate out each component would be almost impossible. Consequently, I assign points to each test, paper, and other assignment, and give grades on the basis of the total percentage of points earned by the student over the term. This at least avoids the detrimental effects of grading students' performance relative to one another and probably approximates the outcomes described by Travers.

WHAT ABOUT THE STUDENT WHO WANTS A GRADE CHANGED?

If you have kept students informed of their grades on tests, papers, and other graded work during the term, you will have avoided most complaints. But there still may be some. My basic strategy is the same as that used in returning tests or papers: listen first, then go over the criteria used. Try to understand the student's reasoning. This may be a learning experience for both of you.

If students are worried about their grades in connection with their admission to a specialized school or because they are on probation, I may offer to write a letter to their advisor or other authorities describing their work in detail and pointing out any extenuating circumstances that may have influenced the grade. This may serve to cushion the refusal to change the grade.

In addition, of course, you may try to explain to the students the rationale of grades. Usually this doesn't seem to do much good. Both students and faculty sometimes confuse two possible criteria on which grades may be based. One of these is the relative amount of *progress* the student has made in achieving the goals of the course; the other is *achievement of the goals of the course* at the end of the term. In most classes, research has demonstrated a relatively low correlation between these two criteria. If you were to mark solely on progress, the students who came into the course with the least background might still be the poorest students in the class at the end of the course and get an A for their progress. Most employers, registrars, and professors interpret a grade in terms of achievement of course goals; hence professors who grade solely on the students' progress may send the students into advanced courses or jobs for which they lack the requisite skills and knowledge.

However, progress is also relevant to prediction. A student who has made a great deal of progress despite a poor background may do as well in a further course or job as someone with somewhat better performance at the end of the course who made relatively little progress. My own solution is to assign grades primarily in terms of achievement of course goals (total performance), but when a student's total points or overall performance is close to the boundary between grades, to assign the higher grade if there has been much progress.

No matter how you grade, some student will be unhappy. Be sympathetic, but beware! If you begin changing grades, the jungle drums of the campus will soon spread the word. Be sure that you understand your institution's regulations with respect to grade changes. Check, too, on procedures that students may use to appeal capricious grading.

Don't finish reading this chapter with your own anxiety aroused by the dangers of grading. It is proper that good teachers should be humble as they see how great is the power they have over the happiness of their students by printing a simple A, B, C, or D. Nevertheless, one of the real satisfactions of teaching is giving a good grade to an ordinarily average student who has come to life in your course.

A List of Don'ts

These may look absurd, but they have all happened. Avoid making the same mistakes.

1. Never give students any idea of what their grades are before the final examination. The shock of seeing an F as the final grade will so stun them that they'll be incapable of protest. Or, better yet, tell them they had A's all the way through the course and got an A on the final, but you have given too many A's, so you're giving them B's.

(cont.)

2. Tell students that you really think they deserved a higher mark, but that you had to conform to department grading policies and hence had to grade them lower.

3. Tell students that their grades on the final exam were higher than their final grades in the course. (Of course they'll understand that the final examination is only one part of the total evaluation.)

4. Even though your school doesn't record pluses, tell students that their grades were D+, C+, or B+. They'll gladly accept the fact that the C–, B– or A– was only a few points higher and will be proud that they did better than anyone else who got a D, C, or B.

5. Tell a student that grades are really very arbitrary, and that you could have split the B's from the C's in many different places, and that grades are so unreliable that you really can't distinguish your top B student from your low A student. He'll appreciate the aesthetic value of your choice of a cutting point.

RELEVANT RESEARCH

Not only do instructors control the pleasantness or unpleasantness of a good many student hours, but because of their power to assign grades they can block or facilitate the achievement of many important goals. The importance of this aspect of the teacher's role is indicated by studies of supervision in industry. In one such study it was discovered that workers were most likely to ask a supervisor for help if the supervisor did not have responsibility for evaluating his subordinates (Ross, 1957). This implies that, as long as students are anxious about the grades the instructor will assign, they are likely to avoid exposing their own ignorance.

Students' anxieties about grades are likely to rise if their instructor's procedures make them uncertain about what they must do in order to attain a good grade. For many students, democratic methods seem unorganized and ambiguous. In an ordinary course students know they can pass by reading assignments and studying lecture notes, but in an extremely student-centered class they may find that the instructor doesn't lecture, doesn't make assignments, and doesn't even say which student comments are right or wrong. The student simply doesn't know what the instructor is trying to do. Thus, if your teaching or grading procedures differ from those your students are used to, you need to be especially careful to specify the procedures and criteria used in grading.

Some instructors have thought that the grade problem might be licked by using a cooperative system of grading. Deutsch (1949) found no differences in learning between students in groups graded cooperatively and those graded competitively, although the cooperative groups worked together more smoothly. Following up Deutsch's work, Haines and McKeachie (1967) also found no significant achievement advantages for students working cooperatively versus those working competitively for grades, but did find marked differences in group morale. Haines's work suggests that cooperative grading in the discussion can be successfully combined with individual grading on achievement tests. (The chapters "Assessing, Testing, and Evaluation" and "Active Learning" also discuss grading groups.)

IN CONCLUSION

1. Grades are communication devices. Instructors cannot unilaterally change their meaning without distorting the communication process.
2. Grading standards differ from college to college and department to department, but there is some shared sense of the meaning of grades.

Supplementary Reading

What grades mean to faculty, parents, personnel directors, and students is described in O. Milton, H. R. Pollio, and J. Eison, *Making Sense of College Grades* (San Francisco: Jossey-Bass, 1986).

A fine vignette about the problem of assigning grades is Linc Fisch's "Students on the Line," in *The Chalk Dust Collection* (Stillwater, OK: New Forums Press, 1996), pp. 132–134.

Barbara Davis describes a number of systems for determining grades and gives sensible advice in her chapter "Grading Practices," in *Tools for Teaching*, 2nd ed. (San Francisco: Jossey-Bass, 1993).

Another good resource is B. E. Walvoord and V. J. Anderson, *Effective Grading: A Tool for Learning and Assessment* (San Francisco: Jossey-Bass, 1998).

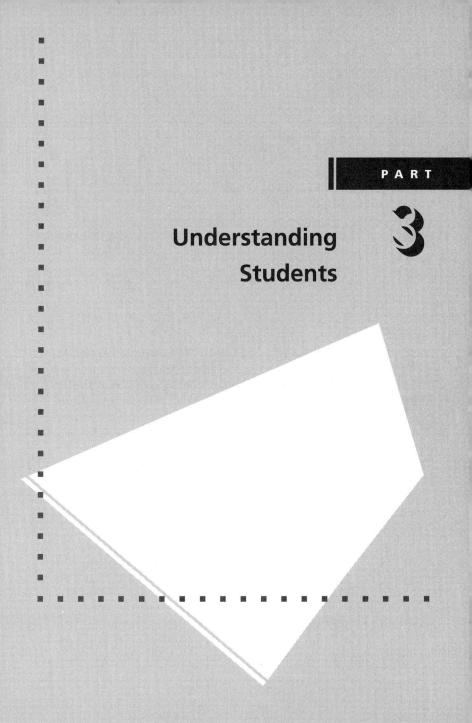

PART

3

Understanding
Students

9 Motivation in the College Classroom

▪ ▪ ▪ ▪ ▪ ▪ ▪ ▪ ▪ ▪ ▪ ▪ ▪ ▪ ▪ ▪

Few topics concern teachers at all levels as much as the motivation of students. We worry over any who appear disengaged and may disparage students who appear to care only about grades. We delight in the students eager to ask intelligent questions, whose hands fly into the air, who not only prepare for class but also seek us out to learn more. We marvel when we learn that these behaviors sometimes describe the same student—but in different courses. How can we better understand the motivational patterns of our students and shape courses that foster the motivation to learn? The research and knowledge base on student motivation is strong and can provide a framework for fostering student motivation in the college classroom.

We all want students who are motivated to learn. These are the students who choose to attend class regularly, participate constructively, persist when learning is difficult, make the effort to prepare for class and to study effectively, solicit help when they need it, and translate all this into academic success. Knowing more about how students are motivated and what you can do to structure a class that positively affects student motivation can make a significant difference in student engagement and learn-

This chapter was written by Barbara Hofer of Middlebury College.

ing. A classroom of motivated learners affects *our* motivation as well and can make teaching a more satisfying experience for the instructor.

MOTIVATION THEORY

Researchers typically consider three indices of motivation: choice, effort, and persistence. Students who are motivated to learn will choose tasks that enhance their learning, will work hard at those tasks, and will persist in the face of difficulty in order to attain their goals. Why students vary in their motivation is a persistent question, and there are several theoretical frameworks that help us interpret this. Some students may be driven by a high *need for achievement* (McClelland et al., 1953). This may be characterized as an individual trait or a disposition, and it is likely to be the outcome of early environments in which parents set high standards and rewarded achievement. In general, students differ from one another in the degree to which achievement for its own sake is meaningful to them. Motivation is also contextual, however. A particular student may exhibit a striving for achievement on the soccer field but not in your class, or perhaps is more motivated to achieve in some disciplines than in others. Classroom context can foster certain types of motivation over others, as can the overall climate of an educational institution.

Autonomy and Self-Determination

Many psychologists believe that human beings have a fundamental need for autonomy and self-determination (Deci & Ryan, 1985). Most individuals want to be in charge of their own behavior and value a sense of control over their environment. We can enhance students' sense of control by offering choices and supporting their autonomy, which in turn enhances motivation. The importance of "stage-environment fit" in motivation (Eccles et al., 1993) might well be applied to the needs of late adolescents and adults in colleges and universities. We can provide educational environments that meet developmental needs by giving students meaningful opportunities for choice, accompanied by accountability for their actions. Quite often these can be relatively small steps on the part of the faculty member, such as offering a choice of paper topics or reading assignments, yet they go a long way in acknowledging a student perspective.

Intrinsic and Extrinsic Motivation

Instructors at the college level often complain of student preoccupation with grades, typified by the perpetual classroom question: Will that be on the test? These *extrinsically motivated* students are likely to engage in the course for reasons of external rewards, such as grades, recognition, or the approval of others (notably, instructors and parents). Individuals who are *intrinsically motivated* are those who engage in an activity for the value of the activity itself, rather than for an external reward. Can a student be both intrinsically and extrinsically motivated? The answer is a resounding "yes," so it is useful to understand how both motives operate and to know something about the relationship between them in order to maximize student motivation.

Students who are intrinsically motivated are those who learn for the pleasure of learning and who have a sense of self-determination about their educational path. Intrinsic motivation has been shown to foster conceptual understanding, creativity, involvement, and a preference for challenge. Research on college student learning indicates that students with an intrinsic orientation are more likely to use cognitive strategies such as elaboration and organization, resulting in a deeper processing of the material (Pintrich & Garcia, 1991).

Although the image of a classroom of intrinsically motivated learners might sound ideal, students are also driven by the desire for grades, approval, and other rewards, and understandably so. Intrinsic and extrinsic motivation exist not on a single continuum, but on two separate ones, and students may often have multiple goals for the same course. A student enrolled in a required course, for example, may be deeply interested in the material, but may also see it as a step in her professional development and may desire to earn an A so that she will be likely to gain admission to graduate or professional school. Even students who initially appear only extrinsically motivated to take a course, perhaps viewing it merely as a requirement toward graduation, can become more intrinsically motivated by your arousing their curiosity, providing appropriate levels of challenge, and offering them choices that enhance their control (Lepper & Hodell, 1989).

Although studies have indicated that external rewards may diminish intrinsic motivation by undermining self-determination (Deci & Ryan, 1985), recent research seems to support the judicious use of external rewards as a complement to other motivational approaches. Extrinsic rewards may be particularly useful when intrinsic motivation is lacking—and it is reasonable to assume that students are not always going to be intrinsically motivated to learn everything they are expected to learn during the college years. Students may also find extrinsic rewards to be productive during the early stages of learning a new subject, before they feel they can begin to master it and when the necessary nature of the tasks (such as memorizing vocabulary in a foreign language or learning a large number of terms in the sciences) may not be intrinsically interesting. There is also some evidence from a study of intrinsic motivation in college undergraduates that the pursuit of grades may not be incompatible with subject matter appreciation (Covington, 1999). In particular, those students who attain their grade goals and whose achievement is not driven by the desire to avoid failure may increase their interest in the subject.

Furthermore, extrinsic rewards are most beneficial when they contain informative feedback and enable students to focus on improvement. Thus grades alone are less helpful than those accompanied by narrative feedback that addresses specific directions for change.

Expectancy × Value Theory

Students typically direct their behavior toward activities that they value and in which they have some expectancy of success. From this social cognitive perspective, motivation is viewed as the outcome of multiplying these two forces; if either one is absent, the resulting product is zero. Instructors can benefit by knowing that they need to foster both. Students need to feel that there is a reasonable possibility of success and that the work is of value. Thus even students who believe they can do well in an introductory course might not continue with the subject if they do not see that the material is of value. Likewise, even those who entered with professional ambitions dependent on the course may not persist in the field if they think that they cannot expect success.

Mastery Versus Performance Goals

Motivated behavior is directed toward goals, and goals related to learning tend to reflect two broad types of purposes. Although there have been different terms used to categorize the two types of goal orientations, a useful distinction is *mastery goals* versus *performance goals*. Students who adopt mastery goals are those whose primary desire is to understand and master the material. By contrast, students with performance goals are more likely to focus on their own achievement relative to that of others. The classrooms we create may implicitly foster a particular type of goal, depending on grading practices, classroom climate, and other such factors.

In a classroom that is mastery focused, instructors generally use criterion-referenced grading rather than normative (grading on a curve); foster a supportive climate where students can take intellectual risks; and provide opportunities for students to demonstrate improvement. A mastery orientation may be visible in classroom discussions when students ask genuine questions to which they do not already know the answers, driven by a desire to better understand the material, rather than to impress their peers and instructor. Mistakes are viewed as an opportunity for learning. In a class that is focused on performance, instructors often use normative grading practices (which imply that only a percentage of students are likely to succeed) and provide no opportunities for revising and improving written work. Student questions may be formulated to present the inquirer in the best light and to gain recognition and reward. In contrast to students with mastery goals, students who are ego involved with their performance may compare grades with one another and take academic shortcuts, such as avoiding more effort than is necessary to acquire the desired grade. Fostering a mastery orientation in the classroom begins with syllabus construction and can be considered throughout a course.

Attribution Theory

When individuals need to seek an explanation for unexpected outcomes, they make attributions about the probable causes. In academic motivation, this often arises when students fail to perform well on a test or get a grade that differs from what they might have expected. Typical attributions are effort ("I didn't study hard enough"), ability ("I'm just not good at this subject"), or luck ("The test emphasized the material I actually studied!"). Attributions can be categorized along three dimensions—locus, stability, and responsibility—which refer, respectively, to whether the cause is internal or external, stable or unstable, and controllable or not (Weiner, 1986). Students who explain their disappointments with internal, controllable attributions ("I know I didn't prepare adequately for the test") are likely to do better next time, because they believe they can affect the outcome. Students who attribute failure to stable, uncontrollable causes ("The teacher is biased against me" or "I will never understand statistics") are less likely to be motivated for improvement and may be pessimistic about future outcomes. Instructors can assist students in making adaptive attributions, particularly by helping them attribute failure to effort rather than to ability, as well as by communicating their own positive attributions about students' capabilities for learning.

Social Goals and Social Motivation

Students are obviously motivated by more than academic achievement. For example, they also have social goals that are operative in the classroom: they want to be socially responsible and to form intimate social relationships with peers (Patrick et al., 1997). Although most studies of the relationship between social goals and academic motivation and achievement have been conducted with younger adolescents, certainly no college instructor would doubt that social goals are operative in the college classroom. Enabling students to meet some of those goals in conjunction with academic goals in your classroom may enhance student motivation to attend class and participate in academic work. For example, brief opportunities to discuss a question with a partner work well from a cognitive perspective because they foster elaboration and retention and provide opportunities for clarification. But they also give students an opportunity to get to know one another.

PUTTING MOTIVATION THEORY INTO PRACTICE

Although there are many ways you can structure classes that foster student motivation to learn, here are a few suggestions:

1. In planning assignments, consider issues of choice and control. If you would like students to write three papers during the term, provide assignments during four time periods and let them choose which three to complete. This enables students to take charge of planning their work in the context of requirements from other courses and allows them to select issues of greatest interest. (This also has the advantage of spreading out the grading that you will need to do.) Similarly, provide a choice of topics for each assignment and consider a range of options that engages interest. Foster initiative by allowing students to propose alternative topics that meet the intent of the assignment.

2. Foster mastery by encouraging students to revise their writing. Although it might not be reasonable for you to read drafts of every paper, you might do this for the first written assignment and then create peer review groups for additional papers. Or you can vary this process by responding to outlines for one paper and then reading drafts of opening paragraphs for the second. You can further foster mastery by uncoupling feedback and grading, so that early drafts receive written comments but no grades.

3. Adopt a criterion-referenced approach to grading rather than a normative one. Outline course requirements so that the point value for each assignment is clear from the beginning and students know what they need to do to succeed—and know that

they can succeed without worrying about their standing relative to others in the course. This fosters a sense of control, creates a cooperative rather than a competitive climate, and appeals to both intrinsically and extrinsically motivated students.

4. Test frequently enough that students become accustomed to the format and have opportunities to learn from their mistakes; at the very least, consider a similar format for the midterm and final. Allow students to justify and elaborate on their multiple-choice answers, which enhances control, and give partial or full credit for acceptable and reasonable justifications of alternative answers. Provide choices of essay questions to answer ("Answer five out of the following six questions"). Consider providing one of the essay questions in advance, particularly one that might require more thoughtfulness and preparation.

5. When grading tests, create a frequency distribution of responses and consider dropping questions missed by a large number of students—and then reteach the material after you return the tests. This sense of shared responsibility for the learning process heightens student awareness that you are committed more to their mastery of the material than to penalizing them for what they do not yet know.

6. Consider scheduling two test-taking periods for each test, with immediate feedback after the first test and two or three days to study before the next one (an alternate version), and award students the higher of the two grades. This fosters a mastery orientation to learning but also appeals to those students who are externally motivated by grades; the net effect in either case is further studying.

7. Provide feedback to students that is constructive, noncontrolling (for instance, avoid words like *should*), and informative, thus enhancing student desire to improve and continue to learn. View problems as something that can be addressed, not statements about an individual's worth.

8. Learn more about the motivation of your particular students. You might wish to administer the Motivated Strategies for Learning Questionnaire, a research questionnaire that assesses

both motivation and learning strategies, and is designed to be course-specific (Pintrich et al., 1991).

9. Project your own motivation—for the subject matter and for the students. Take opportunities to describe your own intrinsic motivation for both research and teaching and your mastery orientation to learning. Too much of the literature on faculty "rewards" has focused on the extrinsic reinforcement for teaching, neglecting our own intrinsic motivation for academic work. You are a powerful role model for your students as they develop their own passion and motivation for learning as well as for their future professions.

10. In your supervision of teaching assistants, make the motivational implications of your instructional decisions explicit. I am indebted to Paul Pintrich, Bill McKeachie, and Scott Paris, who were extraordinary role models in their design of graduate seminars that fostered student motivation but who also provided me with opportunities as a TA to understand the motivational structure of their undergraduate courses, which I have happily put into practice in my own teaching.

IN CONCLUSION

In review, several key principles about student motivation may be useful to keep in mind as you design your course, think about your instructional methods, and interact with your students.

1. Recognize students' needs for self-determination and autonomy, and provide opportunities for choice and control.

2. Foster intrinsic motivation by arousing curiosity, providing challenge, and offering choices, and provide extrinsic rewards that contain informative feedback and focus on improvement.

3. Make the value of your courses explicit, and take time to help students understand why what they are learning matters.

4. Create conditions that enable students to expect to succeed.

5. Create a classroom environment that promotes a mastery orientation, focused on the development of understanding and

mastery of material and skills, rather than on performance relative to that of others.

6. Foster adaptive attributions: help students value the application of effort and learning strategies, and communicate your belief in their capability.

7. Provide opportunities for students to meet social goals in ways that are compatible with academic goals.

Supplementary Reading

Although the following are directed more toward the motivational issues of K–12 schooling, the theories and many of the suggestions are useful to those who are interested in the issue of motivation in the college classroom.

J. Brophy, *Motivating Students to Learn* (Boston: McGraw-Hill, 1998).

P. R. Pintrich and D. H. Schunk, *Motivation in Education: Theory, Research, and Applications* (Englewood Cliffs, NJ: Prentice Hall, 1996).

D. J. Stipek, "Motivation and Instruction," in D. C. Berliner and R. J. Calfee (eds.), *Handbook of Educational Psychology* (New York: Macmillan, 1996).

10 Valuing Student Differences

Picture a world in which oppression has never existed, a place where snobbery, name calling, stereotyping, hate crimes, and huge discrepanices in income levels never occur. And picture a world in which students are very similar, where they show the same patterns of motivation, learn in the same way, have similar interests and study habits, follow the same lifestyles, and express themselves in a standard fashion, all very much like the style of faculty members, who are also pretty much the same.

Unreal? Of course. Yet this worldview characterizes many of our unconscious assumptions about teaching and learning. In our faculty roles, many of us are focused on the content of our discipline as we have learned it and are continuing to explore it, with very little attention to difference. Ask yourself, "When was the last time I took a very different approach in the content of the courses I teach? Have I introduced the ideas or work of a person who would have been thought marginal years ago? Have I begun to include biographical information in my science classes, talking about how certain theorists struggled to have new ideas accepted, rather than simply presenting the theory? Have I sup-

This chapter was written by Nancy Van Note Chism of Indiana University—Purdue University Indianapolis.

ported students who choose to explore, in a paper or thesis, a topic that is aligned more with their cultural heritage or life situation than with mainstream scholarship in my field?"

Then ask yourself, "When was the last time I taught as though students were different, giving choices about assignments so that they could express their learning in a way that respected their strengths, making sure that I got to know their individual styles, backgrounds, and ways of learning so that I could build on these?"

For most of us, the answer is that we do these things occasionally, but not to the extent that we should, given our future as a multicultural society and the dramatic differences that are occurring in the student body at most colleges and universities today.

A vigorous line of new scholarly research has been documenting the many benefits of student diversity—the ways in which students are different by virtue of their socioeconomic class, race, ethnicity, sex, age, religion, sexual orientation, and physical or learning ability. This diversity, the studies find, benefits individual students, institutions of higher learning, the economy, and society (Milem & Hakuta, 2000). Several studies have documented empirically the ways in which student difference enlarges students' perspectives, increases their critical thinking, and fosters higher intellectual engagement (Alger et al., 2000; Gurin, 1999; Hurtado, 1997; Milem, 2001; Smith et al., 1997; Springer et al., 1996).

Other scholars have provided conceptual arguments for why it is important to attend to student diversity. These reasons are clustered into moral, intellectual, and social grounds (Karenga, 1995; Musil et al., 1999). The moral grounds focus on mutual respect between teachers and learners as people. The intellectual imperative highlights the importance to any intellectual endeavor of multiple perspectives, of seeing things from the fullness of human experience, of growth through challenge and contrast. Socially, the call is for justice and equity among people, both while they are in formal learning environments and as they subsequently live their lives. Sutton (1993), referencing the contributions of Henry Giroux and Paulo Freire, states, "Education is part of a larger ethical, social and cultural enterprise in which teachers are morally responsible to help students engage in a struggle for a more humane world" (p. 163).

Recent surveys (Association of American Colleges and Universities, 2000) show that an overwhelming majority of American citizens believe that (1) understanding of difference will be increasingly important in our society and (2) diversity education is important and effective. A 1998 survey found that more than 90 percent of U.S. faculty members associated an ethnically diverse student body with a better educational experience for all students (Sax et al., 1999).

In addition to these fundamental considerations, the growing diversity of the current and projected student populations is forcing a consideration of the need for attention to a different kind of teaching (Upcraft, 1996). Students who are older than the traditional 17- to 22-year-old range now constitute the majority of the higher education population. Women are now the majority sex at many institutions and nationally account for 56 percent of all bachelor's degrees. Students of color are a greater presence on campus, and the changes in their representation (see Table 10.1) show a marked difference in the past 23 years (*Chronicle of Higher Education*, 2000b). Furthermore, an Educational Testing Services report (*Chronicle of Higher Education*, 2000a) predicts that minority students will account for 80 percent of the growth in the U.S. college population between 2000 and 2015. Students with physical or learning disabilities are attending and self-identifying in higher numbers, reported as 10 percent in 1996 (American Council on Education, 1996), and legislation, such as the Americans with Disabilities Act of 1990, requires educational settings to address the needs of the disabled. Gay, lesbian, and bisexual students (who have heretofore been a largely "invisible" population) are becoming increasingly articulate about their participation. Many students entering college from all of these groups are first-generation college students and students from low-income families. In summary, these trends show that "Whether we are prepared to deal with it or not, it is happening. It does not matter whether we are liberals or conservatives, the future of this country is going to be multicultural" (Hodgkinson, 1995, p. 3).

Group	Percentage of growth, 1976–1997	Percentage of 1997 Total Population (rounded)[a]	
	All Students	Undergraduates	All Students
American Indian	87	9	1
Asian American	34	6	6
African American	50	11	11
Hispanic American	217	8	9
White American	13	71	71
International	113	3	2
Total	32	100	100

[a] Comparison percentages may be slightly skewed by changes in institutions represented in the count.

TABLE 10.1   Racial/Ethnic Composition of the U.S. College Population

Disappointing retention rates and discouragement on the part of many traditionally underrepresented students are indicators that higher education has not been successful in serving new learners. Although financial aid, residential life, and a host of other factors are important, the weight of past research evidence suggests that faculty members are crucial to student educational attainment: positive in- and out-of-class relationships with their teachers can enable students to overcome constraints and achieve academic success (Astin, 1975; Ferguson, 1990; Pascarella & Terenzini, 1991). One step toward helping students from diverse groups to succeed, then, is to become aware of the tremendous influence that we can have on student success. Yet institutional initiatives have far outpaced faculty involvement in diversity efforts (Helton, 2000).

One reason why attention to diversity has been slow to reach the classroom is institutional respect for individual faculty control of content and pedagogy decisions. Yet many of us have clear anxieties with respect to difference in the classroom (Weinstein & Obear, 1992). We wonder whether attention to difference will fragment and irritate social relations and prevent rather than encourage student success. We argue about "canon" issues, fearing a watering down of the curriculum. We may fear that the purposes of social diversity will call on us to treat students preferentially—a practice that we have always been careful to avoid. We may also feel that we are walking on eggshells, that whatever action we take will be misinterpreted (Chesler, 1994). But it is clear that the problems need to be addressed openly. The payoff is not only for our students themselves, but also for our colleges and universities as they profit from truly embracing the opportunity to let previously unheard or unheeded voices enrich and broaden ways of thinking and knowing.

The main teaching issues connected with social diversity fall into two broad categories: curriculum and instructional strategies. The first, curriculum issues, is the most frequently debated. The claim is that the content of most courses very narrowly focuses on the Western intellectual tradition, specifically the experience of the mainstream, European-descended male. Thus students from other cultural traditions feel marginal to the academic experience. They see no role models and feel that their experience is not valued. Second, classroom interactions, academic discourse, cognitive style, and other aspects of teaching and learning also exhibit a male European cultural style that constrains full participation by students from other backgrounds and excludes insights from other cultures. Majority as well as minority students, then, experience an education that is far too narrow, given the possibilities.

The literature on inclusive teaching bears several messages for us to consider: (1) all students need to feel welcome; (2) they need to feel that they are being treated as individuals; (3) they need to feel that they can participate fully; and (4) they need to be treated fairly (Adams, 1992; Border & Chism, 1992; Bowser et al., 1995; Darder, 1996; Lynch, 1997; Prenger, 1999; Saunders & Kardia, 1997; Schoem et al., 1993; Wlodkowski & Ginsberg, 1995).

FEELING WELCOME IN THE CLASSROOM

Feeling included is a key to student motivation to learn (Wlodkowski & Ginsberg, 1995). It is important, then, that students not encounter overt hostility, ignorance, and insensitivity, as well as more subtle messages that their difference is not valued. Although they report that most faculty do not voice such overt hostility, students pick up on more subtle cues, often entangled in our attempts to be humorous, such as jokes about sexual orientation or physical disabilities or women. The message received is that there is an underlying resentment about the presence of students who "don't fit." Many times, well-meaning but ignorant actions are the cause of discomfort. If we address a student with a learning disability with exaggerated enunciation, we can make the student feel that it is assumed he is dull witted. In order to become more sensitive, we must look within ourselves for lingering biases that are a pervasive result of modern socialization. Several publications have good exercises for self-exploration (see the resources listed at the end of the chapter). We must be patient with ourselves and our students while several generations try to unlearn some deep-seated prejudices.

Language is a cue to our stance for many students. Preferences in terminology continue to change as social groups explore their identity. Presently, for example, "gay and lesbian students" is more preferable than "homosexual students"; "Asian" is preferred to "Oriental"; and "women" is preferred to "gals" or other diminutives. Students within broadly labeled categories may prefer their own particular identity, such as "Puerto Rican" rather than "Hispanic" or "Latino." When we listen to the dialog around common terms or ask students about their preferences, we avoid using terms that offend and demonstrate our care and sensitivity.

Welcoming involves not only being personally sensitive as the instructor, but also helping all students to display welcoming behavior toward one another in the classroom. We play a critical role in monitoring classroom behavior and addressing problems as part of the learning experience when they occur. Rather than hurriedly passing over the comment of a student who refers to "colored people on welfare" or "Jewish-American princesses," it is important for us to openly discuss issues surrounding the negative image and language choice of the response, even if embarrassment is a possibility. Failing to stop and take advantage of this "teachable moment" sends a message to students. As one student put it, "Doing nothing is doing something" (Lopez & Chism, 1993). Teaching for diversity is not only being more welcoming to diverse groups, but also increasing the sensitivity of majority students to cultural differences.

First-generation, international, or low-income college students in particular may need to become accustomed to academic customs and lingo (Jones & Young, 1997). Terms and practices that we frequently take for granted, such as *prerequisite, plagiarism, midterm,* and *syllabus,* may be outside the realm of their experience. Because they fear that they are the only ones who need an explanation, first-generation students may be hesitant to ask. It is especially important for those of us who teach introductory courses to realize that we can be helpful by orienting students to the college experience as we teach our courses.

For students from diverse groups to feel valued, we need to go beyond neutrality. Frequently, students experience alienation because their presence is not acknowledged at all. They often use the term *invisible* to describe how they feel. Although majority students sometimes describe the same feeling, it is experienced more deeply by students who are from a group that has traditionally experienced exclusion, because they are more likely to wonder if the action is related to their group membership. To avoid having students interpret the impersonal, businesslike behaviors of the traditional classroom as instances of personal rejection, we can take care to call students by name, engage in formal greetings or "small talk" before moving on, or allow for the personal to enter the domain of the scholarly as appropriate. When we acknowledge diversity at the beginning of a course by indicating that we welcome different perspectives and want to accommodate different needs, we set the tone for students to feel respected and free to communicate with us.

One of the biggest problems with helping underrepresented students feel welcome is large class size. They can feel lost and may also feel that the peer environment is more likely to get out of hand because classroom management is more of a challenge.

Students of color, for example, often say that they are very hesitant to speak out on issues about people of color in large group settings because they fear physical violence and slurs that the instructor will not witness. International or second-language students may worry that their speech patterns will be ridiculed or that they will be asked to repeat themselves several times in front of the large crowd. Our attempts to manage large class environments well and to increase personal contact with students by walking throughout the room, scheduling out-of-class visits with students, or working closely with small groups of students on a rotating basis are especially important gestures that can be made to students experiencing the "outsider" syndrome. The use of collaborative learning, peer teaching, focus groups, and other methods can help students feel included (Wlodkowski & Ginsberg, 1995). Simply asking students to turn to another person to discuss an issue can occasionally help to make a large class smaller.

Technology use is also a potential barrier. First-generation and lower-socioeconomic-status students may have less access to computers and less familiarity with them than others. Students from "high-touch" cultural backgrounds may not find "high-tech" methods inviting. To be inclusive, we should ensure that students have access to the equipment and training they need, and we should use instructional technology in ways that will encourage active participation and interaction.

Feeling Welcome Through the Curriculum

Alienation also occurs frequently when students look in vain for mention of their social group or evidence of their perspective throughout the curriculum. For example, works by or about people of color or gay, lesbian, or bisexual people should not be noticeable only by their absence. Often we do not realize the effect of emphasizing only traditional content. In data collected for a study of gay and lesbian issues in the college classroom (Lopez & Chism, 1993), one gay student reported looking forward to the day when his American history instructor would lecture on a section of the text that dealt with the gay pride movement, only to hear the instructor say that he would not deal with the "so-called

Stonewall Riots." Another student in the same study reported that a human sexuality instructor said that the class would skip the chapter on homosexuality because the course was only about "normal" sexuality. The students reported that examples used in classes and assignments consistently presumed a heterosexual orientation. When such things happen, students feel that their point of view, their culture, their heritage are not welcome. They look for role models of scholars, practitioners, and artists in their field of study and find few examples that would encourage them to persist in school. Simple attempts at inclusion can be of enormous importance to students seeking validation. They can also increase the breadth of exposure of majority students.

As many scholars have noted, rethinking the curriculum often begins with including references to or about scholars or issues connected with socially diverse groups, but ultimately it involves a transformative approach whereby the entire assumptions and content of a given field are reconsidered from the perspectives of diverse people (Gay, 1995; Kitano, 1997; Sleeter, 1991; Toombs & Tierney, 1992). Transformation in sociology, for example, could begin with attention to eliminating stereotyped references or including mention of the work of some current sociologists of color, but would move on to rethink some basic ways of doing or thinking about sociology in light of feminist epistemology or other paradigms. Transformation also involves what Darder (1996, p. 139) calls "an emancipatory view of authority." She suggests that, because "knowledge as a historical and cultural product is forever in a state of partiality," classrooms should be seen as settings for open inquiry and the challenge to existing ideas that diverse perspectives can bring. Often the scholarship necessary to revise courses is hard to access or undeveloped. It takes both personal and institutional commitment and much original scholarship to do this work. Excellent advice on curriculum transformation is now available in such works as *Creating an Inclusive Curriculum* (Friedman et al., 1996).

The rewards of investing in curriculum change are powerful: enrichment of the scholarship as well as the increased engagement of students from diverse social groups. And if we wish to create a welcoming climate, we can

■ Display authentic concern for students and avoid patronizing behaviors.

■ Attend to terminology preferences of social groups by reading and listening to discussions as well as asking directly.

■ State explicitly that diversity is valued in the classroom and deal promptly with biased student comments rather than ignore them.

■ Personalize classroom interactions as much as possible by engaging in informal discussion before class, using students' names, and encouraging students to visit during office hours.

■ Enrich course content by drawing on perspectives, examples, references, and ways of knowing that reflect the fullness of human inquiry.

Being Treated as an Individual

Although students from diverse groups are very eager that members of their group feel welcome on campus, they also want to be treated as individuals. One barrier that prevents this is stereotyping. Images of the African-American student as a "dumb jock" or "special admissions" student; of the Muslim student as a "terrorist"; of the female sorority student as a "fluffhead"; or of the lesbian student as an "argumentative dyke" influence our expectations, often in unconscious ways. Stereotypes that are ostensibly positive, such as the "math whiz" Asian American or the "wise" older student, are also problematic because they may place unrealistically high expectations on some students. We do not have to voice these stereotypes for students—they often get the message indirectly. For example, we may lavish excessive praise on an American Indian student, causing the student to feel that the expectations for him are low because of his ethnicity. We might consistently ask female students, rather than males, to take notes for students who are ill or ask males, rather than females, to head up lab groups. Because early socialization into these stereotypes is very powerful, we are often unaware of the biases we exhibit. Attending to these requires that we engage in a continual process of "unlearning" through careful reflection on our past assumptions in light of present understandings. It is also important to realize that within-group differences are sometimes very large. Terms used to describe categories of difference, such as "Hispanic/Latino" and "Asian American," are very broad and encompass multiple subgroups with important differences. The way of life for people from Hawaii, for example, is very different from that for the Inuit or someone whose parents came from China, yet all are in the "Asian-American" category.

Tokenism, paying attention to a person solely because of a chosen demographic characteristic of interest, can also get in the way of treating students individually. Students feel uncomfortable when we say such things as "John, how do disabled people feel about this issue?" John may not have an opinion; he may feel that there is likely to be a range of opinions on the topic across students with disabilities; and he might feel put on the spot. While it is understandable that we might want to include the student in the treatment of a topic and hear the voice of the "local expert," most students want to be respected as individuals and to contribute on their own volition when these issues are addressed.

Individual nurturing through mentoring relationships is also important, yet women and students of color report much lower instances of being mentored than male European Americans (Blackwell, 1990; Hall & Sandler, 1982). In commenting on the reasons for the lack of mentoring and graduate associateships reported by minority graduate students, Blackwell concludes that faculty do not choose students who are different from themselves, because there is a "tendency for faculty members to consciously or subconsciously attempt to reproduce themselves through persons chosen as their protegées" (p. 8). Keeping an open mind about having work go in a new direction or appreciating stylistic differences as potentially complementary or liberating are often involved in mentoring previously underrepresented students.

In sum, to treat students as individuals, we can

- Look beyond stereotypes to appreciate individual characteristics.

- Allow students to volunteer opinions rather than asking them to serve as representatives of their social group.

■ Cultivate mentoring relationships with students from under-represented or marginalized groups.

FULL PARTICIPATION IN LEARNING

Valuing people who think and act in ways that are consistent with the traditional culture of the institution often leads to inadvertent or deliberate exclusion of those who are different. Most of us are unaware that we are operating within a cultural perspective, because the dominant culture is taken for granted. As Adams (1992) describes, whereas this culture is natural and invisible to some, it is uncomfortable for many students from socially diverse groups because in its most extreme form it is "narrow in that it rules out nonverbal, empathic, visual, symbolic, or nuanced communication; it neglects the social processes by which interpersonal communication, influence, consensus, and commitment are included in problem solving; it overlooks the social environment as a source of information . . . ; it ignores the values and emotions that nonacademics attach to reasons and facts" (p. 6).

The gap between the dominant classroom culture and the culture of other students can be large. For students who have not had a great deal of mainstream culture experience and whose native language is not English, the differences are enormous (Collett & Serrano, 1992; Jones & Young, 1997). Many scholars have enumerated differences between particular cultures and academic culture. Hofstede (1986), for example, talks about differences in whether the individual or the group is valued, whether there are large or small power distances between people, whether the culture seeks certainty or tolerates ambiguity, and whether the culture stresses the "masculine" characteristics of material success and assertiveness or the "feminine" characteristics of quality of life and interpersonal relationships. He describes the classroom culture as very different from the cultural expectations of many groups. Much has been written about the differences between an afrocentric and a eurocentric worldview (Asante, 1987, 1988; Karenga, 1995). These studies portray the afrocentric worldview as stressing harmony, egalitarian social relations, a fluid notion of time and space, the social world, nonverbal communication, holistic thinking, intuitive reasoning, and approximation; the eurocentric worldview as stressing competition, power, numerical precision, abstract thinking, verbal communication, analytical thinking, logic, and quantitative accuracy. This literature portrays American classrooms as placing an almost exclusive emphasis on the eurocentric worldview.

Learning Style Dimensions of Full Participation

There is not a clear consensus on whether one can draw implications on learning styles from cultural styles or whether particular learning styles are associated with particular groups. In the case of some of the populations being discussed, such as gay, lesbian, and bisexual students, there is no present evidence to indicate that there are clear patterns. For some other groups, such as students with learning disabilities, there are clear differences (by definition) connected with the disability. In some of the remaining categories of students, such as nontraditional-age students, women, and students of color, several studies suggest that there are patterns. These descriptions must be viewed with caution, because talking about broad patterns across groups of people who have many intragroup differences can lead to stereotyping and overgeneralization. On the other hand, if descriptions of styles are considered as tools to illustrate differences rather than as applicable to every individual in the categories described, they can be helpful. Irvine and York (1995) provide an excellent overview of this topic.

When scholars talk about major differences in cognitive and social-interactional styles across various cultures, they often use the work of learning style theorists and apply their constructs, which are usually polar opposites, such as abstract versus concrete thinking, to a particular cultural group. Anderson and Adams (1992), for example, use Anderson's categories of relational and analytical, and Witkin and Moore's (1975) categories of field independence and field dependence (also termed "field sensitivity") to illustrate differences in style. They argue that women from the European-American culture and men and women from

American Indian, Hispanic-American, and African-American cultures often exhibit a style that is relational and field dependent. They suggest that many people from these groups are more improvisational and intuitive than sequential and structured; more interested in material with social or concrete content than abstract material; more holistic than analytical; and more cooperative than competitive. Most European-American males (most faculty members) and Asian-American males would tend to fall into opposite categories. They have been socialized through their culture and the academic tradition to value analytic, structured, abstract approaches. The danger that this research warns against is that we might view differences from the traditional norm as deficits, devaluing the work of some students and preventing them from learning well. An additional danger is that overreliance on the mainstream style leads to stale scholarship.

Similarly, a body of literature on cognitive development discusses patterns in the way in which women take in and process information (Baxter Magolda, 1992; Belenky et al., 1986). These studies have looked closely at epistemological development, resisting the strict association of one pattern with male students and one with females, while at the same time identifying contrasting styles that are gender related. They find that development in the women they studied culminates in levels of thinking that are as complex as those described in studies of men, but qualitatively different at each stage in gender-related ways. Baxter Magolda, for example, describes four levels of epistemological reflection: absolute, transitional, independent, and contextual knowing. Within each of the first three levels, however, students demonstrate contrasting approaches, generally termed "relational" and "abstract." For example, transitional knowers, the most prevalent type of knowers among traditional-age college students, demonstrate two patterns: the interpersonal pattern, found more frequently in women, and the impersonal, found more frequently in men. Although both genders are transitional knowers in that they view knowledge as uncertain, at least in some areas, and understanding as more important than acquiring and remembering information, they demonstrate the different gender-related patterns shown in Table 10.2.

Interpersonal	Impersonal
Want to exchange ideas with others	Want to debate ideas
Seek rapport with the instructor	Want to be challenged by the instructor
Want evaluation to take individual differences into account	Want fair and practical evaluation
Resolve uncertainty by personal judgment	Resolve uncertainty by logic, judgment, and research
Source: Baxter Magolda, 1992.	

TABLE 10.2   Gender-related Patterns of Thinking in Traditional-Age College Students

One area of research that documents how different ways of knowing affect classroom learning is the literature on classroom participation. Several researchers have found in empirical studies that in classroom discussion white males speak more frequently and for longer periods than white females and males and females of color, and that they are treated deferentially by teachers (Allen & Niss, 1990; Knoedler & Shea, 1992; Sadker & Sadker, 1992; Trujillo, 1986). Clearly, the style associated with European-American males is dominant in many American college classrooms, making it difficult for others to participate.

Physical and Learning Disabilities

Students with mobility impairments, problems with vision or hearing, and learning differences because of attention issues, dyslexia, or a host of other characteristics must also be allowed full participation. Although such students are encouraged to speak with instructors about their needs, teachers can pave the way for this interaction by opening each course with a general statement on caring about students' individual needs and inviting students to speak with them about these, as well as inserting statements about alternative formats and practices in the syllabus for each course. Rojewski and Schell (1994), Prenger (1999), and the Center for Teaching and Learning (1998) suggest specific ways in which instructors can adapt or modify their teaching to serve students with disabilities. Instructors who cultivate a good relationship with the campus units that serve students with disabilities can make good recommendations and provisions for full participation.

Age Differences

Full participation for students older than the traditional 17 to 22-year-old college student can be fostered by attending to students' need for relevance to their life experiences and by being flexible when the personal responsibilities of students with child care issues or workplace pressures call for different learning arrangements. When the age of the student entails some physical limitations, such as hearing loss or diminished memory, provisions similar to those extended to students with physical disabilities, such as alternative formats, permission to audiotape class, or extended time for tests, can be offered. Excellent advice for teaching nontraditional-age students is contained in Siebert and colleagues (2000).

Increasing Opportunities for Full Participation

There are several ways that we can increase opportunities for participation. First, we can be aware that different cultural and learning styles exist. We can reflect on our own styles and on the extent to which our preferences for a style or grounding in a culture leads to teaching practices that exclude others. Similarly, we can be alert to these differences among our students.

Second, we can use varied instructional approaches. Moving between lecture, discussion, small-group work, experiential learning, simulations, and other strategies allows more possibilities for students to find learning opportunities and for all to expand their own stylistic repertoires. Similarly, we can use redundancy in teaching modalities and provide for options in assignments.

Third, we can evaluate work from multiple perspectives. For example, rather than viewing a personal narrative by a nontraditional-age student as "subjective, emotional, and unscholarly," we can see it as an alternative kind of contribution to the traditional footnoted and impersonal paper, each valuable in a different way.

Increasing Motivation

In addition to attending to differences in style, culture, and physical ability, a very powerful way that we can enable full participation in learning is to attend to the motivational aspects of learning. Refer to the previous chapter for an extended discussion of motivation theory. Wlodkowski and Ginsberg (1995) enumerate ways in which this can be done:

- *Establishing inclusion* focuses on conveying a sense of respect for the student and working to connect students through communicating a sense of confidence in the student and encouraging collaboration and ownership. Practices that foster inclusion include collaborative and cooperative learning, peer teaching, writing groups, and exercises that create opportunities for reframing knowledge from different perspectives.

- *Developing attitude* speaks to the importance of students' need for personal relevance and self-determination. Strategies that attend to attitude include engaging students in goal setting, allowing choices in learning, and encouraging experiential learning.

- *Enhancing meaning* stresses the need for engagement and challenge through promoting higher-order thinking in real-world applications. Meaning can be enhanced through the use of critical questioning, decision-making exercises, research on student-generated questions, and creative activity.

- *Engendering competence* addresses a central finding of motivation theory research, the need for the learner to feel that success is possible. Here the focus is on multiple ways to represent knowledge and on effective assessment methods, including frequent feedback, self-assessment on the part of the learner, and alternatives to pencil-and-paper tests—alternatives grounded in the context of the skills or knowledge being assessed.

BEING TREATED FAIRLY

Egalitarian treatment of students is a very valued norm in American higher education. Grading anonymously, giving all students the same amount of time to complete a test or assignment, and requiring the same number and type of assignments by each student are common practices. We often say, "I treat all students the same." Yet a closer look reveals that we do not treat all students the same, nor should we. Students with disabilities are often allowed more time for exams, the help of a reader, or a special setting for taking the test. Nonnative speakers may be allowed to use dictionaries during test taking, and their work may be graded more for content than for expression of ideas. Some students may be excused from class for religious holidays that other students do not observe. Equal treatment involves not necessarily same treatment, then, but treatment that respects the individual circumstances of particular learners.

Although we may readily accept different treatment for students who are disabled or are nonnative speakers or are older students who have hearing impairments or work slowly, we might find it much more difficult to justify different treatment based on gender, socioecomic status, or cultural characteristics. Once again, however, beginning with the individual student is important. It is important to have expectations that are appropriate to the student. Some disjuncture between the student's point of entry and the dominant culture may occur, and balance should be sought. For example, students coming from cultures where time is viewed fluidly may have difficulty understanding that due dates will be interpreted literally or that class begins promptly on the hour. Most students have learned to be bicultural and to operate under different sets of assumptions based on the cultural context. Others, however, may need help. It may be necessary to have individual conversations with such students, emphasizing the expectations or giving reminders about due dates. It may be important to tolerate a few mistakes before penalizing students or to rethink the cultural embeddedness of the rule. A discussion—at the start of the course—on expectations and standards, coupled with a clear syllabus, can help communication immeasurably.

We can also consider cultural or gender-related issues that may affect class discussion. Many female students or students of both genders from American Indian or Asian-American backgrounds have been socialized to value listening more than speaking. For them, a class participation grading scheme based on number of contributions in class may be problematic. Fair treatment might be based on quality of comment rather than on quantity or on performance in dyad or small-group, rather than whole-class, conversation. The teacher can help students who are from cultures more reflective than spontaneous by giving the class time for silent thought before responses are solicited. They may need to learn the culture. Conversely, students from the dominant culture may learn from them, incorporating the strengths of silent reflection into class routines. Myra and David Sadker (1992) recommend that teachers ask an observer to record participation levels in their classes, to give them a sense of the patterns that are occurring so that they may avoid the pitfall of unequal discussion.

Inherent in all discussions about fairness is mutuality. The need for order and routine must be balanced by appreciation for variation and richness of perspective. Strongly forcing students from nontraditional backgrounds to acculturate to the institution in order to succeed prevents the institution from learning and expanding its potential. Pervading considerations of social diversity are issues involved in the ongoing revitalization of colleges as places of learning.

IN CONCLUSION

As faculty, we play a crucial role in the success of students from socially diverse groups. To help these students get the most from their education and to help the institution benefit from the talents and perspectives the students bring, we can

1. Help to make the students feel welcome by displaying genuine interest, personalizing our interactions with them, and honoring and including their perspectives and experiences.

2. Treat students as individuals, rather than as representatives of social groups.

3. Ensure that students from diverse social groups have ample opportunity to participate fully through providing options for different learning styles and modes of expression.

4. Strive for fair treatment by communicating appropriate expectations and making instructional decisions with inclusion in mind.

Supplementary Reading

L. B. Border and N. V. N. Chism (eds.), Teaching for Diversity [Special issue]. *New Directions in Teaching and Learning,* 1992, *49.* This collection of essays treats the following topics: the culture of the classroom, learning styles of diverse learners, gender equity in the classroom, feminist pedagogy, and developing programs to promote inclusive teaching. Descriptions of successful programs and a resource guide are included.

A. I. Morey and M. K. Kitano (eds.), *Multicultural Course Transformation in Higher Education: A Broader Truth* (Needham Heights, MA: Allyn and Bacon, 1997). This collection contains a very comprehensive set of chapters that deals not only with curricular transformation but also with pedagogy and assessment issues.

D. Schoem, L. Frankel, X. Zúñiga, and E. A. Lewis (eds.), *Multicultural Teaching in the University* (Westport, CT: Praeger, 1993). This collection of thoughtful essays explores the meaning and function of multicultural teaching in higher education, through conceptual pieces as well as reports of the actual experiences of instructors from various disciplines and perspectives working to enact new curricula and teaching practices.

R. Wlodkowski and M. Ginsberg, *Diversity and Motivation: Culturally Responsive Teaching* (San Francisco: Jossey-Bass, 1995). The authors approach multicultural teaching from the perspective of motivation, identifying norms and structural conditions that will help students feel included, establish a productive attitude toward learning, derive meaning from their learning, and feel competent as learners.

Several teaching and learning centers have wonderful handbooks on inclusive teaching. Many of these are on the World Wide Web. Particularly comprehensive treatments have been done by the Universities of Michigan, Nebraska at Lincoln, North Carolina at Chapel Hill, and Virginia.

11 Problem Students (There's Almost Always at Least One!)*

Periodically during my weekly meetings with teaching assistants, I suggest that we discuss problem students or situations in their classes as an agenda item for the next week. I have never found that the next week's discussion ended early for lack of examples. It is reassuring to know that one is not alone in having a particular problem and that it is probably not due solely to one's inadequacy as a teacher. This chapter will discuss some of the common problems that have been raised by my teaching assistants and will suggest some strategies to try. But first a word of general advice.

It is human nature for us to perceive the problem as the student; but before focusing on changing the student's behavior, take a few moments to look at what you are doing that might be related to the student's behavior. Interpersonal problems involve at least two people, and in many cases the difficulties are not one-sided.

---

* Note that strategies for dealing with some problems are discussed in other chapters; for example, students who don't do their share of the work are discussed in the chapter on active learning, emotional students in the chapter on facilitating discussion, and cheaters in the chapter on cheating.

ANGRY, AGGRESSIVE, CHALLENGING STUDENTS

Every once in a while, a class will include one or more students who seem to have a chip on their shoulder—who convey, both verbally and nonverbally, hostility toward you and the whole enterprise. Sometimes the attitude is not so much hostility as a challenge to your authority. What can you do?

Probably the most common strategy we use is to try to ignore them. This strategy often succeeds in avoiding a public confrontation and disruption of the class. However, it may not result in better motivation and learning for the student.

I try to become better acquainted with the student. If I have had students turn in minute papers or journals, I read the angry student's writings more carefully to try to understand what the problem is. I may ask the student to come in to see me and discuss the paper, leading to questions about how the student feels about the course, what things he enjoys, what topics might be interesting to him. (I use the male pronoun because these students are most likely to be males, although I have also encountered hostile female students.) Sometimes you will feel in such a conversation that you have to drag each word from the student, yet the student will accept your invitation to come in for another discussion. Sometimes you may need to invite a small group of students to meet with you (including the hostile student) in order to make the situation less threatening for the hostile student who hides fear with aggressiveness.

Whatever your strategy, it seems to me important to let the student know that you recognize him as an individual, that you are committed to his learning, and that you are willing to listen and respond as constructively as possible.

What about overt hostility—the student who attacks your point of view during a lecture or class discussion, or the student who feels that your poor teaching or unfair grading caused students' poor performance on a test?

First of all, *listen* carefully and respectfully. Nothing is more frustrating than to be interrupted before your argument or complaint has been heard. Next, acknowledge that there is a possibility that the student may be right or at least that there is some logic or evidence on his or her side. Recognize the student's feelings. Then you have at least two or three alternatives:

1. State your position as calmly and rationally as you can, recognizing that not everyone will agree. If the issue is one of substance, ask the class what evidence might be obtained to resolve or clarify the issue. Don't rely on your own authority or power to put the student down or to make it a win-lose situation. If the issue is one of judgment about grading, state your reason for asking the question, what sort of thinking you were hoping to assess, and how students who did well went about answering the question. Note that your judgment may not be perfect, but you have the responsibility to make the best judgment you can, and you have done so.

2. Present the issue to the class. "How do the rest of you feel about this?" This has the obvious danger that either you or the aggressor may find no support and feel alienated from the class, but more often than not it will bring the issues and arguments for both sides into the open and be a useful experience in thinking for everyone. This might be a place to use the two-column method described in the chapter "Facilitating Discussion," listing on the board, without comments, the arguments on both sides.

3. Admit that you may have been wrong, and say that you will take time to reconsider and report back at the next class session. If the student really does have a good point, this will gain you respect and a reputation for fairness. If the student's argument was groundless, you may gain the reputation of being easy to influence, and have an increasing crowd of students asking for changes in their grades.

What about the student who comes into your office all charged up to attack your grading of what was clearly a very good exam paper?

Again, the first step is to listen. Get the student to state his or her rationale. As suggested in the chapter "Assessing, Testing, and Evaluating," you may gain some time to think if you have announced that students who have questions or complaints about grading of their tests should bring a written explanation to your office of their point of view and the rationale for their request for a higher grade.

But, once again, don't be so defensive about your grading that you fail to make an adjustment if the student has a valid point. I have on rare occasions offered to ask another faculty member to read the paper or examination to get an independent judgment.

If you don't feel that the student has a valid point and your explanation is not convincing, you may simply have to say that, although the student may be right, you have to assign the grades in terms of what seem to you the appropriate criteria. If you have been clear about the rubric you use in grading, both before giving the assignment or test and when you returned the papers, grievances should be rare.

ATTENTION SEEKERS AND STUDENTS WHO DOMINATE DISCUSSIONS

In their book *The College Classroom*, Dick Mann (1970) and his graduate students describe eight clusters of students, one of which is "attention seekers." Attention seekers talk whether or not they have anything to say; they joke, show off, compliment the teacher or other students—they continually try to be noticed (Mann et al., 1970).

At the beginning of the term, when I am trying to get discussions started, I am grateful for the attention seekers. They help keep the discussion going. But as the class develops, both the other students and I tend to be disturbed by the students who talk too much and interfere with other students' chances to talk. What do I do then?

Usually I start by suggesting that I want to get everyone's ideas—that each student has a unique perspective and that it is important that we bring as many perspectives and ideas as possible to bear on the subject under discussion. If hands are raised to participate, I call first on those who haven't talked recently.

If the problem persists, I may suggest to the class that some people seem to participate much more than others and ask them for suggestions about what might be done to give all students a chance to participate.

Alternatively, I might ask two or three students to act as "process observers" for a day, to report at the end of the class or at the beginning of the next class on their observations of how the discussion went, what problems they noticed, and what suggestions they have. (I might even ask the attention seeker to be a process observer one day.) Or you might audiotape or videotape a class and play back one or more portions at the next class period for student reactions.

If all else fails, I ask the student to see me outside class and mention that I'm concerned about the class discussions. Much as I appreciate his involvement it would be helpful if he would hold back some of his comments until everyone else has been heard.

In the preceding comments I may have assumed that the attention seeker was not making good, helpful comments. There are also dominant students who are knowledgeable, fluent, and eager to contribute relevant information, contribute real insights, and solve problems. We prize such students; yet there is still the potential danger that other students will withdraw, feeling that there is no need to participate, since the dominant student is so brilliant or articulate that their own ideas and questions will seem weak and inadequate. Here subgrouping may help, with the stipulation that each student must present his or her question, idea, or reaction to the task of the group before beginning a general discussion.

In his newsletter *The University Teacher* Harry Stanton (1992), consultant on higher education at the University of Tasmania, suggests that each student be given three matches or markers at the beginning of the class. Each time they speak they must put down one of their markers and when their markers are gone, their contributions are over for the day. Perhaps subgroups could pool their markers or one could borrow or bargain for an extra marker for a really good idea that needs to be presented at this time.

INATTENTIVE STUDENTS

Periodically I have a class in which two or three students in the back of the classroom carry on their own conversations. This is annoying not only to me but to students sitting near them. What to do?

Think back to my first word of advice. Is the lecture material too difficult? Too easy? Is the topic of discussion one that arouses anxiety? Assuming that the answer to these questions is "no" and the behavior persists despite changes in topic or level of difficulty, what next?

My first attempt is typically to break the class into buzz groups assigned to work on some problem or to come up with a hypothesis, and to move around the class to see how the groups are progressing, making sure that I get to the group including the disruptive students to see that they are working on the group task. Usually this works, and sometimes this gets the students reengaged in the class for the rest of the class period.

But suppose that in the next class period the same problem recurs? This time I might have the class write minute papers and call on one of the inattentive students to report what he or she has written, or alternatively call on someone seated near the inattentive group, centering activity toward that part of the classroom.

Another possibility is to announce that, because research evidence indicates that students who sit in front get better grades (and you can explain why seeing an instructor's face and mouth improves attention and understanding), you have a policy of rotating seats periodically so that next week you will expect those sitting in the back row to move to the front row and all other rows to move back one row.

If all else fails, I might have a general class feedback discussion on what factors facilitated and what factors might have interfered with learning in the class thus far in the term. Alternatively, I might ask one or more of the students to see me outside of class to ask about their feelings about the class and to express my concern about not being able to teach in a way that would capture their attention.

UNPREPARED STUDENTS

There are often good reasons why students come to class unprepared, but there are also students who are chronically unprepared for no apparent reason. What can we do? I'll elaborate on the suggestions made in the chapters "Facilitating Discussion" and "How to Make Lectures More Effective."

In my introductory course I try to communicate from the beginning that I expect students to read the assignments before class by announcing that I will give a brief quiz the second day of class based on the first lecture or discussion and the assignment for the next class. I give the quiz and then ask students to correct their own papers, indicating that this quiz had two purposes: to start the habit of reading the assignment before class, and to give them an idea of whether or not they were getting the main points of the assignment. I give a second quiz a week later and a longer one three weeks later. By this point I hope that my students have established a routine for keeping up with their assignments.

Such a procedure assumes that students know what is expected of them. One of the most common causes of under-preparation is that students don't really know what is expected. Often instructors say something like, "You might want to look at the next chapter of the book before the next class," or they state that the next lecture will be on topic X, without indicating that this is also the topic of the next reading. Giving students some questions to think about as they study the next assignment can help, as will announcements of an activity in the next class that depends on the assignment. One of the advantages of a well-written syllabus is that it communicates your expectations. You also need to communicate expectations by frequent use of such phrases as "As your assignment for today demonstrated" or questions such as "What does X (the textbook author) say about . . . ?" or "What evidence from the assigned readings would support (or not support) your position?"

THE FLATTERER, DISCIPLE, CON MAN (OR WOMAN)

If one is new or somewhat insecure, it is tempting to respond positively to anyone who tells you that you are the best teacher he or she has ever had, or who is impressed with the depth of your knowledge and wants to learn more about your special research interests. In fact, one does not need to be new or insecure; we all relish compliments and interest in our work. More often than not such interest is genuine and can be genuinely enriching for both you and the student; but there are students for whom such an approach is a conscious strategy for winning better grades or getting exceptions from deadlines for papers or other requirements.

The real danger presented by such students is that you will begin to mistrust all students and lose compassion for students who really need an extension of time or some other indication of flexibility. I would rather be conned a couple of times than to turn off by cold rigidity a student who is in real need. Thus my advice is to start with an assumption of honesty; nonetheless, in general, don't change the rules of the game unless you are willing to change them for everyone or unless you are convinced that there are reasonable grounds for a special exception.

DISCOURAGED, READY-TO-GIVE-UP STUDENTS

Often after the first few weeks you will spot some students who seem depressed and discouraged. Sometimes they come to class late or miss class; often their papers are constricted and lack any sense of enthusiasm or creativity. In my introductory classes, some students begin with great enthusiasm and energy and a few weeks later seem to have lost their energy; interestingly, we spot the same phenomenon in our proseminar for beginning Ph.D. students.

In both cases the transition to a new level of education brings demands greater than those students have experienced in the past. Often their familiar supports from family and friends are no longer available; they begin to doubt their own ability to achieve their goals.

There is a magic elixir for this problem that research has demonstrated to be surprisingly effective. This is to bring in students from the previous year who describe their experiences of frustration and self-doubt during their first year and report that they surmounted them and survived. The theory explaining why this works basically states that the task is to convince the discouraged students that their problems need not be attributed to a lack of ability that cannot be changed but rather is a temporary problem. By developing more effective strategies, investing more effort, or simply becoming less worried, better results are likely to follow (Van Overwalle et al., 1989; Wilson & Linville, 1982).

STUDENTS WHO ARE STRUGGLING

Not all discouragement is temporary. Some students are having trouble that requires additional help. I give quizzes and tests early in the term largely to help students identify and diagnose their difficulties. I invite those who have not done as well as they had hoped to come in to see me.

First I ask them for their own assessment of the cause of their difficulty and try to offer helpful suggestions. Usually I will also ask more specific questions:

"Have you missed any classes?"

"Do you study the assignments before class?"

"How do you study?" (This may lead to a discussion of learning strategies; see the chapter on learning strategies.)

"What kind of notes do you take?" (I usually ask to see them.)

"Do you discuss the class with classmates—asking questions, explaining, summarizing?"

Sometimes I refer the student to other resources on campus, such as a reading and study skills center. I check with the student later to see whether he or she has tried any of my suggestions, and I watch later performance to see if further help is needed.

STUDENTS WITH EXCUSES

As indicated earlier, I believe that it is better to be taken in by a fraudulent excuse than to be seen as unfair in response to a legitimate excuse. Nonetheless, one doesn't want to be seen as so gullible that students come to rely on excuses rather than doing their assignments. Caron, Whitbourne, and Halgin (1992) studied excuse making and in their sample found that about two-thirds of their students admitted having made at least one false excuse while in college. From these students' reports it appears that fraudulent excuses were about as frequent as legitimate ones. In most cases the excuse was used to gain more time for an assignment.

The Caron et al. data do not give many clues about what one can do to prevent or detect false excuses. If the problem is one of time, one might build in checks on the progress of a paper or other assignment to reduce the tendency to put off work until the last minute—you could, for example, have students turn in an outline or bibliography some time before a paper is due.

Sometimes I have announced in the syllabus that there would be a graded series of penalties depending on how late a paper was, indicating that this was to make up for the advantage the late students had in having extra time to look up more sources, get comments and feedback from other students, and so forth. An alternative that I have not used, which might be more advantageous psychologically, would be to offer a bonus for papers turned in early.

It might also be wise to put in your syllabus that you want to be flexible on deadlines and recognize that unforeseen events may prevent students from being able to meet a deadline. But in making exceptions you will require evidence supporting the request for an extension.

STUDENTS WHO WANT THE TRUTH AND STUDENTS WHO BELIEVE THAT EVERYTHING IS RELATIVE

You have just given a superb lecture comparing two competing theories. A student comes up after class and says, "That was a great lecture, but which theory is right?"

All too many students feel that the teacher's task is to tell students the facts and larger truths and the student's task is to listen to the truth, learn it, and be able to give it back on exams. This conception seemed to William Perry of Harvard University to be particularly common among first-year students.

Perry (1981) suggested that individual differences in student responses to teaching may be conceptualized in terms of student stages of cognitive development. Students at the lower stages are characterized by a dualistic view of knowledge. Things are either true or false, right or wrong. The teacher knows the truth; the student's job is to learn the truth. Students in the middle stages have learned that authorities differ. There seems to be no settled truth; everyone has a right to his or her own opinions. This stage is succeeded by the recognition that some opinions and generalizations are better supported than others. The student's task is to learn the criteria needed for evaluating the validity of assertions in different subject matter fields. The final stages involve student commitment to values, beliefs, and goals with the recognition that despite the lack of complete certainty one must make decisions and act on one's values. Barbara Hofer (1997) found that dualists are now rare. Rather, college students are more likely to believe that multiple perspectives are equally valid. So what should teachers do?

Perry and Hofer would agree that teachers need to help students understand how knowledge is arrived at in their own disciplines, what counts as evidence, and how to read critically and evaluate knowledge claims. For development in such epistemological beliefs students need to debate and discuss issues in which competing ideas are challenged and defended; they need to write journals and papers that are responded to by the teacher or by peers.

STUDENTS WITH EMOTIONAL REACTIONS TO SENSITIVE TOPICS

In almost every discipline there are some topics that will arouse strong feelings in some of your students. In a psychology class it might be "group differences in intelligence"; in biology it might be "evolution" or "animal experimentation"; in sociology it might be "the role of birth control and abortion in population policy." Often we are hesitant to open such topics up to discussion.

But if the topic is relevant and important, it is probably wise to acknowledge the sensitivity of the topic and to admit that it may be hard for some members of the class to feel free to contribute their ideas. Explain why the topic is relevant to the goals of the course. Comparing alternative approaches, perhaps by using the two-column method described in the chapter "Facilitating Discussion," may help students see the complexity of the issue.

In conducting the discussion it is important to stress that each student should listen to other students with respect and try to understand their positions. You might ask a student to put into his or her own words what other students have said. If feelings are running high, you might cool things off by asking students to write for a couple of minutes—one thing they have learned or one point that needs to be considered. Having students write a short essay advocating a position opposed to their own is effective in opening their minds.

Be sure to allocate enough time for adequate discussion. Students may be reluctant to participate until they feel that it is safe to speak honestly. Such fear of rejection also suggests that you schedule controversial topics late enough in the term to ensure that students have developed trust in you and their classmates.

IN CONCLUSION

1. Don't duck controversy.
2. *Listen*, and get students to listen to one another.
3. Keep your cool. You don't have to respond immediately.
4. Talk to colleagues. Ask what they would do.
5. Remember that your problem students are human beings who have problems and need your sympathy and help—no matter how much you would like to strangle them.

Supplementary Reading

An excellent review of the attributional retraining research dealing with motivation of discouraged students is R. P. Perry, F. J. Hechter, V. H. Menec, and L. Weinberg, *A Review of Attributional Motivation and Performance in College Students from an Attributional Retraining Perspective,* Occasional Papers in Higher Education, Centre for Higher Education Research and Development, The University of Manitoba, Winnipeg, Manitoba, Canada R3T 2N2.

A helpful source is Mary Deane Sorcinelli's chapter, "Dealing with Troublesome Behaviors in the Classroom," in K. W. Prichard and R. M. Sawyer (eds.), *Handbook of College Teaching: Theory and Applications* (Westport, CT: Greenwood, 1994).

Barbara Hofer and Paul Pintrich review the various theories about epistemological beliefs and learning in "The Development of Epistemological Theories: Beliefs About Knowledge and Knowing and Their Relation to Learning," *Review of Educational Research*, 1997, *67*, 88–140.

Counseling, Advising, and Educating

COUNSELING*

Some of your most effective teaching may occur during office hours. As my hair has been turning to white, I have felt that students were more reluctant to impose upon me and come to my office. Thus, when I have a class of no more than 30 students, I pass around a signup sheet and ask every student to sign up for a half-hour "get acquainted" office visit either alone or with other students who have signed up for the same time. This at least breaks the ice so that they know where my office is and presumably find it not to be forbiddingly uncomfortable. My hope is that they will then feel freer to use my office hours and to make appointments to see me.

In this chapter I will first deal with the most common reason students come to talk to you—problems with the course. Next we move to academic advising (helping students plan their

---

* I use the word *counseling* as a generic term covering helping students with problems with your course, advising students about academic programs, and psychological counseling about personal problems.

programs), then to serious problems that may need the help of professional psychological counselors, and finally to individualized teaching.

I should warn you that a student's ostensible reasons for coming to you may be quite different from the real reasons. Often students ask about a study problem when their real desire is to know the instructor better. They complain of inadequate study habits when underneath there may be difficulties with their home life. I do not mean that you should disregard the problems the students actually present, but if you are aware of possible underlying factors, you may be more understanding and more effective as a counselor.

Counseling need not be restricted to the office. Arriving early and talking to students after class can meet some needs. Out of the classroom you may be able to get to the real problem more easily over a Coke in the student union than in a more formal office visit.

The most common student problem is worded something like this: "I study harder for this course than for all my other courses, but I just can't seem to pass the tests." In handling this problem I usually encourage the students to express their own ideas about their difficulties. Sometimes their diagnosis and plans for improvement will be much more accurate than any I can give them. If the student has no idea what to do, ask the student to describe in detail how he or she has spent time during the previous week and studied for your course. Frequently, simple information on budgeting time, on how the students can ask themselves questions about the assignment, or on getting an overview of a chapter before reading it can be of much help.

In general, the key is to get the students away from reading passively or trying to memorize and instead to question, relate, and think more actively about the assignment and lectures.* Sometimes you can help by getting the students to use the study guide often published as an ancillary to the textbook or by

---

* For further help you might suggest Paul Hettich, *Learning Skills for College and Career,* Walter Pauk, *How to Study in College,* or Tim Walter and Al Seibert, *Student Success.*

referring the student for reading and study skills to an agency providing training. Even better may be to encourage peer teaching. See the chapter on active learning.

E-MAIL

Much communication that formerly would have occurred in office hours is now carried on by e-mail. This may facilitate communication with some students who are reluctant to take the teacher's time as well as with those who don't want to make the effort to go to a faculty office. Although this may take more of your time, the benefits generally outweigh the costs. Your prompt response can communicate your interest in being helpful. Saving your e-mail can be a useful way to update yourself on preceding interactions and may be helpful if a grievance is filed. Sending a copy to a colleague or administrator of your response to antagonistic or overly personal interactions may also be helpful.

ADVISING AND PROGRAM PLANNING

The modern university is a complex organization. The student's path through this organization is supposedly mapped by handbooks and catalogues. Unfortunately, most of these documents are, at best, forbiddingly dull and confusingly written. In too many instances they are less than adequate road guides because almost every curriculum has its unwritten requirements. These are preferences for certain sequences of courses or for the choice of one of several alternatives that are so strongly adhered to by the department or college that they become, in effect, requirements for graduation. At the same time, because they are not formal requirements, they exist as part of the folklore rather than as part of the written law.

This state of affairs means that, where students are left on their own to select courses, there is great danger of having to extend the normal four-year program because of mistakes in curricular planning. This has given rise to the faculty counselor who is given the responsibility for guiding the students through the intricacies of their chosen curriculum.

The university usually places on this faculty counselor the responsibility for the enforcement of various other regulations governing the students' curricular activities—for example, the number of credits students may elect in a given period, the fulfillment of prerequisites, and the meeting of general requirements for graduation where they exist. The result is that relations between students and faculty are often strained, for the students going to see the faculty members become part of a bureaucratic, impersonal processing that they are impatient to pare down to its irreducible essentials.

DEALING WITH PSYCHOLOGICAL PROBLEMS

At some point you will suspect that a student needs psychological counseling. Some of the signs are belligerence, moodiness, excessive worry, suspiciousness, helplessness, emotional outbursts, or depression. Sometimes you will spot symptoms of drug or alcohol abuse. How do you get the student to the help needed?

The first step may be to get the student to talk to you. Usually this can be handled by asking the student to come in, perhaps to discuss a paper or test. Typically the student will be aware that things aren't going well, and you can simply ask, "How are things going?" or "What do you think is the reason for your problems?" Listen rather than intervening. After listening and expressing concern, you might then say, "What do you think you can do?" One alternative, probably the best, is to seek professional help.* If the student agrees that this might be a good idea, I've found that it helps to pick up the phone and say, "I'll call to see when they can see you." In fact, most such agencies will at least carry out an initial interview with any student who walks in. But

---

* Be sure you know what resources are available.

the sense of commitment involved when a faculty member has called seems to make students more likely to follow through than if they simply agree that they'll go in. Even if the student does not immediately get professional help, your concern and support will be helpful, and awareness of the availability of professional help may be valuable later.

POTENTIAL SUICIDES

The increasing concern with suicide risk among college students prompts a few words on the early recognition of the kinds of depressed states that accompany such risks. If you were to notice a sudden falling off of a particular student's faithfulness in attending class, you might want to inquire further, especially if you noted signs of neglect of personal grooming and hygiene, lethargy, and any marked weight changes, or a facial expression atypically gloomy or distressed. Your interest in the student should include concern with any other changes he or she has been experiencing, including major separations or losses and mood states. You should listen for talk of death or references to suicide or to getting one's personal and legal affairs in order. Your major concern should not be to reach an accurate assessment of suicide risk. A student manifesting any of these characteristics is surely troubled and should be urged to seek whatever professional counseling is available. Once I walked with a student to the clinic to be sure that he got there. On a couple of occasions when the student seemed unlikely to seek help, I have asked the university health service to call the student in.

INDIVIDUALIZED TEACHING AND MENTORING

I discuss one-on-one teaching in the chapter on using project methods. Here I want to discuss interactions with students dealing with larger issues of their educational and personal development. The potentially most fruitful and most appropriate interpretation of educational counseling is the one least often defined explicitly and most neglected. Even in classes of 40 to 60 students, it is difficult for the learning process to include the meeting of a maturing and a mature intellect. Too frequently students must be content to listen to lectures and pursue readings aimed at some abstracted image of a student.

In out-of-class interactions with students or as a student's academic advisor, you can supplement their course-related learning with personalized learning that facilitates their adjustment to college. This is particularly necessary for first-year students, to whom new intellectual spheres are being opened, usually at a time when they have taken a big step away from their family and community roots. This is likely to be a time when a great many new assumptions and new ways of dealing with important ideas need to be digested. Educational counselors, because they have no commitment to covering a specific subject matter, can provide students with an opportunity to digest and integrate the intellectual experiences they have been having. Far from being a chore to be assigned to the least successful faculty member, such a demanding responsibility is best undertaken by persons of broad intellectual interests and foundations who, at the same time, have strong pedagogical commitments.

This time, when students are making big strides toward greater independence from family and are trying to seek out models who can represent innovations of the adult role to which they aspire, is a time when there should be opportunities for close relationships with faculty members. The very characteristics of the large university throw obstacles in the way of such an experience. Educational counseling is one of the important means for achieving it. It seems probable that the most effective pattern for doing this would be for counselors to plan small-group meetings with the students assigned to them for counseling to provide an opportunity for the groups of new students coming from different parts of the state and country to exchange with each other and with a person of some intellectual maturity the impacts of their initial university experiences. A number of colleges and universities group first-year students into interest groups or seminars that meet regularly during the first term to help establish both academic and social support systems. We often think first of mentoring graduate students, but mentoring is a role you will have for students at all levels.

The problems of the older student entering college are in some ways similar despite the obvious differences in life experience. While both younger and older students often feel some anxiety about their ability to carry out academic work successfully, the older students may have even greater concerns than younger students about their ability to adapt to the college environment and to form helpful relationships with peers (most of whom are much younger and experiencing quite different social and recreational lives).

IN CONCLUSION

1. Listen carefully.
2. Try to empathize.
3. Paraphrase, question, and summarize but delay suggesting alternatives until you are confident that you understand.

Supplementary Reading

In A. W. Chickering, *The New American College* (San Francisco: Jossey-Bass, 1988), the chapter by Jane Shipton and Elizabeth Steltenpohl provides a useful perspective on the broad issues faced by academic advisors. The typical schedule of 15 minutes per advisee is clearly insufficient for planning an academic program in relationship to lifelong goals.

In *Tools for Teaching* (San Francisco: Jossey-Bass, 1993), Barbara Davis offers good practical advice in Chapter 44, "Holding Office Hours," and Chapter 45, "Academic Advising and Monitoring Undergraduates."

Also see A. G. Reinarz and E. R. White (eds.), Teaching Through Academic Advising [Special issue], *New Directions for Teaching and Learning,* 1995, 62.

Chapter 7, "One-on-One Interactions with Students," in Anne Curzan and Lisa Damour's book *First Day to Final Grade* (Ann Arbor: University of Michigan Press, 2000) provides good advice on counseling students with a variety of problems.

Adding to Your Repertoire of Skills and Strategies for Facilitating Active Learning

13 Teaching Students to Learn Through Writing: Journals, Papers, and Reports

When I began teaching, most courses in the social sciences and humanities required a term paper. Ordinarily papers were graded for the quality of the content and original thinking, disregarding the quality of writing (if this is possible). All too often, students looked at the grade on the term paper returned at the end of the term and paid little attention to helpful comments by the professor. The "writing across the curriculum" revolution taught us that thinking as well as writing is improved by the opportunity to get feedback on a first draft before turning in a paper for a grade. Thus more and more teachers are assigning several shorter papers with multiple drafts evaluated by peers or the teacher.

A LITTLE THEORY

Why does writing improve thinking? Skill in thinking is like musical and athletic skills. It takes practice to improve—particularly practice that enables one to see what works and what doesn't. Much of our thinking remains in our minds, where it is not exposed to review. The very process of putting thoughts to paper forces clarification; seeing them on paper (or on the computer screen) facilitates our own evaluation; and receiving comments from peers or a teacher provides further help. Note that most of these educational gains do not require that writing be graded. Writing is to facilitate learning and thinking. Thinking in turn results in class discussions that are animated and thoughtful.

LOW-STAKES WRITING

One of the lessons I learned from training in "writing across the curriculum" is that students can learn a lot from low-stakes writing—writing that doesn't count for a grade. In fact, grading writing may interfere with learning. The "minute paper" described earlier is a good example of low-stakes writing. Like the minute paper, much writing is now done in class—not just in papers written outside class. Thus I begin this chapter with low-stakes writing and conclude with the traditional graded paper.

THE STUDENT LOG OR JOURNAL

One example of low-stakes writing is a log or journal. Originally my journal assignment dealt only with readings chosen by the students outside the required assignments, but more recently I have encouraged students to write about anything in other courses or outside class that relates to the course. In my syllabus I say:

> The journal or log is not to be a "paper" in any formal way. It should demonstrate that you have thought about what you have read and experienced. How did it relate to other material of the course? Don't just summarize a reading. Write down your reactions, questions, comments, criticisms, and insights. Did you enjoy it?

Journals are turned in several times during the term. Students exchange journals the class period before each due date. The reader of the journal is encouraged to act as a coach rather than a critic. I write extensive comments both on the log and on the comments of the coach, pressing for active thinking. Thus the journal becomes a three-way dialog between the two students and me, as

I give the pairs of students time to read each other's comments and mine when I return them.

Journals are not graded, but a specified number of points is allocated for writing the journal. However, I do tell students that full credit for the journals depends on an amount of reading and writing that is appropriate in relation to other course requirements (in my course, two to six hours a week). Over the course of the term, journals clearly improve in their quality of thinking, and I hope that the active observation and reading carries over to other courses and experiences after my course is over. Research evidence indicates that journals, as well as other writing, produce gains in learning, thinking, and motivation (Beach & Bridwell, 1984; Hettich, 1990).

THE PAPER THAT COUNTS TOWARD A GRADE

Although journals, minute papers, and other low-stakes writing accomplish important educational goals, there is still a place for the traditional paper written out of class:

1. To provide an opportunity for students to go beyond conventional course coverage and gain a feeling of expertise in some area. This is an important way in which students learn to value learning.

2. To give students an opportunity to explore problems of special significance to them, thus boosting their motivation.

3. To help students gain skills in finding and using informational sources (such as libraries and technology) that will be useful in later learning both in higher education and after graduation.

As noted in the chapters, "Motivation in the Classroom" and "Valuing Student Differences," giving students a choice of topics helps deal with diversity of student backgrounds and increases intrinsic motivation.

When undergraduates are required to write a paper, they seem to face three alternatives:

1. Copy one from the World Wide Web, or borrow one from a friend or fraternity or sorority file.

2. Find a book in the library that covers the needed material. Copy it with varying degrees of paraphrasing and turn it in.

3. Review relevant resources and, using powers of analysis and integration, develop a paper that reveals understanding and original thinking.

Most teachers prefer that their students adopt the third alternative. Few of us, however, have evolved techniques for eliminating the first two.

I start with the assumption that most students would rather not plagiarize. When they plagiarize it is because they feel trapped with no other way out. Typically in this situation the student feels that it is almost impossible to write a paper that will achieve a satisfactory grade. This may be because of self-perception of lack of ability or background. More often it results from a lack of planning; the student has arrived at the time the paper is due with little preparation. The only way out seems to be to find an already-written paper.

How can one help students avoid such a trap? By pacing the student.

I try to break the process of writing a term paper into a series of easy steps, such as

1. Finding a topic.

2. Gathering sources, data, or references.

3. Developing an outline. (I give my students a handout with an outline of the major sections to be included.)

4. Writing a first draft.

5. Rewriting.

In addition to an overall outline, I usually give my students advice about how to think about their paper. For example, I might ask students to choose an issue being discussed in the media to discuss from a psychological perspective. In this case I would say, "In writing your paper, first state the issue and explain its importance. Then assume that you are a prosecuting attorney presenting arguments and evidence for choosing one side of the issue. Then assume you are a defense attorney arguing the other side.

Finally imagine that you are the judge stating your conclusions and the basis for them."* I set deadlines for handing in a report at each step. When time permits, I meet with the student to discuss the paper at one of the early steps. In the meeting I not only provide guidance, but also offer encouragement and motivation for doing well (and I can sometimes spot and discourage impending signs of plagiarism). Other techniques I've used for discouraging plagiarism are:

1. Including on a test some questions that require each student to use knowledge gained in preparing his or her term paper.

2. Having students give oral reports on their papers and answer questions from the class.

Dealing with Plagiarism

If, despite your preventive techniques, you suspect plagiarism, what should you do? Here you are in a conflict situation. Typically you don't want to reward plagiarism, yet it may be very difficult and time consuming to locate the original source. So should you forget it? No.

I recommend a conference with the student. You may use the indirect approach of discussing or questioning the student about the content of the paper to assess the student's knowledge, or you may be direct in expressing your suspicions. In many cases the student will admit plagiarism; in some cases you will encounter blustering anger. In any case you will need to arrive at a decision about (1) turning the case over to college discipline procedures, (2) permitting the student to write another paper, or (3) giving the paper full credit. Often I tell the student that I will consult my department chair or a respected colleague before making a final decision.

Giving a failing grade is probably the most frequent alternative chosen by teachers, but also the most problematic. The teacher is then vulnerable to a legal challenge of the grade for not following the college rules for disciplinary action.

In conclusion, *prevention is preferable to punishment.*

---

* I'm indebted to a British professor who described this in a faculty workshop I conducted at Oxford.

Other Possibilities for Writing Assignments

1. A letter to the editor (or to a member of Congress)
2. A dialog (either between two students or a simulated dialog between two theorists or others being studied)
3. Two versions of the same paper for different audiences
4. A collaborative paper by a pair or group
5. Writing an argumentative paper and dealing with responses to the paper by other students
6. Writing to a sibling, parent, or a friend describing and explaining something interesting in the course

TEACHING WRITING, GIVING FEEDBACK, AND CORRECTING PAPERS

"I'm teaching physics (or psychology or history). It's the job of the English Department to teach writing. It would be unfair to my students to evaluate their writing. Moreover, I've never had any training in teaching writing. I'm not even sure when to insert a comma in my own writing."

In addition to concerns about competence, faculty members have concerns about the time required. If one asks students to write more, how can one conscientiously comment on that writing without an impossible increase in time spent grading?

Here are some suggestions:

1. The professor is not the only person who can provide help on writing. Often peers can provide useful suggestions on their classmates' papers. To help students know what to look for, you can provide models—of well-written papers on a given topic as well as of papers with your own comments about some common problems. Form subgroups of four or five students, and have each group read and comment on each other's papers. Giving feedback on peers' papers can help develop skill in self-evaluation.

2. A ten-page paper is not necessarily twice as valuable as a five-page paper. Short papers can be evaluated in less time than long

papers and may provide sufficient stimulus for student thinking and sufficient opportunity for feedback.

3. Encourage students to revise their papers before turning them in, even if what is submitted is only a draft rather than the final paper. Developing the habit and skill of revising is worthwhile, and word processors make it easy. (And if the student takes time to revise, your time will be saved.)

4. Encourage students to submit a draft for feedback before submitting the paper for a grade. Having a chance to try out ideas without risk helps free up students to be more thoughtful and creative. Hillocks (1982) found that focused teacher comments facilitate learning, but their effect is twice as great if students have a chance to revise their papers.

When students submit their drafts, Barbara Cambridge (1996) asks them to attach three questions about what they'd like to know about the draft or what aspects they would like to improve. I like this because it encourages students to develop the ability to evaluate their own writing, and it gives us guidance about where to focus our comments.

5. Up to a point, more comments, and more specific comments, lead to greater learning. There are three kinds of qualifications to this statement:

a. A student can be overloaded with feedback. There is a limited number of things a student can be expected to learn and remedy at one time.

b. Motivation for improvement is affected by the balance of encouragement versus criticism. Feedback can be either helpful or detrimental (Kluger & DeNisi, 1996). A heavy dose of criticism may cause a student to quit trying to improve. Give students hope that they can improve.

c. The type of comment makes a difference. Simply noting errors is not helpful if the student doesn't know how to correct the errors. Helpful comments provide guidance about how to improve.

d. If your feedback is primarily about grammar, spelling, or minor points, be sure to comment on the major ideas as well.

6. Here are some examples of comments that might help:

"I don't quite follow your organization. Could you give me an outline along with your revision?"

"You state your position strongly, but you are weak in covering other positions. See if you can find others in class with a different position and listen to their arguments." "In class we discussed X; do you think X is relevant to this point?"

WHAT TO DO WHEN A PAPER IS TO BE GRADED

To help students learn to write and think, grades are of little value. Students need more information. Try to make your criteria clear. A good example of such a statement of criteria is the outline developed by Gary LaPree of Indiana University (LaPree, 1977) and contained in the box that begins below.

Criteria for Evaluating Term Papers

A. Content

1. Introduction
   a. Is the topic novel and original?
   b. Does the author state purpose, problem, or question to be considered?
   c. How does the author convince the reader that the paper is worth reading?
2. Body
   a. How are the statements made warranted? (Is there evidence that data collected have been analyzed and the literature reviewed? Are the assumptions logical?
   b. Presentation of evidence
      1. Is contradictory evidence dealt with adequately?
      2. Are multiple sources considered if available?
      3. Is the evidence discussed relevant to the purpose stated?

(cont.)

    4. Is the argument internally consistent? In other words, does one point follow from another?

    5. Is the argument plausible?

    6. Are the methods chosen for testing the argument convincing?

c. Suitability of paper's focus

    1. Is the problem chosen focused enough to be adequately covered in the space of the paper?

    2. Is the problem chosen too specific for the author's sources of information?

d. Background information

    1. Is enough information given to familiarize the reader with the problem?

    2. Is unimportant background material included?

e. Is the presentation easy to follow and well organized?

f. Does the author deal with the problem set up in the introduction?

3. Conclusion

    a. Does the author summarize findings adequately?

    b. Is the conclusion directly related to the questions asked in the introduction?

    c. Does the author suggest areas where further work is needed?

B. Connections to class

1. Evidence that class materials have been read and understood

2. Application of lecture materials and assigned readings to paper

C. Form

1. Spelling

2. Grammar

3. Appropriate use of words

4. Paragraph form: Are ideas presented in coherent order?

5. Footnotes and bibliography: Are borrowed ideas and statements given credit? Is the form of the footnotes and bibliography understandable and consistent?

LaPree's list of criteria is not intended to be something one considers only after reading a paper, but rather is a guide to the teacher's active thought processes while reading student papers and for suggestions to be made to the student. Just as we teach students to read actively—questioning, relating, synthesizing—so we should be actively questioning the writer's thinking and expression as we read. Giving the students copies of such a rubric in advance will help them write better papers and save you time in giving feedback and grading.

WHAT ABOUT DEADLINES AND STUDENTS WHO MISS THEM?

One of the banes of a teacher's existence is the paper or journal turned in after the due date. Some teachers refuse to accept late papers; more commonly we apply a sliding scale with increasing reduction of the grade the later the paper. Roberts and Semb (1990) let students choose their own deadlines, a method that should help motivation even though it failed to result in fewer late papers. I have sometimes asked the class to discuss the issue of deadlines and late papers, setting a due date that takes account of their schedules and mine. Regardless of the method you use, you need to explain your rationale and you need to leave yourself room for exceptions. Grandmothers sometimes really do die.

PORTFOLIOS

If you require more than one paper (perhaps short ones), you may want to reserve the grade for a portfolio (as I described in the chapter "Assessing, Testing, and Evaluating") rather than grading each paper separately. This gives the students a chance to show their development throughout the course.

IN CONCLUSION

1. Make sure that your students understand the value of writing for both your low-stakes and your graded assignments.

2. Writing facilitates learning, memory, and thinking.
3. Development depends on feedback that provides guidance.
4. Feedback on nongraded writing or drafts of papers to be graded later contributes more to development than assigning a grade.
5. Prevent, in order to avoid punishing, plagiarism. If punishment is indicated, follow the procedures required by your institution.
6. Providing feedback takes time. Save time by encouraging peer feedback, self-evaluation, and shorter papers.

Supplementary Reading

Useful analyses of writing processes and implications for teaching may be found in:

L. W. Gregg and E. R. Steinberg (eds.), *Cognitive Processes in Writing* (Hillsdale, NJ: Lawrence Erlbaum, 1980). Note especially the chapter by Hayes and Flower.

E. P. Maimon, G. L. Belcher, G. W. Hearn, B. F. Nodine, and F. W. O'Connor, *Writing in the Arts and Sciences* (Cambridge, MA: Winthrop, 1981).

Ross MacDonald helpfully summarizes the research on feedback in "Developing Students' Processing of Teacher Feedback in Composition Instruction," *Research in Developmental Education*, 1991, 8(5), 1–5.

Writing to Learn: Strategies for Assigning and Responding to Writing Across the Disciplines [Special issue], *New Directions for Teaching and Learning*, 1997, 69, edited by Mary Deane Sorcinelli and Peter Elbow, offers help on everything from types of assignments to grading.

E. M. White, *Teaching and Assessing Writing* (San Francisco: Jossey-Bass, 1994).

Reading as Active Learning

14

While professors like to think that students learn from professors, it seems likely that students often learn more efficiently from reading than from listening. In the chapter on learning strategies Claire Ellen Weinstein describes skills and strategies to improve learning and retention from reading. The journals and papers described in the chapter on writing illustrate one way to get students into the library and reading primary sources. Nonetheless textbooks are still a basic tool for teaching most courses, and you can teach students to be active readers of textbooks.

TEXTBOOKS

For decades the demise of the textbook has been eagerly predicted by advocates of each of the new panaceas for the problems of education. First television, then teaching machines, then the computer—each was expected to revolutionize education and free students and teachers from their longtime reliance on textbooks. But each of the new media has settled into its niche in the educational arsenal without dislodging the textbook. In fact, the greater availability of a wide variety of printed materials is probably as important as the technological revolution.

The introduction of open-stack libraries, paperback books, inexpensive reprint series, and the photocopier has given the college teacher the opportunity to choose from sources varying in style, level, and point of view. Many teachers are substituting paperback books, reprints, and collections of journal articles for the textbook as the sources of the basic information needed by students. But in most undergraduate courses there is little hope that bits and pieces will be integrated by students into a meaningful whole despite the valiant efforts of instructors to give assistance.

Learning is facilitated by organization. Lacking organization, facts and concepts become subject to interference, quickly forgotten and inaccessible. With input from field experience, discussion, paperbacks, reprints, the World Wide Web, and other sources, the student needs, more than ever, some frame of reference within which to assimilate the boomin', buzzin' confusion of points of view present in a modern course. Ideally, the textbook can provide such a structure.

Certainly, modern teachers should provide a variety of learning experiences for students. If individual differences are to be attended to, students need an opportunity to learn in laboratory settings, field experiences, discussion, lectures, or reading from diverse sources. Textbooks are an important part of the teacher's compendium of tools, and the newer teaching methods and aids supplement rather than supplant reading. In fact, a goodly part of higher education is education in how to read—how to read poems, how to read social science, how to read legal briefs, how to read the literature of our culture and our professions.

HOW DO YOU GET STUDENTS TO DO THE ASSIGNED READING?

The main reason students come to class unprepared is that they don't see what difference it makes. In many courses, textbook assignments and lectures are independent parts of the course, sometimes overlapping, sometimes supplementary, but often not perceived as interdependent. Thus the first strategy for encouraging reading is frequent use of the phrase "As you read in your textbook assignment for today, . . ." or the question "What was your reaction to [the author of the textbook]'s discussion of . . .?"

A second strategy is to have students write a minute paper at the beginning of occasional class periods on "The most important idea (or two or three ideas) I got from the assignment for today." Alternatively, you can have students write a question—either something they would like explained or something that was stimulated by the reading.

The basic problem often may be found in the meaning of the word *read*. To many, "read" is simply to pass one's eyes over the words as one does in reading a story. One has completed the assignment when one has reached the end of the assignment.

We need to teach students how to read—how to read nonfiction with understanding, how to think about the purpose of the author, about relationships to earlier learning, about how they will use what they've read.

Research on Learning from Reading

A number of classic studies have compared printed materials with lectures, and the results—at least with difficult materials—favor print (Hartman, 1961).

Study questions intended to guide the students' reading are often helpful. Marton and Säljö (1976b) found that questions designed to produce more thoughtful, integrative study were more effective than questions of fact.

Nevertheless, study questions do not automatically guarantee better learning. Students sometimes tended to look only for answers to the questions while disregarding the other content of the chapter (Marton & Säljö, 1976a). Andre (1987) reviewed meta-analyses and other studies of study questions and concluded that questions generally do aid learning and that higher-level questions, rather than low-level factual questions, increase the effectiveness of student processing of the reading. Similarly, Wilhite (1983) found that prequestions focusing on material at the top of the organizational structure facilitated learning, especially

Examples of Study Questions to Encourage Thought

Your assignment for Monday is to study the next chapter, "Memory." Here are some study questions:

1. How would you apply the idea of "depth of processing" to your learning from this chapter?

2. How does the limited capacity of working memory affect your learning in lecture classes?

3. How is the approach taken by researchers in memory like, and how is it different from, that taken by the researchers in learning you studied in the last chapter?

for the less able students. You need questions that get students to *think* about the material. One way to encourage thoughful reading is to ask students to write a half-page answer to a thought-provoking question and to bring multiple copies to class to share with peers in small groups. Discussion after the students have read one another's papers is usually lively.

Teaching Students to Learn More from Reading

We saw in the chapter "Assessing, Testing, and Evaluating" that students' study methods and learning were influenced by the sort of test questions they expected. Thus many students can read thoughtfully if tests require deeper understanding and thinking. But other students faithfully read and reread regardless of the type of assignment, memorizing definitions and facts without thought of the goal of the author and the relationship of this reading assignment to their previous learning. You can help by discussing with the students why you chose the reading and how they should read it.

Recently I have put the students in my introductory psychology class into small groups on the first day of class to discuss what characteristics of textbooks help their learning. Then each student chooses two introductory psychology textbooks to compare before the next class meeting. At the next class the students report their findings, and each student chooses the textbook he or she prefers. This means that for the rest of the semester I need, in preparing for each class, to scan the three to six books that have been chosen, but this enriches the class discussions and seems to increase the meaningfulness of the students' study.

There is ample evidence that students do benefit from specific instruction in selecting main ideas, asking themselves questions, looking for organizational cues, and attempting to summarize or explain what they have read. Particularly in introductory classes you will help learning if you make explicit reference to your goal in assigning a particular chapter and discuss ways in which students can best achieve that goal (McKeachie et al., 1985; Weinstein & Mayer, 1986). Suggest that your students

1. Look at topic headings before studying the chapter.

2. Write down questions they would like to answer.

3. Make marginal notes as they read.

4. Underline or highlight important concepts.

5. Carry on an active dialog with the author.

For a fuller description of ways to help students become better learners, see the chapter on learning strategies.

IN CONCLUSION

1. Reading is an important tool for learning.

2. To facilitate learning, a teacher needs not only to choose appropriate reading materials but also to help students learn how to read them effectively.

3. Despite the availability of photocopies, coursepacks, paperbacks, and the World Wide Web, textbooks are still useful tools for teaching.

4. If material students need to learn is in print, in a form conveniently accessible for them, they will probably learn more efficiently from reading than from listening to you.

Supplementary Reading

T. M. Chang, H. F. Crombag, K. D. J. M. van der Drift, and J. M. Moonen, *Distance Learning* (Boston: Kluwer-Nijhoff Publishing, 1983), Chapter 4.

R. G. Crowder and R. K. Wagner, *The Psychology of Reading: An Introduction*, 2nd ed. (New York: Oxford University Press, 1992).

F. Marton, D. Hounsell, and N. Entwistle (eds.), *The Experience of Learning* (Edinburgh: Scottish Academic Press, 1984).

C. E. Weinstein and R. E. Mayer, "The Teaching of Learning Strategies," in M. Wittrock (ed.), *Handbook of Research on Teaching* (New York: Macmillan, 1983), pp. 315–327.

Active Learning: Cooperative, Collaborative, and Peer Learning*

One of the recurring criticisms of higher education is that it hasn't increased its productivity at the same rate as industry. By "productivity" critics typically mean that colleges should turn out more students using fewer teachers—as if colleges were factories producing shoes, automobiles, or soap.

The bottleneck in educational efficiency is that learning to think requires thinking and communicating the thinking through talking, writing, or doing, so that others can react to it. Unfortunately a professor can read only one paper at a time, can listen to only one student's comments at a time, and can respond with only one voice.

The problem is not one of communicating knowledge from professors to students more efficiently. Printed materials

---

* I use the term *peer learning* to include "collaborative" and "cooperative" learning. Some authors distinguish collaborative from cooperative learning, but both involve peer learning in which there is interdependence of students working toward a common goal. Similarities in and differences between collaborative and cooperative learning are discussed in Matthews, Cooper, Davidson, and Hawkes (1995).

have done this very well for years, and for most educational purposes are still superior to any of the modern alternatives. The problem is rather one of interaction between the learner and teacher. Fortunately, interactions that facilitate learning need not be limited to those with teachers. Often those with peers are more productive.

PEER LEARNING AND TEACHING

The best answer to the question: What is the most effective method of teaching? is that it depends on the goal, the student, the content, and the teacher. But the next best answer may be: Students teaching other students. There is a wealth of evidence that peer learning and teaching is extremely effective for a wide range of goals, content, and students of different levels and personalities (Johnson & Johnson, 1975; Johnson et al., 1981). Moreover, skill in working cooperatively is essential for most vocations. Miller and Groccia (1997) found that cooperative learning produced positive results in ability to work with others as well as better cognitive outcomes.

Here are some tips that may be helpful in initiating a variety of types of cooperative learning methods:

1. Have students discuss what contributes to effective group functioning. Explain why working together is important and valuable.

2. Make sure students know what their task is; for example, if it involves out-of-class work, give teams a few minutes before the end of the class period to make plans. At this time they should also report to you what they plan to do and when and where they will meet.

3. For in-class group work, move around and listen in to be sure students are not lost and confused. Use this time to get and keep them on the right track.

4. Help students develop the skills they need for working together effectively.

Suggestions for Students: How to Be an Effective Group

1. Be sure everyone contributes to discussion and to tasks.
2. Don't jump to conclusions too quickly. Be sure that minority ideas are considered.
3. Don't assume consensus because no one has opposed an idea or offered an alternative. Check agreement with each group member verbally, not just by a vote.
4. Set goals—immediate, intermediate, and long-term—but don't be afraid to change them as you progress.
5. Allocate tasks to be done. Be sure that each person knows what he or she is to do and what the deadline is. Check this before adjourning.
6. Be sure there is agreement on the time and place of the next meeting and on what you hope to accomplish.
7. Before ending a meeting, evaluate your group process. What might you try to do differently next time?

STUDENT-LED DISCUSSIONS

In pioneering experiments in educational psychology and general psychology, Gruber and Weitman (1962) found that students taught in small, student-led discussion groups without a teacher not only did at least as well on a final examination as students who heard the teacher lecture, but also were superior in curiosity (as measured by question-asking behavior) and in interest in educational psychology. Similar results have been found in many more recent studies. Webb and Grib (1967) found in their research that students report that the sense of freedom to ask questions and express their own opinions is a major advantage of the student-led discussions.

How to Use Student-led Discussions

Do you just assign students to lead discussions with their peers when you don't have time to prepare? No. Student-led discussions don't give you a lot more free time. If the groups are to achieve the good results reported by researchers, you need to meet with the leaders to discuss issues that may arise, suggest possible discussion-eliciting questions, and make it clear that their status as leaders does not mean that they now have to play the role of experts. Questions that are not resolved can be referred back to you, to reading, or to World Wide Web resources.

PEER TUTORING

"Pay to be a tutor, not to be tutored" is the message from studies of peer tutoring. For example, Annis (1983a) compared learning of students who read a passage and were taught by a peer and students who read the passage and taught it to another student.

The results demonstrated that teaching resulted in better learning than being taught. A similar study by Bargh and Schul (1980) also found positive results, with the largest part of the gain in retention being attributable to deeper studying of material when preparing to teach. These results fit well with contemporary theories of learning and memory. Preparing to teach and teaching involve active thought about the material, analysis and selection of main ideas, and processing the concepts into one's own thoughts and words. However, this does not mean that those being tutored fail to learn. Peer tutoring also helps those being tutored (Cohen, Kulik, & Kulik, 1982; Lidren, Meier, & Brigham, 1991). Hartman (1990) provides useful suggestions for training tutors. Peer tutoring need not be one on one. Group tutoring is also effective.

THE LEARNING CELL

One of the best-developed systems for helping pairs of students learn more effectively is the "learning cell" developed by Marcel Goldschmid of the Swiss Federal Institute of Technology in Lausanne (Goldschmid, 1971). The learning cell, or student dyad, refers to a cooperative form of learning in pairs, in which students alternate asking and answering questions on commonly read materials.

1. To prepare for the learning cell, students read an assignment and write questions dealing with the major points raised in the reading or other related materials.

2. At the beginning of each class meeting, students are randomly assigned to pairs, and one partner, A, begins by asking the first question.

3. After having answered and perhaps having been corrected or given additional information, the second student, B, puts a question to A, and so on.

4. During this time, the instructor goes from dyad to dyad, giving feedback and asking and answering questions.*

A variation of this procedure has each student read (or prepare) different materials. In this case, A "teaches" B the essentials of his or her readings, then asks B prepared questions, whereupon they switch roles. Research by Goldschmid and his colleagues demonstrated that the learning cell is effective in a variety of disciplines (Goldschmid, 1975; Goldschmid & Shore, 1974). Training students to generate thought-provoking questions enhances learning (King, 1990; Pressley et al., 1992). To recapture student attention and stimulate deeper processing, I often ask students to think about a problem for a minute, write for a minute, and then share their thoughts with a neighbor (Think-Pair-Share). Students then feel more free to participate in a general discussion of the problem. Pairing can also be effectively used for interviews, discussion of an issue or questions, analyzing a case or problem, or summarizing a lecture or assigned reading.

TEAM LEARNING: SYNDICATE AND JIGSAW

The term *syndicate* has a faintly evil connotation in the United States, but in Great Britain and other countries, *syndicate* is used to describe a team-based system of learning that has proved to be effective. In syndicate-based peer learning, the class is

---

* Students can also use the learning cell technique outside of class. My students use it in preparing for tests. A similarly structured method is "Ask to Think—Tell Why" (King, 1997).

divided into teams (or syndicates) of four to eight students. Each syndicate is given assignments (perhaps three or four questions). References are suggested, and members of the syndicate may divide up the readings. The findings may then be discussed by the various syndicates as they meet in small groups during the regular class period. The syndicate may then make a written or oral report to the class as a whole.

I have found that I get more interesting reports when I remind students that they have probably sometimes been bored by student reports. Hence they need to plan not only the content of the report but also how to make it interesting. I'm impressed by student creativity; my students have developed graphic and audio aids, skits, class participation, and other devices for motivating their classmates.

Hartman (1989) reports increased student motivation and student perceptions of deeper understanding as a result of the use of this method.

The *jigsaw* method, first developed by Elliot Aronson, begins like the syndicate by dividing a class into groups which are given assignments. Members of each group report back to their group, which agrees on what and how to present to the rest of the class. However, instead of a presentation to the entire class, each member of the group next meets in a new task group with one member from each of the other groups. In this new task group each student is responsible for teaching the students from the other groups what his group has learned. Since every student is thus in a group in which every group is represented, all students have the opportunity to learn the essence of all the assignments.

STUDENT CHARACTERISTICS AND PEER LEARNING

Peer learning works better for some students than others, but learning is increased for most students and does not hurt the learning of others.

When dealing with ability differences, heterogeneity may be better than homogeneity. Larson and colleagues (1984) found that cooperative learners with partners with dissimilar vocabulary scores recalled more main ideas after studying a textbook passage not only on the passage studied cooperatively but on a passage studied individually.

WHY DOES PEER LEARNING WORK?

Motivationally, peer learning has the advantages of interaction with a peer—an opportunity for mutual support and stimulation. (One piece of evidence for the motivational value of peer learning [Schomberg, 1986] is that it reduces absenteeism.) Knowing that your teammates are depending on you increases the likelihood of your doing your work. Cognitively it provides an opportunity for elaboration—putting material into one's own words—as well as a chance to begin using the language of the discipline. It communicates that the locus of learning is in the students' heads. An effective partner can act as a model of useful strategies as well as a teacher.

Several of the effective peer learning techniques involve alternating between listening and summarizing or explaining. Structures of peer learning such as the learning cell that reduce the chance that one participant is simply a passive recipient seem likely to be better for both motivation and learning.

The task of the successful student in peer learning is to question, explain, express opinions, admit confusion, and reveal misconceptions; but at the same time the student must listen to peers, respond to their questions, question their opinions, and share information or concepts that will clear up their confusion. Accomplishing these tasks requires interpersonal as well as cognitive skills—being able to give feedback in nonthreatening, supportive ways, maintaining a focus on group goals, developing orderly task-oriented procedures, and developing and sustaining mutual tasks. It is little wonder that peer learning sometimes fails; the wonder is that it so frequently works. And it does.

Students are more likely to talk in small groups than in large ones; students who are confused are more likely to ask other students questions about their difficulties or failure to understand than to reveal these problems with a faculty member present. Students who are not confused must actively organize and reorganize their own learning in order to explain it. Thus both the confused and the unconfused benefit.

IN CONCLUSION

1. Students may learn more from interacting with other students than from listening to us. One of the best methods of gaining clearer, long-lasting understanding is explaining to someone else.

2. This does not mean that we can be eliminated or have time to loaf. More of our time will be spent in helping students work together effectively, less time in preparing lectures.

Supplementary Reading

Two comprehensive books on cooperative learning are D. W. Johnson, R. T. Johnson, and K. A. Smith, *Active Learning: Cooperation in the College Classroom* (Edina, MN: Interactive Book Co., 1991), and B. Millis and P. Cottell, *Cooperative Learning for Higher Education Faculty* (Phoenix: ACE & Oryx Press, 1998).

One of the preeminent scholars of cooperative learning in higher education is Jim Cooper, who in 1991 initiated the newsletter *Cooperative Learning and College Teaching,* an excellent source of ideas for different ways of using cooperative learning. You can subscribe by writing:

Network for Cooperative Learning in Higher Education
Dr. Jim Cooper
HFA-B-316
CSU Dominquez Hills
1000 E. Victoria St.
Carson, CA 90747

A goldmine of helpful information is found in Philip Abrami's book *Classroom Connections: Understanding and Using Cooperative Learning* (Toronto: Harcourt Brace, 1995).

In his book, *Collaborative Learning: Higher Education, Interdependence and the Authority of Knowledge* (Baltimore: Johns Hopkins Press, 1993), Kenneth Bruffee takes the position that knowledge is socially constructed. Whether or not you accept the social constructivist view, Bruffee's book is worth reading.

Cooperative learning does not imply absence of controversy. D. W. Johnson, R. T. Johnson, and K. A. Smith describe the use and value of controversy in their book *Academic Controversy: Enriching College Instruction Through Intellectual Conflict* (Washington, DC: ASHE/ERIC, 1997).

16 Problem-based Learning: Teaching with Cases, Simulations, and Games

■ ■ ■ ■ ■ ■ ■ ■ ■ ■ ■ ■ ■ ■ ■ ■ ■

PROBLEM-BASED LEARNING

Problem-based learning is (along with active learning, coopera-tive/collaborative learning, and technology) one of the most important developments in contemporary higher education. The ideas embodied in problem-based learning have a long history, ranging back at least to the use of cases in Harvard Medical School in the nineteenth century and extending through John Dewey's philosophy, Jerry Bruner's discovery learning, and the develop-ment of simulations in the 1960s. The current surge of interest, I believe, stems partly from McMaster University where, in 1969, the medical school replaced the traditional lectures in first-year basic science courses with courses that started with problems pre-sented by patients' cases. A chemical engineering professor at McMaster, Don Peters, developed a problem-based approach for his courses, and another engineering professor, Charles Wales of West Virginia University, had a little earlier developed a problem-based method called "guided design." In a few years, courses and curricula in various disciplines in universities all over the world were using similar problem-based methods: In this chapter, I will describe guided design, the case method, and simulations—all variants of problem-based learning.

Steps in Problem-based Learning (Guided Design)

1. State the problem and establish a goal that will be pursued in resolving it.

2. Gather information relevant to defining the problem and understanding the elements associated with it.

3. Generate possible solutions.

4. List possible constraints on what can be accomplished as well as factors that may facilitate getting a solution accepted.

5. Choose an initial or possible solution using criteria that an acceptable solution must meet. The criteria can include tangible and monetary costs and benefits, the likely acceptance of the solution by others, and discipline or other standard criteria normally applied to such problems.

6. Analyze the important factors that must be considered in the development of a detailed solution. What has to be done, who does it, when it should happen, and where the solution would be used are possible factors to explore.

7. Create a detailed solution.

8. Evaluate the final solution against the relevant criteria used earlier, to ensure that it meets at least those requirements and others that now appear to be necessary.

9. Recommend a course of action and, if appropriate, suggest ways to monitor and evaluate the solution when it is adopted.

Based on Wales and Nardi (1982). Used by permission.

Problem-based education is based on the assumptions that human beings evolved as individuals who are motivated to solve problems, and that problem solvers will seek and learn whatever knowledge is needed for successful problem solving. Even in cultures where students do not expect to participate actively in classes, problem-based learning can be successfully implemented; Marjorie McKinnon (1999) describes the introduction of problem-based learning at the University of Hong Kong in her article "PBL in Hong Kong." Thus if a realistic, relevant problem is presented before study, students will identify needed information and be motivated to learn it. However, as in introducing any other method, you need to explain to students your purposes.

The steps involved in "guided design," described in the box "Steps in Problem-based Learning," are representative of those likely to be involved in many variations of problem-based learning. Note the emphasis on assessment of constraints, costs, benefits, and evaluation of the final solution. Helping students develop skills of self-assessment is an important goal of education.

Problem-based learning does not mean that you can sit back and relax once you have presented the problem. Check on each group's progress. If you have set a time when groups must report, you may have to help a group clear up a misconception or get out of a blind alley. It's frustrating to start a problem and not have a chance to finish.

In the McMaster model of problem-based learning, students meet in small groups with a tutor who acts as a facilitator. Although the facilitator is typically a faculty member, teaching assistants or peers can also be successful if trained. Typically, after the students have presented their recommendations, classroom discussion summarizes the learning that has occurred and integrates it with students' prior skills and knowledge.

THE CASE METHOD

As indicated earlier, the case method has been widely used in business and law courses for many years and is now being used in a variety of disciplines. Generally, case method discussions produce good student involvement. Case methods, like other problem-based methods, are intended to develop student ability to solve problems using knowledge, concepts, and skills relevant to a course. Cases provide contextualized learning, as contrasted with learning disassociated from meaningful contexts.

Cases are often actual descriptions of problem situations in the field in which the case is being used; sometimes they are syntheses constructed to represent a particular principle or type of problem. For example, in medicine a case may describe a patient and the patient's symptoms; in psychology the case might describe a group facing a decision; in biology the case might describe an environmental problem. Whatever the case, it typically involves the possibility of several alternative approaches or actions and some evaluation of values and costs of different solutions to the problem posed. Usually cases require that the students not only apply course content but also consult other resources.

Finding the Right Cases

You can write your own cases, but you may be able to find cases already written that are appropriate for your purposes and are motivating for your students. For example, Silverman, Welty, and Lyon (1994) have published cases for teacher education. Other cases can be found on the Internet.

Typically the case method involves a series of cases, but in some case method courses the cases are not well chosen to represent properly sequenced levels of difficulty. Often, in order to make cases realistic, so many details are included that beginning students lose the principles or points the case was intended to demonstrate. Teachers attempting to help students learn complex discriminations and principles in problem solving need to choose initial cases in which the differences are clear and extreme before moving to more subtle, complex cases. Typically, one of the goals of the case method is to teach students to select important factors from a tangle of less important ones which may nevertheless form a context to be considered. One does not learn such skills by being in perpetual confusion, but rather by success in solving more and more difficult problems.

The major problem in teaching by cases involves going from the students' fascination with the particular case to the general principle or conceptual structure. In choosing a case to discuss, the teacher needs to think, "What is this case a case *of*?"

Tips for Teaching with Cases

Usually cases are presented in writing, but you can use a videotape or you can role-play a problem situation. (Role playing is like a drama in which each participant is assigned a character to portray, but no lines are learned. The individuals portraying specific roles improvise their responses in a situation—a situation that presents a problem or conflict.)

Whatever method you use to present the problem, you should allow class time for students to ask questions about the process they are to use and to clarify the nature of the problem presented. You should clarify ways of going about the case study, such as:

1. What is the problem?
2. Develop hypotheses about what causes the problem.
3. What evidence can be gathered to support or discount any of the hypotheses?
4. What conclusions can be drawn? What recommendations? Make it clear that there is no one right answer.

Very likely you will want to form teams (as described in the chapter on active learning) and take time during class for the teams to agree on when to meet and to determine what they will do before their meeting. Some problems may involve work extending over several meetings in class and out of class.

When the teams report, your role is primarily to facilitate discussion—listening, questioning, clarifying, challenging, encouraging analysis and problem solving, and testing the validity of generalizations. You may want to use a board, overhead, or computer to keep a running summary of points established, additional information needed, and possible ethical or value considerations. Don't to forget to include the evidence supporting alternative approaches.

If the case is one that actually occurred, students will want to find out what actually was done and how it worked out. You can have a productive discussion about how the actual process, variables considered, or strategies used differed from those in the class. Sometimes you might bring in someone working in the field so that the students can see how an expert analyzes the case, and also ask questions about what really happens in practice.

GAMES AND SIMULATIONS

An educational game involves students in some sort of competition or achievement in relationship to a goal; it is a game that both teaches and is fun. Many games are simulations; for example, they attempt to model some real-life problem situation. Thus there are business games, international relations games, and many others. Whatever the topic, the planner of the game needs to specify the teaching objectives to be served by the game and then plan the game to highlight features that contribute to those objectives. Early educational games often involved large-scale simulations in which participants played the roles of individuals or groups in some interpersonal, political, or social situation. Now many simulations are available on computers. Research and laboratory simulations are available for courses in the sciences, and interactive social simulations can be used to teach foreign languages. Computer simulations are often more effective in teaching research methods than are traditional "wet labs."

As with other teaching methods, the effectiveness of simulations depends to some extent on the degree of instructional support or structure. Research on traditional as well as nontraditional teaching has shown that students with low prior knowledge tend to benefit from a higher degree of structure than students with greater knowledge or intelligence (Cronbach & Snow, 1977). Veenstra and Elshout's research (1995) on computer simulations in heat theory, electricity, and statistics found even more complex relationships. Structuredness made little difference for high-intelligence students; more structure enhanced learning for students with low intelligence and low metacognitive strategies (poor analysis, planning, evaluation, and work methods). But more structure impaired learning for low-intelligence students with high levels of metacognitive strategies.

The chief advantage of games and simulations is that students are active participants rather than passive observers. Students must make decisions, solve problems, and react to the results of their decisions. Lepper and Malone (1985) have studied the motivational elements in computer games. They found that key features are challenge, self-competence, curiosity, personal control, and fantasy.

There are now a number of well-designed games that have been used in enough situations to have the kinks worked out. Some use computers to implement the complex interaction of various decisions. One classic example is SIMSOC (Gamson, 1966), a sociology game in which students are citizens of a society in which they have economic and social roles; for example, some are members of political parties, and some have police powers. Games like this are useful in getting students to consider varied points of view relevant to the issues addressed in the game. Like the case method, an educational game may be either too simple or complex to achieve the kind of generalization of concepts or principles that the teacher desires. The biggest barrier to the use of games is logistic. Often it is hard to find a game that fits the time and facilities limitations of typical classes. Devising one's own game can be fun but also time consuming. Nonetheless, games are potentially useful tools for effective teaching.

IN CONCLUSION

Whether one uses cases, games, simulations, or other problems, problem-based learning is a valuable part of one's armamentarium of teaching strategies. In fact, even if you don't use problem-based learning in its traditional forms, the general principle that students like to solve problems that offer a challenge but are still solvable is important. And motivation isn't the only reason to use problems. If students are to learn how to think more effectively, they need to practice thinking. Moreover, cognitive theory provides good support for the idea that knowledge learned and used in a realistic, problem-solving context is more likely to be remembered and used appropriately when needed later.

There is a good deal of research on problem-based learning in its various forms, including case methods and simulations. My summation of the results is that, compared with traditional methods of teaching, problem-based learning may sometimes result in less acquisition of knowledge but typically shows little, if any, decrement. However, retention, application, and motivational outcomes are generally superior to those in traditional methods of instruction.

Supplementary Reading

Guided design is fully described in C. E. Wales and R. A. Stager, *Guided Design* (Morgantown: West Virginia University, 1977).

Donald Woods has published three useful books on problem-based learning: *Problem-based Learning: How to Gain the Most from PBL* (written for students), *Helping Your Students Gain the Most from PBL* (written for teachers), and *Resources to Gain the Most from PBL*. All three are published by Donald R. Woods, Department of Chemical Engineering, McMaster University, Hamilton, ON L85 4LT, Canada.

Practical help in using problem-based learning and in using role playing may be found in A. Grasha, *Teaching with Style* (Pittsburgh: Alliance Publishers, 1996).

LuAnn Wilkerson and W. H. Gigselaers (eds.), Bringing Problem-Based Learning to Higher Education: Theory and Practice [Special issue], *New Directions for Teaching and Learning*, 1996, *68*, has articles describing problem-based learning in a variety of courses.

Diana Laurillard has a good discussion of computer-based simulations in her book *Rethinking University Teaching: A Framework for the Effective Use of Educational Technology* (London: Routledge, 1993).

The Harvard Law and Business Schools were pioneers in using the case method. The following two references provide a good description of the methods they developed.

C. R. Christensen and A. J. Hansen, *Teaching and the Case Method* (Boston: Harvard Business School, 1987).

M. McNair (ed.), *The Case Method at the Harvard Business School* (New York: McGraw-Hill, 1954).

A sophisticated description of the use of the case method in medical education as well as two experiments on activating and restructuring prior knowledge in case discussions may be found in H. G. Schmidt, *Activatie van Voorkennis, Intrinsieke Motivatie en de Verwerking van Tekst* (Apeldoorn, The Netherlands: Van Walraven bv, 1982). (Don't worry. Despite the Dutch title, the text is in English.)

A helpful general introduction to the case method is R. A. Weaver, T. J. Kowalski, and J. E. Pfaller, "Case Method Teaching," in K. W. Prichard and R. McL. Sawyer (eds.), *Handbook of College Teaching: Theory and Applications* (Westport, CT: Greenwood Press).

Linc Fisch's article "Triggering Discussions on Ethics and Values: Cases and Innovative Case Variations," *Innovative Higher Education*, 1997, *22*, 117–134, has lots of practical tips.

Samford University has played a leading role in problem-based learning. They have a web site with a newsletter: www.samford.edu/pbl.

17 Technology and Teaching

■ ■ ■ ■ ■ ■ ■ ■ ■ ■ ■ ■ ■ ■ ■ ■ ■

As network computing and tools for learning, teaching, and administration gain more power and accessibility, integrating technology into the educational process is becoming a major initiative for most colleges and universities. Some instructors are embracing technology wholeheartedly, whereas others feel puzzled or left behind. Because of concerns we've heard from instructors, we believe the essential questions of technology integration are threefold: (1) How will technology enhance teaching and learning? (2) What should be considered when teaching with technology? and (3) What are the effects of technology on teaching? In this chapter we will address each of these issues.

HOW WILL TECHNOLOGY ENHANCE TEACHING AND LEARNING?

When instructors ground their choice of technology tools in individual course goals, personal teaching philosophy, and disci-

This chapter was written by Erping Zhu and Matthew Kaplan of the University of Michigan's Center for Research on Teaching and Learning.

pline-specific values, technology tools are capable of enhancing teaching and learning. Technology can make increased learning productivity possible if it is coupled with changes in pedagogy and implementation (Berge, 2000; Johnstone, 1992; Oppenheimer, 1997; Twigg, 1992). Communication technologies, for example, offer increasing opportunities for online conferencing and collaboration (Harasim, 1993). Murphy, Drabier, and Epps (1997) assert that the very nature of computer conferencing promotes a collaborative approach to learning.

Technology, especially learner-centered technology, can activate principles of learning theory on both the cognitive and the metacognitive levels (Bonk & Cummingham, 1998). When an instructor creates a technology-enriched learning environment that places tools in the hands of learners to build, browse, link, draw, juxtapose, represent, and summarize information, the learners are engaged in an intentional process of constructing meaning from information and experience (Lehrer, 1993). Technology-enhanced learning environments can also have a positive influence on student motivation, through factors such as novelty, curiosity, control, personal choice, and effort. For example, the intrigue of answering questions posted by peers in a foreign country or the delight of posting one's ideas and work on the web can build a personal sense of pride and ownership into academic assignments (Harasim, 1990). These technologies can also allow instructors to diversify course content so that students are exposed to materials from cultures and perspectives different from their own (see the chapter "Valuing Student Differences" for more on diversity). In addition, technology-enriched learning environments such as Carnegie Mellon Online **(http://online .web.cmu.edu/)** have the potential to support diverse learners by moving beyond the traditional constraints of time and place. (See the distance education chapter for more detailed information.)

Wager and McCombs (1995) summarize the potential benefits of technology-enhanced instructional environments. Such environments can provide greater opportunities to experience learning activities that are internally driven and constructed, goal oriented and reflective, personally meaningful and authentic, collaborative and socially negotiated, and adaptive to individual needs and cultural backgrounds.

TEACHING WITH TECHNOLOGY

When considering technology in their teaching, many instructors begin with questions about various technology tools: Should I use PowerPoint? Do I need to create a course web page? What programs are best for getting started? Although there is some validity to jumping into the world of technology in order to experiment and develop one's repertoire of teaching strategies, we would like to begin our discussion by stepping back and taking a more systematic approach to technology integration. In our view, the use of instructional technology is more likely to be effective and appropriate, facilitating student learning and increasing your own productivity, if there is a careful examination of the various factors involved in the teaching and learning process rather than a focus solely on types of technology.

From a systems approach, teaching with technology involves four major components: the students, the instructor, course content, and technology tools (see Figure 17.1). An examination of each component raises a set of issues that we need to consider in order to make technology integration as successful as possible. For example, content can be examined in terms of learning outcomes and the discipline being taught. Instructors can think of their own experience with technology, the amount of time they have for planning and teaching, and their role in the teaching and learning process. We need to think carefully about our students, their exposure and access to technology, as well as their preferred learning styles. Finally, we can turn to the technology itself and analyze it according to its functions. This approach to teaching and learning with technology assumes that the four component parts are integrated and that changes in one part will require adjustments to the other three in order to achieve the same goals.

Course Content

When considering any technology tools for instruction, you need to examine your instructional goals: What do you expect students to learn from the class? What skills and knowledge do you want them to acquire by the end of the term? What teaching strategies

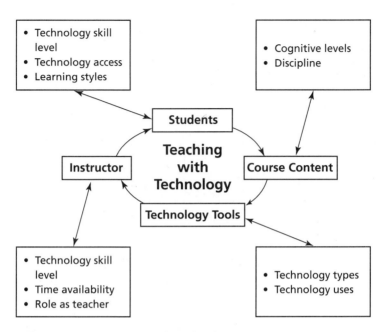

FIGURE 17.1 Teaching with Technology

(lecture, discussion, group work, case studies) will best help students achieve these goals? (See the chapter "Countdown for Course Preparation" for more information on the process of course design and planning.) Once you have answers to these questions, you can choose the appropriate technologies to support your goals and design appropriate learning activities to incorporate those technologies into your course.

When the learning objectives are at the knowledge or comprehension level (Bloom, 1956), you may use technology tools that support information delivery or programs that reinforce and help apply the knowledge that students have learned. On the other hand, when the instructional goals are at the application/analysis or synthesis/evaluation levels (Bloom, 1956), it is appropriate to provide students with a complex technology-enhanced learning environment, in which they can apply, integrate, and make sense

TECHNOLOGY CAPABILITY

Presentation & Distribution	Drill & Practice Integration	Interaction & Communication	Creation & Manipulation

Knowledge Comprehension	Application & Analysis	Critical Thinking Collaboration	Synthesis & Evaluation

LEARNING OBJECTIVE

FIGURE 17.2   Technology and Learning Objectives

of what they have learned. Figure 17.2 briefly illustrates the basis for selecting technology in accordance with learning objectives.

For example, if your goal is for students to record and remember factual material effectively, you might want to improve readability of lecture topics and outlines, and find an easy way to give students copies of those outlines. Microsoft PowerPoint is one of the tools that can help you achieve this goal. However, if you also wish to promote critical thinking through active learning during lectures, PowerPoint alone may not be the best choice; presentation software can lead to a teacher-centered and student-passive mode of instruction (Creed, 1997). To avoid placing students in a passive learning mode, you will need to incorporate activities that engage students in active thinking, reflecting, and performing tasks. In this case, although you might still want to incorporate PowerPoint slides, you could use the peer instruction teaching method (Mazur, 1997) in lecture, to reinforce students' understanding and engage them in thinking. With this approach, an instructor poses a conceptual question, students discuss possible answers in pairs, and then they vote electronically for the correct answer. The instructor then has immediate feedback about how well the students have understood the concept. You could also extend student thinking beyond the class by setting up an online class discussion using a web-based conferencing program.

The discipline you teach, as well as the goals you set for student learning, will affect your decisions about which technologies are most appropriate for a given course. In some disciplines, technology is a standard part of professional work in the field, and decisions about technology integration need to take these realities into account. For example, students learning statistics in the social sciences will need to have experience with spreadsheets and other statistical software. Which program to choose could depend on which package allows students to perform the most relevant operations. Similarly, there are many applications specifically designed to support student learning in foreign language classes. In other areas, however, discipline-specific software is not as common, and instructors will need to use more generic technology tools and tailor them to their specific course goals.

The Instructor

Once you have a clear view of the course content and how technology can support your instructional goals, you will need to ask some questions about your own skills and attitudes: (1) How skilled and experienced are you in using technology? (2) How much time do you have for course planning and preparation? and (3) How do you think of your role as a teacher?

If you have relatively little experience using technology, it might not make sense to move to a technology-rich environment even if your course goals would support such a shift. Instead, you can start slowly with tools that are established and easy to use so that you build your confidence and support your students' learning. You will probably want to seek out support from colleagues in your department, as well as from instructional technology support offices on your campus. You might find out what tools your colleagues are using in their courses, what skills you will need to develop in order to be comfortable teaching with this technology, and what workshops or consultations are available to support your efforts.

The time you have available for course planning, skill development, and the teaching process should also influence the extent to which you undertake technology integration in your courses. As we stated previously, the selection of technology tools should be based on a course's goals and objectives rather than on the availability and newness of technology tools. As a result, you will need to spend time on course design and technology selection before a course starts. You will also need to guide and mentor students in using the technology while the course is being taught. Guiding and mentoring students involves much more interaction than just presenting, distributing, and explaining course content. It may take more time than you expect or wish to spend on teaching. You need to be aware of this and be well prepared and ready for such a time commitment when you make the decision to integrate technology into your courses. Using technology to teach without adequate preparation and time commitment could have a negative impact on your teaching and student learning.

For novices this might mean starting small, planning for courses well in advance, and waiting for junctures in your career when you can devote time to more significant technology projects. Even expert users need to think carefully about whether they can afford to begin a major technology initiative. Search for support, both technical and pedagogical. Many campuses now have teaching centers and offices of instructional technology with consultants who can work with you and help you plan effectively. In addition, you can look for graduate and undergraduate students who have experience working with technology and might be able to provide support and assistance.

One final issue we need to consider in this category is how the instructor views his or her role in the teaching process and how technology integration can support or conflict with that view. As we stated in the first section, technology-rich learning environments are often most successful when students are actively engaged. In this case, teaching with technology will involve guidance, mentoring, and coaching of students (once you move beyond simple applications such as presentation software and e-mail). If you see your main role in teaching as that of an expert, an authority in a given field whose main task in teaching is to convey information, the shift to guide or coach may be disconcerting. In some cases you might even find that your students know more about and are more comfortable with the technology than you are. It is best to think carefully about your own view of teaching and students, how your use of technology might change the dynamics in your class, and whether you are willing to make that shift. For some instructors this might be an opportunity to reinvigorate their teaching; for others it might be an exercise in frustration.

Students

As you integrate technology tools into your course, the background and preparation of the students you teach will play an important role in your decision making. In particular, you will need to consider students' previous experience with technology, their access to technology, and the variety of learning styles they bring to your course.

Many instructors report that student comfort and experience with technology seem to increase each year. Data from national studies confirm that, overall, Americans are gaining greater access to technology. In August 2000, over 50 percent of American households had computers, a 58 percent increase from December 1998. Similar increases were found in the percentage of households connected to the Internet (up from 26.2 percent to 41.5 percent of all households). If present trends continue, over 50 percent of Americans will be connecting to the Internet sometime in 2001 (Shapiro & Rohde, 2000). Moreover, exposure to computers is by no means limited to the home. Access to computers in the public schools has been a national priority since 1994, and the results have been striking. By 1999, 95 percent of public schools and 63 percent of all instructional classrooms in public schools were connected to the Internet, up from 35 percent and 3 percent, respectively, in 1994 (Williams, 2000).

Despite these encouraging statistics, there is still a digital divide in this country, by both race and income level. African-American and Hispanic households are about half as likely to have connections to the Internet as the national average (23 percent). In the public schools, far fewer classrooms had Internet access in areas with high poverty: 39 percent versus 62 to 74 percent of classes in areas with lower concentrations of poverty (Williams, 2000). Although it is important not to assume that all students have had the same exposure to technology, it is also important for instructors to avoid making assumptions about who has had access and who has not. To avoid such assumptions, you can conduct a brief survey at the beginning of the semester to find out where your students stand. Even students who come from houses with computers might not have spent much time with them and might not be familiar with the applications you expect them to use.

To help, you can develop a brief orientation to the technology or some tasks early on that will allow students to learn the technology and accomplish some course-specific goals. Finally, find out where students can go for help and tell them about the resources available.

Unless your campus requires students to have computers (a policy that is growing in popularity), you also need to consider the extent to which students have access to the technology tools you intend to use. On some campuses this will be more of an issue than on others. But even at universities that are very well outfitted with technology, courses requiring students to spend a lot of time in computer labs can be seen as a burden. Explaining why you have incorporated technology into the course—and being able to frame your explanation in terms of improving student learning—can help. As you decide the extent to which you will pursue technology integration, you might also need to balance your own enthusiasm with the realities of your campus infrastructure.

Aside from issues of exposure and access to technology, you will want to take into consideration the fact that students will come to your class with a variety of learning styles and preferences. Individuals differ in their general skills, aptitudes, and preferences for processing information, constructing meaning from it, and applying it to new situations (Jonassen & Brabowski, 1993). Some learners enjoy collaborative learning, some prefer independent learning, and still others like more traditional, directive learning (Grasha & Yangarber-Kicks, 2000). Technology tools offer great flexibility in creating learning activities and environments to meet various learning styles and needs.

Just as technology has the potential to change the role of the instructor from centralized dispenser of knowledge to guide or mentor, it can also shift the student's role from passive recipient to active participant. Active participation requires students to take on new responsibilities, such as monitoring their own learning goals, setting priorities, and controlling the pace of their own learning. Some students may not be ready for the instructor to place these responsibilities on them. Students can even be resentful of the new expectations and challenges, because they are used to learning in a passive and responsive way rather than being active and taking initiative. When an instructor takes a more student-centered approach, some students might see this as an abdication of responsibility rather than as a positive development. As you more toward greater student involvement and responsibility, you will need to explain why you are taking this approach and build in enough structure so that students do not feel lost. The following suggestions should help:

- Discuss options for support should students encounter difficulties.
- Provide opportunities for feedback about the class, so that you can make minor adjustments when problems arise.
- Be clear about your expectations for using technology and for any projects and assignments.
- Build in multiple milestones for independent or group projects, so that you can check student progress.

Technology Tools

Now that we have carefully considered the context of teaching and learning, we can turn to an examination of the technology itself. How can technology facilitate teaching and learning? Not all tools are the same. Some can assist learning in one content area only; others are useful for a range of disciplines. Some technology tools are built with specific instructional goals in mind; others are not. For example, computer-assisted instruction and software programs for language learning and mathematics are usually designed to accommodate specific instructional goals and objectives. On the other hand, "worldware" (Ehrmann, 1995) and learner-centered technology (Bonk & Cunningham, 1998) represent another group of technology tools that were not designed with any specific instructional goals and objectives in mind and, in some cases, were not even developed to support instruction. Such technology includes electronic mail, electronic conferencing programs, the web, databases/spreadsheets, and programs like Hyperstudio, Authorware, and Director. Instructors can adopt any of these tools in their teaching and use it as a partner to support student learning and enhance critical thinking (Jonassen, 2000).

To examine the appropriate uses of these various technologies, we can categorize each tool according to its functions and uses (see Table 17.1). For example, a large group of tools can be used

TABLE 17.1 Tool Types, Examples, and Instructional Uses

Type	Example	Instructional Use
Communication Technology		
• One-to-one • One-to-many • Many-to-many	E-mail, telephone Bulletin board, listserv, teleconference, videoconference Web conferencing software, Internet Relay Chat (IRC)	Presenting information Integrating information Interacting and collaborating
Organization and Presentation Technology		
• Text • Text/graphic • Text/graphic/ animation	PowerPoint, Inspiration, SmartDraw Semantic networking tools Gif Construction/ Builder, Firework, Flash	Presenting information Integrating information
Information Search and Resource Management Technology		
• Information searching (local and worldwide access) • Information managing	Web, Internet Electronic database, such as MathSci Database, Wilson Indexes, and ERIC database Procite, EndNotes	Presenting, integrating, and manipulating information
Audio and Video Technology		
• Analog • Digital	Audio/videotape Compact audio/ videodisc Digital audio/video Streaming audio/ video	Presenting information Integrating information

Type	Example	Instructional Use
Web-based Course Management Systems		
• Commercial product	Blackboard WebCT	Presenting information Integrating information
• Noncommercial product	Web-Course in a Box TopClass UM.CourseTools[a]	Interacting and collaborating
Creation and Manipulation Tools		
• Simple text and graphic	Databases and statistical packages	Presenting, integrating, applying, manipulating,
• Multimedia	ToolBook, Authorware, Director, HTML editors	and making sense of information/data Interacting and collaborating
Discipline-specific Software Programs and Tutorials		
• Arts and sciences	Math, science, and language software programs	Presenting, integrating, reinforcing, and applying information
• Humanities and others		
Distance Learning Systems		
• Television-based	Interactive television conference	Presenting information and delivering
• Internet-based	Web-based audio/ videoconference	instruction to remote learners

[a] UM.CourseTools is a customizable web-based classroom management tool used at the University of Michigan.

to help students communicate and interact with one another or the instructor. Software programs such as Inspiration, SmartDraw, and PowerPoint assist users in organizing information and displaying it in text or graphic format. The web, the Internet, electronic databases, and other information management tools enable users to search, gather, manipulate, and use information. Tools such as Logos, ToolBook, Macromedia Authorware and Director, and HTML editors allow users to create learning artifacts and environments. Table 17.1 briefly summarizes common categories of technology, provides examples, and lists the instructional purposes for each tool.

Communication technology enables users to communicate with one another in three different modes. One-to-one communication via telephone or e-mail allows comparatively private conversations between a student and an instructor. One-to-many teleconferences or listservs offer the means to broadcast information to a group. Many-to-many communication, such as threaded electronic discussions, allows students to exchange ideas and opinions and collaborate with one another on learning tasks. For example, students can ask the instructor questions via e-mail and receive answers and explanations electronically. Students can extend or carry on a class discussion online using a threaded discussion program. And students can integrate knowledge, construct understandings, and work collaboratively on learning tasks with the support of various communication tools.

Organization and presentation technology allows instructors to organize and present information as text, graphic, or animation. With programs like Microsoft PowerPoint instructors can display visual outlines for a lecture or a professional presentation. Software programs such as Inspiration and SmartDraw enable the instructor to explain the hierarchical relationship in a system or a unit. The use of graphic and visual images can facilitate student understanding of physical processes that are difficult to explain in words.

Information search and resource management technology helps users search, locate, and manage information. Skills in searching, locating, and evaluating information and resources are crucial to teaching and learning across disciplines. The web and other Internet-based electronic databases make it possible for users to search for and gather information worldwide. Intranet-based or restricted electronic databases give users access to resources such as Lexis-Nexis (Lexis-Nexis Academic Universe) and ABI/ INFORM (Business and Management Index). Bibliographic management programs such as ProCite and Endnotes offer users tools for organizing information and resources for future retrieval.

Audio and video technology has a long history of instructional uses, and analog audio and videotapes in particular are ubiquitous. With the development of computer technology, audio and video can be transmitted not only in analog format, but also in digital and even in streaming media format. The compact disc has increased the storage and quality of the audio and video, but digital versatile disc (DVD) provides another new standard of quality and data storage. Streaming audio and video can be played in real time without downloading files entirely, whereas most other audio and video files must be fully downloaded before playing. Audio and video are powerful tools for instruction, especially in areas such as music and film studies. Video is capable of bringing real-life cases into classroom environments and demonstrating procedures for performing kinesthetic tasks. Videotaped interviews and vignettes, for example, can help students in the health sciences explore the issues involved in caring for patients from diverse cultural backgrounds.

Web-based course management systems usually provide a set of tools, allowing the instructor to create and manage course web sites without using HTML editors or other programming languages. A web-based course management system usually includes space for a syllabus, a schedule or calendar, announcements, assignments, online discussions, and group work. Some systems are built with an assessment component, allowing the instructor to give students online quizzes or tests. Most web-based course management systems are constantly adding and improving features. A number of instructors in colleges and universities across the country are using web-based course management systems such as Blackboard, WebCT, or UM.CourseTools to manage courses online. Instructors use these systems to distribute course assignments, manage course-related resources electronically, and engage students in collaborative learning activities.

Creation and manipulation tools allow users to create and design learning activities, modules, or learning environments. Popular tools include Macromedia Authorware and Director, ToolBook,

HTML editors such as Macromedia Dreamweaver and Adobe GoLive, statistical packages, and other programming tools. Instructors can use these tools to create computer-assisted instructional modules for drill and practice, interactive tutorials, self-assessing tests, simulations or games for skill application, and virtual learning environments. They are also great tools for instructors to engage students in creating learning activities or in peer-teaching modules. These types of technology applications enable students to learn by doing, an important principle for learning in general and particularly relevant to learning with technology (Schank et al., 1999).

Discipline-specific software programs and tutorials offer instructors a wide range of software to support learning in specific disciplines. Symbolic algebra programs such as MACSYMA and MAPLE, and Perseus project (including CD, videodisc, and the Internet version), are examples. Some of these programs are built with instructional goals and objectives, whereas some, like Perseus, have left the decision to the instructor. Perseus has been used for interdisciplinary studies in history, literature, art, archaeology, and mythology. Before adopting a particular piece of discipline-specific software, instructors need to preview the program to be sure it suits the goals and objectives of the course in question.

Distance learning systems can include all the technology tools previously listed. In addition, distance learning courses can be delivered via videoconference systems (one- or two-way audio and video) and Internet-based audio and videoconference software programs. Technology aside, instructors teaching courses to students at a distance via audio- and videoconferencing will confront a set of instructional decisions that they don't usually face in traditional classrooms. For more information on teaching distance learning courses, see the chapter on distance education.

Although the systems approach to teaching with technology that we've discussed here can serve as a model or framework for planning technology integration, tips on using technology may help you manage technology-supported teaching more effectively, avoiding some of the traps in which other instructors have been caught. For tips on using the most common technology tools, see Figure 17.3.

FIGURE 17.3   Tips for Using Common Technology Tools in Teaching

PowerPoint

- Use fonts 24 points or larger.
- Use dark type and light background.
- Use the slide as a guide for the talk rather than reading from it.
- Face the audience when showing the slide.
- Distribute or encourage students to download a copy of the slide.
- Keep the room lights on and avoid showing slides in a dark room for more than 15 minutes.
- Avoid putting students in a passive mode of receiving information by combining the slide presentation with chalkboard/whiteboard use or any other learning activities.
- Have a backup plan in case of a power outage or equipment failure.

E-mail

Set up rules for using class e-mail; for example:

⇨ establish convention for naming message titles and subtitles (e.g., ECON 101—Assignment and ECON 101—Request for Appointment).

⇨ clarify wait time for the instructor's response (e.g., a student who sends an e-mail at 3 A.M. can't expect a timely response from the instructor).

⇨ ask students to use consistent attachment formats (e.g., saving documents in RTF or Text format).

- Keep a copy of important correspondence yourself.
- Don't assume that your students will keep all the messages you send.

Online Conferencing/ Discussion

- Define clear goals and objectives for the online discussion.
- Organize the online conference clearly by category and topic ahead of time.
- Provide detailed instructions for students, including student roles and responsibilities.
- Set rules for appropriate and inappropriate behaviors before starting discussions.
- Set a clear starting and ending time for each discussion topic.
- Set clear expectations and standards for assessing student performance in the online discussion.
- Direct students to training classes, online tutorials, and any other assistance when necessary.
- Create a comfortable atmosphere for the online discussion; for example:

⇨ be a participant rather than an instructor;

⇨ challenge the students without threatening them;

⇨ use personal anecdotes when appropriate;

⇨ bring your own experiences to the discussion;

⇨ don't dominate a discussion or let a few students dominate it.

- Ask questions at different levels (e.g., knowledge, comprehension, application, analysis, synthesis, and evaluation).
- Paraphrase a message if it is not clear.
- Encourage active student participation.
- Bring an online discussion to a closure (e.g., summarizing learning points).
- Energize the online discussion if needed (e.g., using role-plays, simulations, pros and cons).

(cont.)

FIGURE 17.3 *(cont.)*

Teaching with the Web

Course Web Pages

• Allow plenty of lead time for planning the course.
• Be sure that the course web pages are functional.
• Have a backup plan for lectures (e.g., print or save the web pages on your local hard drive).
• Be well prepared for your web lecture; for example:

⇒ check the classroom setup (e.g., browser, software, computer memory, monitor, and audio).
⇒ verify links, especially the external links.
⇒ check the room lighting to see if it is suitable for both viewing the projected screen and taking notes.
⇒ arrange for a technical support staff to be in your classroom at the start of class to help with the setup and get you off to a good start.
⇒ always know whom to call for help if technical problems occur.

• Emphasize the need for filtering and interpreting information on the web when encouraging students to use the web resources.
• Remind students that only a smaller fraction of the whole archive of knowledge is available on the web.

Web-based Course Management Systems

• Have a clear idea of what features you will use and why you are using them.
• Start with manageable features if you are a first time/novice user of the system.
• Hide features that are not in use if possible.
• Rethink how to organize and present course materials effectively through the use of a web-based course management system.
• Prepare students for the use of the system and arrange student training if necessary.
• Be aware that creating web-based courses and modules requires at least as much or more effort and time as traditional courses.

WHAT ARE THE EFFECTS OF TECHNOLOGY ON TEACHING?

Assumptions about technology and its effects vary among technology users. Some proponents of technology believe that instructors can automatically take advantage of the technology to teach well, and students can learn well if they get the right hardware and software in the classroom. Others believe that hardware and software used in the class are irrelevant to student learning. These two opposing positions actually reflect the debate of medium and message in the field of educational technology (Clark, 1994a, 1994b; Kozma, 1994). The research studies collected in *No Significant Difference Phenomenon* by Tom Russell (1999) do indicate that the vehicle—the technology used for providing information—does not significantly affect student learning outcomes. However, other researchers, such as Kozma (1994), argue that we have not sufficiently used and examined the attributes and specific functions of individual technologies or explored and compared their effectiveness in instruction. We cannot, therefore, expect to find that technologies make a difference until we can exploit the unique capabilities of the medium. Both opinions suggest useful directions for examining the effects of educational technology on learning and teaching. For practical and useful research into teaching with technology, questions should be directed toward exploring what the best teaching and learning strategies are and how technologies best support those strategies (Ehrmann, 1995; Kozma, 1994).

IN CONCLUSION

As we mentioned previously, the successful integration of technology entails the careful consideration of course content, the capabilities of various technology tools, student access to and comfort with technology, and the instructor's view of his or her role in the teaching and learning process. The use of technology may change teaching methods and approaches to learning as well as attitudes, motivation, and interest in teaching and learning the subject. These changes may in turn have an impact on the effectiveness of teaching and learning. As you think about the effects of technology on teaching and learning, you need to consider the full range of changes technology has brought to a given course or curriculum. The following questions are designed to help you think about how you might evaluate the effect of technology integration on your courses:

■ Are there any changes in student and instructor roles in any of the following areas?

Ownership of learning tasks

Degree of engagement in learning

Control of learning and teaching environment

Sources of information and knowledge

Relationship between the instructor and students and among students themselves

Responsibility for teaching and learning

- Is technology helping students reach the instructional goals and objectives?

Student demonstration of knowledge and skills

Alignment of course goals, technology tools, and assessment methods

- How does the technology affect teaching efficiency?

Use of class time

Use of the instructor's time for course preparation and management

Ability to distribute and present course content

Supplementary Reading

Following are several helpful sources on teaching with technology:

PowerPoint

B. Brown, "PowerPoint-induced Sleep," *Syllabus*, 2001, *14*(6), 17.

T. Creed, *PowerPoint, No! Cyberspace, Yes*, 1999, http://www.ntlf.com/html/pi/9705/creed_1.htm

D. Hlynka, "PowerPoint in the Classroom: What Is the Point?" *Educational Technology*, 1998, *38*(5), 45-48.

R. Mason, "PowerPoint in the Classroom: Where Is the Power?" *Educational Technology*, 1998, *38*(5), 42-45.

T. Rocklin, *PowerPoint Is Not Evil*, 1999, http://www.ntlf.com/html/sf/notevil.htm

E-mail and Online Discussion

C. J. Bonk and K. S. King (eds.), *Electronic Collaborators: Learner-centered Technologies for Literacy, Apprenticeship, and Discourse* (Mahwah, NJ: L. Erlbaum Associates, 1998).

G. Collison, B. Elbaum, S. Haavind, and R. Tinker, *Facilitating Online Learning: Effective Strategies for Moderators* (Madison, WI: Atwood Publishing, 2000).

eModerators provides resources specifically for facilitators and moderators of online discussion at http://www/emoderators.com.

D. Hanna, M. Glowacki-Dudka, and S. Conceicao-Runlee, *147 Practical Tips for Teaching Online Groups: Essentials of Web-based Education* (Madison, WI: Atwood Publishing, 2000).

Teaching with the Web

S. Horton, *Web Teaching Guide: A Practical Approach to Creating Course Web Sites* (New Haven, CT: Yale University Press, 2000).

B. H. Khan (ed.), *Web-based Instruction* (Englewood Cliffs, NJ: Educational Technology Publications, 1997).

G. R. Morrison, S. M. Ross, and J. E. Kemp, *Designing Effective Instruction* (New York: Wiley, 2001).

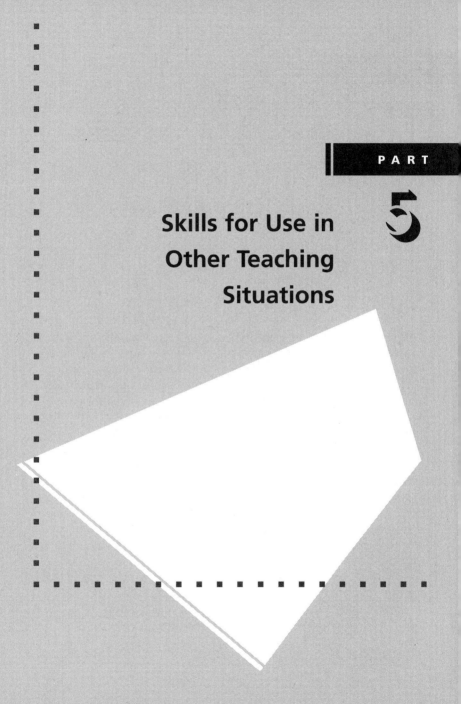

PART

5

Skills for Use in
Other Teaching
Situations

18 Teaching Large Classes (You Can Still Get Active Learning!)

■ ■ ■ ■ ■ ■ ■ ■ ■ ■ ■ ■ ■ ■ ■ ■ ■

When I began teaching in 1946, most first- and second-year courses were taught by lecture in large classrooms or auditoriums. Over the next three decades, research demonstrated that better learning occurred if students had an opportunity to discuss the material. Thus many large courses now supplement lectures with one or two hours of small-group discussion. However, with decreasing government support and increasing enrollments, more and more universities all over the world feel pressure to revert to large classes without small discussion groups or tutorials.

Most of this chapter deals with skills and strategies useful in large groups, whether or not they are supplemented by discussion groups. Before concluding, I will discuss aspects of the teacher's role involved in supervising teaching assistants who lead discussion or laboratory groups.

If you are assigned to teach a large course, you are likely to assume that you must lecture and use multiple-choice or other easily scorable tests, but large classes need not constrain you. You don't need to lecture—at least not all the time.

FACILITATING ACTIVE LEARNING

The most commonly used method of stimulating active learning is questioning and encouraging student questioning, as discussed in the chapters on facilitating discussion and making lectures more effective. But there are many other tools in your active learning kit that are usable in large classes. Remember that, in the chapter on active learning, I reported the research showing that students learn more in student-led discussions, or in learning cells, than they learn in traditional lectures. Thus you can get the advantages of a multisection course by organizing students to meet in class or out of class for discussion. Active learning does not need to be restricted to in-class activity. You can organize study groups. You can use e-mail. The chapter on technology describes ways in which technology can facilitate learning both in and out of class.

Techniques such as buzz groups, problem posting, and the two-column method of large-group discussions were also described earlier. Buzz groups (described in the chapter on facilitating discussion) can be formed and asked to discuss how the material might be used or applied. Simply pausing occasionally to give students a couple of minutes to compare their notes can activate thinking (Ruhl et al., 1987).

Encouraging Student Writing in Large Classes

One of the most important drawbacks of large classes is the lack of student writing. Because grading essays is so time-consuming, most faculty members reduce, or eliminate, writing assignments in a large class. Take heart! You can get some of the educational advantages of writing, and at the same time improve attention to the lecture, without being submerged by papers to grade.

The "minute paper," described earlier, is one valuable tool.* At an appropriate point in the lecture, announce the paper and the

---

* The minute paper need not be one minute; it can be two, three, or as many minutes as needed for a particular topic.

topic or question you want students to address; for example, you might ask the students to summarize the major point or points made so far in the lecture. Or you might give the students a choice of topics, such as a summary, a question, an application, or an example. When the minute is up, you may either collect the papers or break the class into pairs or subgroups to review and discuss one another's papers.

If you wish, you can evaluate and comment on the papers as you would any other student papers. If the class is exceptionally large, you may announce that you'll read and return only a sample of the papers. Students can be motivated to think and write without the threat of grades, and this technique not only gets students thinking actively during the lecture but gives you feedback about what students are learning from the lecture.

Similar to the "minute paper" is the "half-sheet response" (Weaver & Cotrell, 1985). In this technique students tear out a half-sheet of notebook paper to respond to a question or instruction such as:

"What do you think about this concept?"
"Give an example of this concept or principle."
"Explain this concept in your own words."
"How does this idea relate to your own experience?"
"What are some of your feelings as you listen to these ideas?"
"How could you use this idea in your own life?"

Both the minute paper and the half-sheet response can help initiate a large-group discussion.

Other Ways to Maintain Student Involvement

There are a variety of techniques that can help break the deadly routine of lectures day after day: debates, fishbowl, interviews.

In addition to the large-group discussion and subgrouping techniques discussed in the chapters "Facilitating Discussion" and "Active Learning," you can enliven your class with debates either between faculty members or between student teams. If you use student debaters, you need to provide a clear structure, probably using a handout describing the issue, the length of talks, opportunity for rebuttal, and the goal of the debate as a learning device. If the topic is one on which students are likely to have strong biases, you can open minds by assigning groups to argue the side opposite their initial position. You can follow the debate by dividing the class into buzz groups whose task is to find a solution or resolution that takes into account the evidence and values of both sides.

The "fishbowl" can be used in small, as well as large, classes. Tell the students that at the next class meeting you will choose six students (or any convenient number) to be "in the fishbowl." You will then conduct a discussion (based on the work to date) with the students in the fishbowl. The rest of the students are to act as observers and recorders, noting both the process and the content of the discussion. Before the end of the class period, observers will write a brief summary of the discussion and raise questions that remain or answer the question, "What would you have said that wasn't said?"

Another break in lectures can be provided by an interview—perhaps of a colleague with special expertise, someone from outside the university, or one of the students with special experience. A variant might be a dialog on a topic in which you and a colleague have somewhat different views.

Student presentations can enhance the learning and motivation of students who have special interests or expertise and can also be valuable for the other students if presentations are well done. But don't assume that this will be a chance to reduce your own preparation time. If the student simply reads a paper, the audience will be bored. So work with the student on ways of enhancing interest and attention. For some shy students, you may want to conduct the presentation as an interview.

If you plan to have a number of presentations, consider the possibility of a poster session—a method now common in scholarly conventions.

If you use these methods, some students will be frustrated. They came to hear you tell them the TRUTH, which they can then memorize for tests. To handle this frustration, two things may help:

1. Explain how active participation contributes to better understanding and memory.

2. Make sure that your students realize that your tests will require thinking, not just rote memory.

STUDENT ANONYMITY

A major problem of teaching a large class is that students not only feel anonymous, they usually *are* anonymous. And as social psychological research has shown, people who are anonymous feel less personal responsibility—a consequence not only damaging to morale and order but also unlikely to facilitate learning. Moreover, the sense of distance from the instructor, the loss of interpersonal bonds with the instructor and with other students—these diminish motivation for learning.

The larger the group, the less likely that a given student will feel free to volunteer a contribution or question. Yet the students who prefer anonymity may be the very ones who most need to find that others respect their ideas.

What can we do? The fact that with increasing class size it becomes less and less possible to know students as individuals is likely to make us feel that it is not worth trying to do anything. I think this is a mistake. In my experience the students appreciate whatever efforts you make even if they do not take advantage of them. The following box shows some things I've tried.

Reducing Students' Feelings of Anonymity

1. Announce that you'll meet any students who are free for coffee after class. (You won't be swamped.)
2. Pass out invitations to several students to join you for coffee and to get acquainted after class.
3. Pass out brief student observation forms to several students at the beginning of class and ask them to meet you to discuss their observations.
4. Circulate among early arriving students to get acquainted before class starts.
5. Use a seating chart so that you can call students by name when they participate.

6. During your lecture, move out into the aisles to solicit comments.
7. If you can't use regularly scheduled discussion sections, set up an occasional afternoon or evening session for more informal discussion of an interesting question or for review before an examination.
8. Have students fill out an autobiographical sketch with name, hometown, year in college, and what they hope to get out of the course (Benjamin, 1991).

GIVING TESTS IN LARGE CLASSES

In classes of 200 or more, unwary instructors are likely to run into problems they would never dream of in teaching classes with an enrollment of 20 to 30. Most of these problems are administrative. For example, course planning almost inevitably becomes more rigid in a large class because almost anything involving the participation of the students requires more preparation time.

Perhaps you're used to making up your tests the day before you administer them. With a large class this is almost impossible. Essay and short-answer tests that take relatively little time to construct take a long time to score for 200 students; so you may spend long hours trying to devise thought-provoking objective questions for a part of the test. But once you've made up the questions your troubles are not over, for secretaries require a good deal of time to make several hundred copies of a test. Thus spur-of-the-moment tests are almost an impossibility, and by virtue of the necessity of planning ahead for tests, other aspects of the course also become more rigid.

As I indicated in the chapter "Assessing, Testing, and Evaluating," essay examinations are superior to typical objective examinations in their effect on student study and learning. Thus you are likely to regret the loss of the opportunity to give essay tests in a large group. But this loss is not inevitable. To some extent it can be compensated for by greater care in the construction of objective test items. But it is also possible to use essay items without increasing your load beyond reason. In a 500-student lecture course, I regularly included an essay item on the final examination with the stipulation that I would read it only if it would affect the student's letter grade for the course. Since the majority of the students were fairly clearly established as A, B, C, or D students on the basis of other work and the objective part of the final examination, the number of essays I needed to read was not excessive. My subjective impression was that knowledge of the inclusion of an essay item did affect the students' preparation for the exam.

OUTSIDE READING

The testing problem is just one of several factors structuring the conduct of large classes. Another is the assignment of readings in the library. With a small group you can assign library work with little difficulty, only making sure that the materials needed are available and, if necessary, reserved for the class. With a class of several hundred students a library assignment without previous planning can be disastrous. The library's single copy of a book or journal is obviously inadequate. Thus a library assignment must be conceived far enough in advance (usually several months) that enough copies of the book can be obtained, and the librarian can prepare for the fray.

Coordinating Multisection Courses

In any multisection course taught by several different instructors, the problem of coordination inevitably arises. The first approach to coordination is enforced uniformity of course content, sequence of topics, testing, grading, and even anecdotes. Such a procedure has the advantage that students who later elect more advanced courses can be presumed to have a certain uniform amount of background experience. It also is efficient in that only one final examination must be constructed, only one course outline devised, and students can transfer from section to section with no difficulty in catching up.

The disadvantage of this approach is that such uniformity often makes for dull, uninteresting teaching. If the teaching assistants are unenthusiastic about the course outline, they are likely to communicate this attitude to the students. If the course can be jointly planned, this may make for greater acceptance, but may also take a great deal of time.

A second approach to this problem is to set up completely autonomous sections, with all the instructors organizing and conducting their sections as they wish. The effectiveness of giving teaching assistants autonomy depends on how well you train and supervise them.

Training and Supervising Teaching Assistants

Your responsibility begins well before the first class meetings, for your teaching assistants need to know what you are expecting in terms of attendance at lectures, participation in weekly planning and training sessions, testing and grading, office hours, and such. But even more important than the formal requirements are the aspects of preparing the teaching assistants for meeting their first classes, establishing a good working relationship with their students, and developing the skills needed for leading discussions, answering questions, and carrying out other teaching responsibilities.

Here are some suggestions for assisting teaching assistants:

1. Hold weekly meetings to discuss teaching problems and plans.
2. Collect feedback from students early in the term.
3. Observe classes and discuss your observations with the TA.

To get student feedback, you can use simple open-ended questions, such as:

"What have you liked about the class so far?"
"What suggestions do you have for improvement?"

Visiting classes or videotaping can provide useful information about nonverbal characteristics of the teacher and reactions of the students. But observation or videotaping takes time. If you have time, visit classes, but if you are short of time, there is little evidence that videotaping or observation results in significantly greater improvement in teaching than consultation on student ratings collected early in the term (and perhaps repeated a little later). So if you're short of time, invest it in consultation.

IN CONCLUSION

Class size is important.

When taught appropriately, small classes are likely to be better than large classes for achieving long-term goals, such as retention and use of knowledge, thinking, and attitude change. Nonetheless, when dealing with large classes, you can come closer to the outcomes of small classes by

1. Providing discussion sections taught by trained teaching assistants.

2. Using teaching methods that facilitate active, meaningful, learning.

The fact that in a large class you will probably spend some of the time lecturing does not mean that students can now slip into passivity. What is important in active learning is active *thinking*. The techniques discussed in this and preceding chapters can produce active thinking and learning even in large lecture halls.

Supplementary Reading

Because almost every large university now has a program for training teaching assistants, there is a biennial meeting on training, and the papers from the meeting are typically published. The first volume is still one of the best:

J. D. Nyquist, R. D. Abbott, D. H. Wulff, and J. Sprague (eds.), *Preparing the Professoriate of Tomorrow to Teach: Selected Readings in TA Training* (Dubuque, IA: Kendall/Hunt, 1991).

For teaching large classes:

Jean MacGregor, James L. Cooper, Karl A. Smith, and Pamela Robinson (eds.), Strategies for Energizing Large Classes: From Small Groups to Learning Communities [Special issue], *New Directions for Learning and Teaching*, 2000, 81.

R. J. Sternberg (ed.), *Teaching Introductory Psychology: Survival Tips from the Experts* (Washington, DC: American Psychological Association, 1997).

Laboratory Instruction: Ensuring an Active Learning Experience

19

Laboratory instruction is widely accepted as important in order for learners to experience phenomena directly and understand how new knowledge is constructed. Although laboratory instruction derives from the revered apprenticeship model for learning practical arts, it is certainly not limited to the traditional "wet laboratories" of the physical and natural sciences. From psychology and education to the fine and performance arts, instructors create learning environments where students can ask questions and seek answers modeled on the way in which faculty members work.

Laboratory teaching assumes that first-hand experience is superior to other methods of developing the same skills. Laboratory instruction also rightly presumes that the next generation of practitioners will be motivated by an opportunity to participate in practice. The prevailing rhetoric of "learning by doing" characterizes the passionate attachment that faculty have to this form of teaching. The attributes of research, such as hands-on, "mind's-on" work, individualized experimental design, and decision making combined with collaborative tasks, should all theoretically contribute positively to learning. Frequently,

This chapter was written by Brian P. Coppola of the University of Michigan.

though, introductory laboratory instruction does not rise above validating results that are repeated year in and year out all over the country, using rote and lock-step, or "cookbook," procedures. Authentic, research-based laboratory information is hard earned and takes place over extended periods of time, and would appear to be inefficiently gained when compared with abstractions presented orally, in print, or digitally. Thus one would not expect laboratory instruction to have an advantage over teaching methods whose strength lies in rapidly transmitting large amounts of factual information. Rather, one might expect the difference to be revealed in retention, in ability to apply learning, or in actual skill in experimental design, observation, or manipulation of materials and equipment. Unfortunately, few research studies have attempted to measure these kinds of outcomes, a situation exacerbated by the lack of consensus about what the goals of laboratory teaching are.

LABORATORY INSTRUCTION STYLES

In an attempt to define different instructional goals and their corresponding methodologies, Domin (1999) created a taxonomy of laboratory instruction styles which, although originally based in chemistry, hold up well across disciplines. These categories are expository instruction, inquiry instruction, discovery instruction, and problem-based learning.

Expository Instruction

The most popular and most criticized expository instruction features verification of preordained results, an emphasis on manipulation skills, and asking students to follow exactly prescribed directions (or "cookbook" procedures). A prelaboratory session sets out what is to be observed and how to do it. Postlaboratory sessions review and recapitulate the information. In general, the goal for this kind of instruction is for students to develop manipulative or kinesthetic skills. In a classical activity used in both high school and college, students might all receive a block of aluminum and be asked to follow an exact procedure for determining its density, the value of which is provided. Students follow precise directions, often filling in a worksheet with numerical values according to a prescribed script. The presumption is that a student who has successfully followed the procedure and arrived at the expected answer has also learned something about measurement and how it is done. Expository instruction can be done on a large scale with minimal engagement by the instructor, is largely impervious to variation in who does it, and minimizes cost, space, and equipment. Unfortunately, it may also be that virtually no meaningful learning takes place (Hofstein & Lunetta, 1982).

Inquiry Instruction

Without a predetermined outcome, students are asked to formulate their own problem from the information at hand and, in doing so, mimic the process of constructing knowledge. The density activity might begin with a question posed to students who have been given different-sized samples of the same metal: What is the relationship between mass and volume in this material? Different procedures for measuring volume are provided, and the results derived from these different methods are compared. Students have more choice in design and more responsibility in making sense of their results, and they must generally face more directly the importance of reproducibility in making measurements. Followup questions will be either posed by the teacher ("Is density an intrinsic or extrinsic property?") or elicited from the students ("Is the density of all metals the same?"). In a practical sense, it is difficult to keep inquiry laboratories vital because it is difficult to conceal the details of the solutions to these problems from one generation of students to the next without a great deal of effort. Also, the drive to make the teaching process easier can slowly turn these inquiries into exposition.

Discovery Instruction

Discovery instruction is also called "guided inquiry," in which an instructional setting is constructed with a prescribed outcome in mind toward which the teacher directs. Discovery instruction seeks to make knowledge more personal for students and thereby more highly owned. Adapting the density experiment to the discovery mode might begin with a prelaboratory discussion in which the exercise is introduced in the form of a question: What measurements can be made to determine the physical properties of materials? The students are encouraged to make predictions, formulate hypotheses, and then design experiments. All the while, the instructor controls the discussion, steering students toward the information from prior classes, including different mass-to-volume relationships as potentially useful quantities. The instructor also uses these opportunities to evaluate the experimental designs suggested by the students, motivating them with a sense of ownership and curiosity about the undetermined result, and inevitably guiding the discussion toward the preplanned experiment. Students work individually or in a group, with enough variation in their activities for the class to pool their results. Afterwards, the discussion led by the instructor moves the class to the intended lesson. Inquiry-based instruction can invest the student in his or her own learning and can result in deeper understanding.

Problem-based Learning

Problem-based learning (PBL), discussed more fully in the chapter on problem-based learning, creates a context for students to generate their own questions, but does so with a strong foregrounding by the instructor. PBL is popular across many disciplines. An instructor crafts and selects evidence, and then presents the case study to the students, who in turn uncover what the faculty member has in mind as the root lessons.

Meta-lessons about doing research can be abstracted and returned as a PBL framework for collaborative, open-ended exercises (Coppola & Lawton, 1995). Using the density lab, for example, this might begin with concealing even the color of a group of different-shaped metal pieces with black enamel paint. The following principles apply:

1. *An organizing question that students can understand is posed.* They are then expected to design experiments to solve the question. In this case, each student gets a different piece of metal; instead of

asking students to identify the metal, an experiment far outside their experience to design, they are asked to determine who else in class has the same metal they do.

2. *The problem cannot be answered by the work of an individual acting alone,* but requires the class to make group decisions about the experiments they carry out, how they are going to share the information, and what the standards of reasonable comparison need to be. The class might select density as the property to measure. Students will need to decide on units of measurement, how many trials must be done, and what will constitute "the same" versus "different."

3. *Multiple and equally valid strategies can be used to solve the problem* (Mills et al., 2000). The students might ask to do chemical tests on other samples of the metals in order to collect data. They might choose hardness, malleability, color (after scraping), or some combination of these after initial groups have been made.

4. *Experimental procedures are a means to an end.* Exposition and inquiry both have roles in carrying out an individual's work. Procedures for carrying out a known process should be able to be followed. Yet the purpose for collecting information (density) remains focused squarely on the goal (who has the same?) rather than on the measurement for its own sake.

5. *Communication and comparison are key.* The class needs to decide how to share their data and how they will make their conclusions. Samples may be exchanged and tested independently if there are outlying data points or if some students have a hard time reproducing their experiments.

6. *Followup work is implied by the results.* Inquiry inevitably leads to new questions. Once the relative identification is made, and the students have grouped themselves according to the convergence of measured properties, new questions can be posed or elicited. What are the identities of these metals? Is this information enough, or is other information needed?

Relative identification is a strategy widely applicable to making problems. In chemistry, one might ask who has the same solid, liquid, mixture, or concentration of acid. In mathematics, one might ask who has numbers in the same type of series. In psychology, it might be who has the same personality type; in the history of art, who has a painting from the same period; and in English, who has a paragraph with the same structure.

Inquiry, discovery, and problem-based activities are a better way to accomplish expositional goals because they are simply more engaging, permitting higher ownership and self-regulation of learning. Some formal heuristics have been developed for learners in these types of laboratory settings, and they have demonstrated success. One of these is POE (Predict-Observe-Explain; Champagne et al., 1980), and another is the MORE (Model-Observe-Reflect-Explain; Tien et al., 1999) method, which was developed for formal laboratory modules. Case studies are a kind of PBL that begin by posing questions based on a news headline ("Two Would-be Chemists Die in Explosion While Attempting to Make Methamphetamine") and turning it into a structured activity (Bieron & Dinan, 2000).

TURNING NOVICE RESEARCHERS INTO PRACTICING SCIENTISTS

The goals for upper-level laboratories may be quite different from those for lower-level laboratories, where professional development for a specialized work force makes sense. As previously illustrated, traditional verification laboratories can be adapted to more inquiry and open-ended activities. Adaptation can be further extended to capture an even closer flavor of research. Milestones for this process include

1. Defining the higher-level goals to be derived from the exercise. In preparatory chemistry, one of the prescribed criteria is how long a set of reagents is to be stirred together before the reaction is considered to be complete. Monitoring the reaction process while it is occurring and deciding when it is done is a high-level skill that is precluded by providing this information. Instead of providing a complete "cookbook" recipe to follow, the procedure can be truncated or rewritten in order to make this activity an instructional goal.

2. Move from the known as a precedent for exploring the unknown. Once again in preparatory chemistry, it is customary to test out a new procedure on a model compound, perhaps even repeating the procedure on a substrate reported in the literature before proceeding to the new and unfamiliar substrate. The research literature is a wellspring of information for adapting and creating new laboratory exercises. By selecting a new methodological procedure from the recent research literature that appears to be amenable to the time and material constraints of the teaching laboratory, the substrates reported in the literature can be purchased and the recent scientific results used with students. Students become quite engaged when handed a copy of a journal article and access to the substrates. Selecting procedures that can be extrapolated to new, unreported substrates allows students to do actual research and integrates criterion 1 into the lesson (Coppola et al., 1997).

3. Free up time for students to design and carry out new experiments. In many cases, students can suggest new questions about, and adaptations of, experiments they have performed. With careful supervision for safety considerations, such as writing out a proposal and having it subjected to formal approval, students can pursue their own work.

4. Higher-level students can do fundamental experimental design and carry it out. The features of research can be explored with simple problems of which students take nearly complete ownership. This requires extra time and resource support in order to work more individually with students, but this is appropriate for upper- or lower-level honors students. First-year chemistry honors students, for example, can be directed to select a two-step synthetic sequence that represents any part of the subject matter they have studied in the course. They then need to do library or online research to find a proper precedent, make a proposal, keep material costs below a prescribed level, and submit this for approval. Safety data and procedural issues should be included. Upper-level students who have access to better instrumentation or other physical resources can be asked to generate a more open-ended question derived from their entire undergraduate program. Not only can they prepare a proposal, but the class can be asked to peer-review and critique one another's work. After the work is completed (or attempted), the results can be made public via web publication and/or poster sessions to which other students and faculty respond (Henderson & Buising, 2000).

Laboratory instruction also raises an opportunity to incorporate issues that are naturally aligned with practice, such as laboratory safety, which ranges from the manipulation of concentrated chemical substances to issues regarding human participants. Increasingly, formal discussion of research ethics concerning practices such as data handling, laboratory management, authorship, and peer review is being encouraged for beginning and advanced students alike (Coppola, 2000; Kovac, 1999; Sweeting, 1999).

LINK TO COGNITIVE DEVELOPMENT

Instructors can help students develop important thinking and learning skills in laboratory courses which complement the instructional goals for other types of teaching and learning. One set of these skills is described by the Modified Reformed Science Teacher Behavior Inventory (MR-STBI) (Sutman et al., 1998), namely,

1. The use of lower- and higher-level divergent questions.
2. Group-centered cooperative activities.
3. Activities designed to help students reevaluate scientific (mis)conceptions.
4. Laboratory results that are integrated with theories from other disciplines.
5. Instructor-generated discussion related to the laboratory observations.
6. Use of collected data as a primary source of postlaboratory student-teacher interactions.
7. Instructors' use of process terminology (such as classify, analyze, predict, create).
8. Instructors' encouraging students to engage in meaningful discussion with one another.

9. Instructors' encouraging clarification of students' initial responses.

10. Instructors' supervision of laboratory activities by moving from group to group.

WHAT RESEARCH SAYS

Although individual studies make differential claims on the efficacy of one kind of laboratory instruction over another (Arce & Betancourt, 1997; Higginbotham et al., 1998), there is no general consensus about how one design has advantages over another. Gains have been observed when students process information more like experts in a laboratory with an authentic design (Coppola et al., 1997). These students were more intrinsically motivated by the course and developed better strategies for meaningful learning.

IN CONCLUSION

Laboratory instruction is a complex activity which needs to be examined more closely and systematically before broad recommendations can be made. However, perhaps because expository instruction is so poor at promoting engaged and deeper learning, gains are observed with nearly any strategy that promotes more active learning and decision making by students. As is so often true, not only must the goals that one has for an instructional intervention be explicit, but their alignment with the instructional methodology must be carefully managed.

Supplementary Reading

N. A. Glasgow, *New Curriculum for New Times: A Guide to Student-centered, Problem-based Learning* (Thousand Oaks, CA: Corwin Press, 1998) is an easily read and adaptable introduction.

V. L. Lechtanski, *Inquiry-based Experiments for Chemistry* (New York: Oxford University Press, 2000) provides useful, explicit translations of standard experiments to inquiry-based methods.

L. C. McDermott and the Physics Education Group at the University of Washington, *Physics by Inquiry* (New York: Wiley, 1996) have probably the greatest experience in research-based education reform in physics.

Student-Active Science (http://active.hampshire.edu/index) is a rich multidisciplinary resource maintained by leaders in the field.

Facilitating Experiential Learning: Service Learning, Fieldwork, and Collaborative Research

20

One of the valuable residues of the student revolution of the 1960s is the increased use of service learning and field experience as a part of undergraduate education. Not that field education was new. Cooperative education, in which periods of classroom education alternate with on-the-job experiences, had been successfully implemented well before the 1960s by Antioch College and several engineering and other colleges. Disciplines such as marine biology, forestry, archaeology, and geology had routinely required summer fieldwork.

But in the 1960s the educational value of direct experience converged with student idealism and desire for "relevant" meaningful service to produce numerous innovations in experiential education. At my own institution, the University of Michigan, students in service learning courses tutor schoolchildren, conduct recreational programs for patients in a mental hospital, visit and assist the elderly, and work with adolescents who are in detention for illegal activities.

Our department has also had a half-century tradition of involving undergraduates in collaborative research with faculty members. In recent years that program has expanded with university support for such collaborations. Both service learning and undergraduate research programs are becoming a staple feature of college curricula. Service learning, fieldwork, experiential learning, and collaborative research all involve similar faculty-student relationships; the need to balance student independence and faculty guidance; the problem of preventing students from getting lost in the particulars of the project and missing the generalizable concepts, principles, and skills; and the need to give students experiences that build their sense of competence.

EXPERIENTIAL LEARNING

Experiential learning refers to a broad spectrum of educational experiences, such as community service, fieldwork, sensitivity training groups, workshops, internships, cooperative education involving work in business or industry, and undergraduate participation in faculty research. Clearly such experiences require new learning. But is such learning educational? To my mind the criterion is the degree to which the learning is transferable to other times and places. In deciding whether to develop an experiential "course" or to include experiential elements in an existing course, one must, as in making other educational choices, weigh the expected transferable outcomes derived from experience against the outcomes and costs likely from other educational activities. Cognitive and motivational theory point to the likely value of discovering and applying principles and concepts.

WHAT ARE THE GOALS OF EXPERIENTIAL LEARNING?

Experiential learning has both cognitive and motivational goals. Educators hope that abstract concepts will become meaningful when students see that they are helpful in describing and understanding "real-life" phenomena. Similarly, we hope that experiences in the field or laboratory will stir up questions in students' minds that will lead to active learning. Such questions and students' reports of their experiences give students something to talk about in class discussions. Most importantly, actual experience can link learning, thinking, and doing. Teachers hope that field experiences will not only motivate students to learn current course materials but also increase their intrinsic interest in further learning. As a result of the experience, they learn both concepts and how the concepts relate to people; they learn both strategies for learning and strategies for dealing with social situations. Similarly, experience in collaborative research increases intrinsic motivation for research.

An associated goal, important to me, is to increase students' motivation to be of service to others. I am impressed that, even in the materialistic culture of the 1980s, students in my courses found great satisfaction in being helpful to older people, children, their peers, and other human beings.

ARE THESE GOALS ACHIEVED?

Markus, Howard, and King (1993) found positive effects on conceptual learning in a well-controlled study of service learning in political science. In another experiment comparing traditional instruction with the use of service learning, Kendrick (1996) and Brandell and Hinck (1997) found evidence of greater ability to apply course concepts to new situations and greater improvement in social responsibility and personal efficacy. Strage (2000) found improved performance on essay exams when service learning was introduced into a child development course.

There is also evidence that service learning coupled with appropriate discussion can produce greater development in moral reasoning than discussion without service learning (Boss, 1994). Myers-Lipton (1994, 1996) found positive effects on racial prejudice and civic responsibility.

HOW CAN WE GET BETTER OUTCOMES FROM EXPERIENTIAL LEARNING?

Supervising experiential learning requires finding a balance between student independence and teacher control. One needs to give the student sufficient freedom to make, and learn from, mistakes; yet you don't want students to lose so much time and become so frustrated that motivation disintegrates. As in other teaching methods, the ideal is to provide sufficient initial support and guidance so that the student can experience some progress, encouraging more independence as the student surmounts initial problems.

How does one ensure that the experience will be educational? First of all, select placements that are appropriate for your goals. Next, try to ensure that students will actually reflect about the relationship of their experience to relevant concepts and theories. Typically the answer is to require a journal or a written or oral report. The rationale for this is a good one. Generally speaking, research suggests that transfer is enhanced by verbalized concepts or principles. However, the key point, as in all education, is to think about the *goals* of the experience. Are students expected to learn how to apply concepts learned in previous or concomitant education? Are students expected to learn how to distill from real-life complexity generalizations or ideas useful in other situations? Is the experience designed to enhance motivation for learning and to facilitate personality development and altruistic values?

All too often, experiential learning is entered into as something obviously valuable without enough consideration of the values to be achieved or the process for learning. Diana Falk (1995) uses "preflection"—a discussion before beginning a service project in which students imagine what the experience will be like and express their feelings. This is also an opportunity for students to think about what they hope to learn and what they need to do to get the most out of this learning experience. You might develop a contract (which can be revised as the experience develops) specifying the learning expected, the strategies (such as a journal) for achieving the goals, the deadlines, and the ways in which the students as well as the teacher can assess achievement of the goals.

As in the case of laboratories, the educational outcomes depend a great deal on the way field experiences are integrated with other educational experiences. Students in field experiences need to think about the meaning of the experience just as they need to think about their reading, classroom experiences, writing, and other educational activities. Discussions and lectures explicitly tied to field experiences, written reports and journals, oral presentations, and demonstrations are possible techniques for promoting long-term learning from field experiences. As in other learning, feedback is necessary, particularly in the early stages. When service learning becomes an important part of the curriculum, reaching across several disciplines, institutions can have an important impact on their communities.

IN CONCLUSION

Experiential learning, whether in community service or in research, can be a powerful tool for enhancing both motivation and learning. But to be effective it requires careful planning, guidance, and evaluation.

Supplementary Reading

The classic book in this area is Morris Keaton's (with associates), *Experiential Learning: Rationale, Characteristics, and Assessment* (San Francisco: Jossey-Bass, 1976).

The American Association for Higher Education has published an 18-volume series of how service learning has been implemented in each discipline: E. Zlotkowski, *AAHE's Series on Service Learning in the Disciplines* (Washington, DC: AAHE, 1997–1998).

Academic Service Learning: A Pedagogy of Action and Reflection, [Special issue], *New Directions for Teaching and Learning*, 1998, 73, edited by R. A. Rhoads and J. P. F. Howard, is an excellent resource for both beginning and experienced teachers using service learning.

The *Michigan Journal of Community Service Learning* is published annually by the Edward Ginsberg Center for Community Service and Learning at the University of Michigan, Ann Arbor.

21 Using Project Methods, Independent Study, and One-on-One Teaching

■ ■ ■ ■ ■ ■ ■ ■ ■ ■ ■ ■ ■ ■ ■ ■ ■ ■

As we saw in the chapter "Countdown for Course Preparation," most learning occurs outside the classroom. This chapter deals with nonclassroom activities intended to stimulate motivated holistic learning and development.

If one goal of education is to help students develop the ability to continue learning after their formal education is complete, it seems reasonable that they should have supervised experience in learning independently—experience in which the instructor helps students learn how to formulate problems, find answers, and evaluate their progress themselves. One might expect the values of independent study to be greatest for students of high ability with a good deal of background in the area to be covered, since such students should be less likely to be overwhelmed by difficulties encountered. While this expectation contains some truth, motivation and work habits are also important. The material in this chapter is relevant to projects undertaken as part of a course, to senior and honors theses, and to supervision of graduate students.

Experiential learning (described in the previous chapter) also is aimed at the goal of leading students to view learning as going beyond classroom activities. Projects and independent study often include experiential learning experiences.

THE PROJECT METHOD

Independent study programs frequently involve the execution of projects in which a student, or group of students, undertakes to gather and integrate data relevant to some more or less important problem.

Although early research showed that projects did not result in higher performance on conventional factual examinations, Thistlethwaite (1960) found that National Merit Scholars checked requirement of a term paper or laboratory project as one characteristic of their most stimulating course.

The student who completes a project often has a sense of mastery going well beyond that of completing a conventional assignment. Students working on a project have to solve real problems and to use their knowledge in new ways—characteristics of learning situations that both motivate and facilitate more lasting learning.

If we grant that projects sometimes fail to work well, what can we do to increase the probability of success? Here are five suggestions:

1. Make your expectations clear. As in introducing other activities, explain how this is intended to contribute to learning.

2. Be sure the student has a clear question, problem, or goal. This doesn't mean that the goal will necessarily be clear initially, but I do advocate monitoring students' progress in arriving at a goal that represents a problem that is meaningful for them.

3. Help students be explicit about the strategies they plan to use, about their time management, and how they will monitor their progress. This is a chance to get students to develop skills for lifelong learning.

4. Have students compare notes and get feedback on their progress from fellow students. Producing an independent product can be anxiety producing. Peer support can be helpful both substantively and emotionally.

5. Have students keep journals. Writing the journals helps the students reflect on their experience, and reading the journals helps you monitor their progress.

But even if you use these strategies to help students prepare for independent study, a problem remains: your time. Supervision of independent study projects and theses takes time. Is there any way of reducing the time demands? Paradoxically, they involve reducing the one-on-one interactions assumed in independent study and using group strategies. In addition to the peer feedback in suggestion 4, you can do much of the planning and monitoring meetings with small groups of students. In fact, you can make the independent study project a small-group project—an alternative whose value is supported by research.

SMALL-GROUP INDEPENDENT STUDY

Favorable results on independent study were obtained in the experiments carried out at the University of Colorado by Gruber and Weitman (1960). In a course in first-year English in which the group met only about 90 percent of the regularly scheduled hours and had little formal training on grammar, the self-directed study group was significantly superior to control groups on a test of grammar. In a course in physical optics, groups of students who attended class without the instructor but were free to consult him learned fewer facts and simple applications, but were superior to students in conventional classes in difficult applications and learning new material. Moreover, the areas of superiority were maintained in a retest three months later when the difference in factual knowledge had disappeared. In educational psychology, an experimental class of five or six students without the instructor was equal to a conventional three-lecture-a-week class in mastery of content, and tended to be superior on measures of curiosity. See the chapter on active learning for tips on guiding small groups.

RESEARCH ON VARIATIONS IN AMOUNT OF CLASSROOM TIME

Independent study experiments have varied greatly in the amount of assistance given students and in the patterning of instructional versus independent periods. For example, merely excusing students from attending class is one method of stimulating independent study. The results of such a procedure are not uniform but suggest that classroom experience is not essential for learning. However, different kinds of learning may take place out of class than in class.

The experiment reported by McKeachie, Lin, Forrin, and Teevan (1960) involved a fairly high degree of student-instructor contact. In this experiment, students normally met with the instructor in small groups weekly or biweekly, but students were free to consult the instructor whenever they wished to. The results of the experiment suggest that the "tutorial" students did not learn as much from the textbook as students taught in conventional lecture periods and discussion sections, but did develop stronger motivation both for course work and for continued learning after the course. This was indicated not only by responses to a questionnaire administered at the end of the course but also by the number of advanced psychology courses later elected.

The results of the studies in a child development course by Parsons (1957) and Parsons, Ketcham, and Beach (1958) were, in a sense, more favorable to independent study. In the latter experiment, four teaching methods were compared—lecture, instructor-led discussions, autonomous groups that did not come to class, and individual independent study in which each student was sent home with the syllabus, returning for the final examination. In both experiments, students working independently made the best scores on the final examination, which measured retention of factual material in the textbook. The instructor-led discussion groups were the lowest in performance on the final examination. There were no significant differences between groups on a measure of attitudes toward working with children. The authors explain their results in terms of the independent group's freedom from distraction by interesting examples, possible applications, or opposing points of view from those presented in the text.

Although the Parsons, Ketcham, and Beach results were favorable to independent study, they are not very satisfying to the advocate of this method, for they lead to the conclusion that if students know that they are going to be tested on the factual content of a particular book, it is more advantageous for them to read that book than to go to class. But knowledge of specific facts is not the typical major objective of an independent study program. What instructors are hoping for is greater integration, increased purposefulness, and more intense motivation for further study. That independent study can achieve these ends is indicated by the Colorado and Michigan experiments. But the paucity of positive results suggests that we need more research on methods of selecting and training students for independent study, arranging the independent study experience, and measuring outcomes. Note that the Colorado and Michigan results came in courses in which a good deal of contact with the instructor was retained.

TIME IN CLASS

The independent study experiments demonstrate that education is not simply a function of time spent in a class with a teacher. Well-planned activities outside teacher-controlled classrooms can be at least as educational as conventional classes. But merely reducing time in class is not independent study. Generally speaking, the more time spent on learning, the greater the learning. In classic studies, Wakely, Marr, Plath, and Wilkins (1960) compared performance in a traditional four-hour-a-week lecture class with that in a class meeting only once a week to clear up questions on the textbook. In this experiment the traditional classes proved to be superior. Similarly, Paul (1932) found 55-minute class periods to be superior to 30-minute periods, as measured by student achievement.

Shortening class periods, reducing the number of classes, and cutting the length of the academic term may be advisable as part of a planned educational change, but they should not be undertaken with the blithe assumption that the same educational outcomes will be achieved, unless the out-of-class time involves the students in educationally meaningful experiences.

SENIOR PROJECTS

More and more departments require a project as part of a senior capstone course. The major problem departments encounter is a lack of faculty members and faculty time to provide adequate guidance and supervision. Even though senior projects usually involve the writing of individual theses, one can still gain some efficiency by grouping students with similar topics and encouraging cooperative work like that described in the chapter on active learning. Students can cooperate in digging out references for their review of previous research; they can provide frequent feedback to one another; they can support one another when barriers or blocks arise. The tips for term papers included in the chapter on writing, as well as our discussion of projects earlier in this chapter, are also relevant here.

ONE-ON-ONE TEACHING*

Independent study is only one example of teaching individual students. Music, art, physical education, dentistry, medicine, social work, and other fields all involve some individualized teaching one on one, and every teacher has occasions in which skills in tutoring or one-on-one teaching are needed. There is relatively little research on one-on-one teaching methods, but several principles mentioned in earlier chapters are relevant:

1. Students are helped by a model of the desired performance. This may be provided by the instructor's demonstration of the technique, by a videotape, or by observation of a skilled performer. Generally speaking, positive examples are more helpful than examples of what not to do. When instructors perform, they should utilize the same techniques they use in presenting other visual aids, particularly in directing the student's attention to crucial aspects of the technique.

2. Students are helped by verbal cues or labels that identify key features of the skill. Students are likely to be distracted by irrelevant details.

---

* Distance education typically involves much independent study and one-on-one teaching. Much of the material in the chapter on distance education is applicable here, and many of the suggestions in this chapter apply to teaching a distance education course.

3. "Bare bones" simplified simulations or demonstrations are more useful as starting points than complex real-life situations, which may overwhelm the student with too many details.

4. Permit students the maximum freedom to experience successful completion of a task or a part of a task, but give enough guidance so that they will not get bogged down in a rut of errors. This implies that the learning experiences of students go from the simple to the complex, with the steps so ordered that each new problem can be successfully solved.

5. Students need practice followed by feedback.

6. Feedback from the instructor or from peers may provide more information than the student can assimilate. Don't try to correct everything on the first trial.

7. Feedback can discourage students. Try to provide some encouraging feedback as well as identification of mistakes.

8. Feedback that identifies errors won't help if the learner doesn't know what to do to avoid the errors. Give guidance about what to try next.

9. High-level skills are developed through much practice. Simply reaching the point of successful performance once is not likely to achieve the degree of organization and automatization that is necessary for consistent success.

10. Practice with varied examples is likely to be both more motivating and more likely to transfer to later performance than is simple drill and repetition. In clinical teaching with cases, have students note the similarities between cases as well as the unique aspects of particular cases.

11. Coaching is not simply one-way telling and criticizing. Asking the learners about their perceptions of what they are doing and helping them evaluate their own performance is also important. In teaching self-evaluation, you may model the sort of analysis needed. As you evaluate work, verbalize the process you are using and the basis for your evaluation. Like other skills, self-evaluation is learned by practice with feedback. Thus students need many opportunities for self-evaluation with feedback *about their evaluation* as well as about the work being evaluated.

12. Peers can help one another. You don't need to monitor everyone all of the time.

IN CONCLUSION

There is an old saying that the ideal education would be Mark Hopkins on one end of a bench and a student on the other. Individualized instruction can be valuable, and in this chapter I have tried to suggest ways of maximizing its value. But there are many goals of learning that can be achieved as well or better in groups. Thus a good teacher should develop skills for using both.

Supplementary Reading

One of the most interesting, humorous, and wise books on teaching is Linc Fisch's *The Chalk-Dust Collection* (Stillwater, OK: New Forums Press, 1996). Chapter 1, "Coaching Mathematics and Other Sports," has much wisdom.

An excellent reference for project learning at all levels of education is P. C. Blumenfeld, E. Soloway, R. W. Marx, J. S. Krajcik, M. Guzdial, and A. Palinscar, "Motivating Project-based Learning: Sustaining the Doing, Supporting the Learning," *Educational Psychologist*, 1991, *26*, 369–398. Although this article deals primarily with the project method in precollege education, the discussion of why projects help, how projects should be developed, and what kinds of difficulties occur is relevant for college teachers.

Technology issues related to this chapter are discussed in Karen Cardenas, "Technology in Higher Education," in J. Losco & B. L. Fife (eds.), *Higher Education in Transition: The Challenges of the New Millennium* (Westport, CT: Greenwood, 2000).

22 Teaching by Distance Education

Distance education presents one of the most challenging and satisfying forms of teaching. Instead of your efforts evaporating behind you as you grapple with the uncertainties of day-to-day teaching encounters, you can (indeed, must) take the time to think your teaching through, get it right, and then record it for the benefit of many. Distance teaching is an extended act of imagination. Without students around you to observe and respond to, you must construct the entire teaching and learning process in your head. The shift from conventional lecturer to distance teacher is like switching from street performer to playwright. You can no longer develop your act by trying out new lines and dropping the ones that bomb. You have to put yourself on the line— make your investment up front, by plotting the intellectual progress of your students through a series of imagined maneuvers, which you hope will achieve the learning desired.

Distance education encompasses an enormous range of teaching systems whose common feature is that students learn from teachers without having to travel to meet them. A distance education package may involve a few hours of study or several hundred. It may be delivered online, by radio or TV broadcast, or as

This chapter was written by Andrew Northedge of The Open University.

a mail package containing such items as a text, videocassettes, or a CD-ROM. It may be studied entirely independently or be backed up by peer and tutor support through telephone link-ups, online conferences, or face-to-face meetings. Distance education is also developed in very different contexts. I, for example, work within a distance education mass-production system at the UK Open University. Recently I worked full time with a team of eight lecturers and over ten support staff to produce a 600-hour course, which now has over 5,000 students a year. By contrast, many smaller distance education packages are produced by ʕ ˮ two lecturers working around the edges of an existing te⌐   ˏad, with a lot less support.

SKETCHING OUT THE SHAPE OF A COUR

Whatever form it takes, distance education is co⌐   ˏd from a
variety of elements, each of which needs carefuˈ   ˏt. To give
some perspective, let me walk you through a ⱨ   ˏcal example. Let's say you have to produce a 90-hour c⌐   ˏth 6 hours
of study per week over 15 weeks. You look foˈ   ˏle textbook
around which to build the course, but deˈ   ˏead to bind
together your own collection of readings frˈ   ˏrent sources.
You also decide to bring the course to life w   ˏtudies of real
people talking about their experiences (ȷ   ˏr the convenience and cheapness of audio rather than   ˏxperience tells
you that students progress better with pˈ   ˏitor support, so
you opt also for an online conference. Rˈ   ˏassessment, you
decide you will use a mix of comput⌐   ˏl multiple-choice
assignments and written assignments ˈ   ˏy a tutor. To bring
all this together, you will need to writ⌐   ˏone for the course.
You might develop it in the form of a   ˏtext, a CD-ROM, or
a web site. For our purposes here, itˈ   ˏmatter which.
    As with any course, you begin ⱨ   ˏng about what ideas
and knowledge you want to teach. ˈ   ˏe an initial division of
the subject into broad topics whiˈ   ˏllocate over 11 weeks
(having set aside the first and lֈ   ˏs for introductory and
review purposes, and two otherˈ   ˏor assignment writing).
Because they are working in isolֈ   ˏu decide to give students

additional support with assignment writing, working with numerical data, and organizing their studies. You now produce a rough draft of course *objectives* and *outcomes* (see the chapter "Countdown for Course Preparation") and begin to consider how you might set about delivering them within your six hours a week. Table 22.1 models how your course might be structured. Working up from the bottom, we see that every week presents exactly six hours of work. You have decided on two written assignments: one about one-third of the way through the course, to ensure that students start internalizing the ideas of the discipline by putting them to use, then a longer one toward the end, but with enough time for work to be marked, returned, and discussed in the online conference. You put a computer-graded assignment in week 2, so that students get early feedback on whether they are picking up the right messages, another in week 9, and a longer one in week 15 to keep students studying right up to the end of the course. You decide that, if it is to succeed, the online conference must make a substantial contribution and also run continuously throughout the course, so you allocate one hour a week, except during assignment-writing weeks. And you allocate an additional hour in the weeks when assignments are returned, so that the tutor can lead an extended discussion of students' work. There will be two 90-minute audiocassettes, each providing three half-hour segments (or, alternatively, six MP3 files accessed through the course web site). The first five segments present case material; the sixth has an expert reviewing the subject. Studying your collection of readings takes up 27 hours, nearly a third of the course, with the amount varying from week to week. Similarly, working with the text (or CD-ROM or web site) occupies just over a third of the course, the weekly time varying according to the tasks being tackled. To clarify these tasks, we need another table (Table 22.2), this time showing the main teaching and learning activities.

Working up from the bottom again, you have decided to give study-skills support at four points in the course: "getting started" in week 1, "reviewing progress" after tutor-graded assignment 1, "reflecting on strategy" in week 8, and "reviewing personal development" at the end. These half-hour activities will be incorporated within the flow of the text. So will the number skills exer-

TABLE 22.1 Weekly Study Hours for a 15-Week Course

Modes of Study	Week Number															Total Hours
	1	2	3	4	5	6	7	8	9	10	11	12	13	14	15	
Teaching-text/web site	3.5	2	3	2	2	3	1	3.5	2	2.5	1.5		2.5	2	2.5	33
Collection of readings	1	2.5	1.5	3		1.5	3	1.5	2.5	2	3.5		2	2	1	27
Audio material	0.5		0.5			0.5				0.5			0.5		0.5	3
Online conference	1	1	1	1		1	2	1	1	1	1		1	2	1	15
Computer-graded assignment		0.5							0.5						1	2
Tutor-graded assignment					4							6				10
Total	6	6	6	6	6	6	6	6	6	6	6	6	6	6	6	90

TABLE 22.2 Weekly Study Hours Represented as Teaching and Learning Activities

Teaching and Learning Activities	Week Number															Total Hours
	1	2	3	4	5	6	7	8	9	10	11	12	13	14	15	
Framing[a] (text, conference)	2.5			0.5	0.5			0.5			0.5				2.5	7
Teaching narrative (text)	1	1.5	1.5	1.5		1.5	1	1	1.5	2	.5		.5	1.5	1	16
Case studies (text, cassette)	1		1.5			2		1.5	1				1.5	0.5		9
Independent reading	1	2.5	1.5	3		1.5	3	1.5	2.5	2	3.5		2	2	1	27
Online group work (conference)		1	1			1	1	1	1	1			1			7
Working on assignments		0.5			4				0.5			6			1	12
Writing support (text, conference)			0.5	1			2				1.5			2		7
Number skills (text)		0.5			1				0.5				1			3
Study skills (text)	0.5				0.5			0.5							0.5	2
Total	6	6	6	6	6	6	6	6	6	6	6	6	6	6	6	90

[a] See the text for explanations of framing and teaching narrative.

cises, which you have spread across the course to encourage a steady build-up of skill and confidence—choosing weeks 2 and 9 in particular, when tasks within the computer-graded assignments will give students an added incentive. Support for writing tutor-graded assignment 1 consists of an activity in the text in week 3, followed in week 4 by a tutor-led online activity. In week 11, there is similar preparation for tutor-graded assignment 2, in text and online. Assignment post-mortems online fall in weeks 7 and 14. The next row shows assignment work (computer-graded and tutor-graded assignments). The row above shows that you have allocated half the online conference time for structured discussions, with students breaking into miniconferences and then reporting back. (The "Independent reading" row replicates the "readings" row in Table 22.1.) The case studies are based mostly on the audiocassettes, but each is set up in the text and accompanied by activities and discussion. The weeks 8 and 14 case studies are not audio based.

The top two rows of Table 22.2 represent the heart of the course. Here the skilled and imaginative distance education teacher makes it all happen. By "framing," in row one, I mean "'putting in context"—painting the big picture of what the course is all about. We can only ever make sense within frames of reference, and a recurring problem in education is that teachers fail to realize the extent to which students do not share their frames of reference. Consequently, students comprehend little and soon switch off. In distance education, where students and teachers do not meet and are all the more likely to be thinking at cross-purposes, framing is a vital opening maneuver. This does *not* mean talking in grand abstractions. It means starting where the student is and using strong examples to establish the issues the course is setting out to address. For example, after half an hour of preliminaries ("Hello, this is week 1 of a 15-week course" and so on) you might plunge into an exercise using the audio case material to introduce the big themes of the course. These might then be taken up and discussed within the online conference (after initial logging on and introductory rituals have been accomplished). It is important to excite imaginations from the earliest moments. As this book emphasizes throughout, students learn only when they are actively thinking. Having "hooked" them, you will make them ready to grapple with details about how the course works, its various components, and the study activities they will be managing over the weeks ahead. This broad framing needs to be reinforced at times during the course. (Note the extra portions around the first tutor-graded assignment.) In the final week, course review activities constitute the other end of the framing process: closure.

DEVELOPING A TEACHING NARRATIVE

The purpose of the initial framing is to launch a flow of shared meaning, jointly generated by teacher and students (through writing* and reading, respectively)—a flow that must then be maintained throughout the course. The teaching and learning process works only because human beings are able to make meaning together, allowing teachers to lend students the capacity to construct meanings they cannot yet achieve unaided. But whereas in a classroom you can share "live" meaning face to face within the frame of reference of your common surroundings, with distance education you have to resort to other, more "literary" devices, such as stories, pictures, diagrams, and vivid examples. Without these meaning carriers, your explanations are wasted on students. They simply cannot make *your* arguments work in *their* heads. If you link these meaning carriers together, you create a *teaching narrative* that drives and supports your students' thinking as they work through the course.

It's like writing a play. You must have an opening scenario that captures your audience's attention, whatever kind of day they had at home or work. (Distance students usually lead busy lives.) This scenario must pose questions that make your audience curious. (Make your introduction lead up to a short list of *core questions* that your course addresses.) Then there must be incidents that bring in new characters, issues, and questions. These take the form of *examples, case studies,* and *activities* through which you develop a "plot," leading up to a final dénouement. Thus, although you first conceive of your course as a sequence of theoretical expositions, for teaching purposes you need to rethink it as a series of cases and activities which do the job of delivering the

---

* Whether on paper or computer screen.

theoretical argument. These then need to be linked within an overall *story line,* so that students carry their developing thoughts along with them as they address each new case. When courses work like this, students get very involved and learn deeply— indeed, they carry on learning in nonstudy hours and after the course is over.

Achieving this, however, depends on sensitivity to your audience. First, you must be clear who they are. (Write down a description of them.) Then try to imagine them as you write. (Think of someone you know who might take the course.) How can you make your case study so thought provoking that they skip the TV serial and resist family gossip? How can you challenge everyday assumptions and explanations? How can you design a really intriguing activity that is satisfying to complete? (Avoid treating your student as either a moron or a genius— neither "Write down what I just said" nor "Write notes on how you would redesign local government.") Include only activities that are carefully framed and focused and develop your plot. Otherwise, students will soon take to skipping them. (Try writing your own answer to an activity, then refine the task so that it leads directly to that answer and doesn't waste students' time.) And always pick up the thread afterwards, so the activity leads directly into the next plot development. Finally, *summarize* periodically, so that students keep track of the plot and can orient themselves for the next advance. (Succinct bullet points in propositional form impose an excellent discipline, forcing you to be explicit about what you believe has been established.) All this constitutes the *teaching narrative* through which your text/CD-ROM/web site gives coherence and dynamism to the course.

MAKING THE COURSE MANAGEABLE

But you also need to keep the course within bounds. Student dropout is a major issue in distance education. It is so easy—no loss of lifestyle or identity—they just stop. And the most common reason given is feeling overwhelmed by the *workload.* Teachers always underestimate this. They forget that reading takes many times as long with an unfamiliar subject (3,000 words an hour is good going, if a text is challenging your ideas). Teachers also forget to add together all the components of the course. Hence the tables shown earlier. Students can set aside only so many hours per week. If you unthinkingly demand more, you simply force them to drop course elements arbitrarily, or to drop out altogether. Nor is it simply a matter of quantity; it is also a question of clarity and organization. At all times it must be obvious what to do next (simple, explicit instructions; work schedules; calendars). And the course should provide a regular rhythm of study, so students can establish a routine. Naturally their patterns of study will vary greatly, but it is much easier to develop a strategy for fitting study into a busy life when a course has a clear and regular structure.

The other major stumbling block is *difficulty*. Teachers tend to be wildly optimistic about what students can handle. You can, however, bring difficulty levels down dramatically.

- Choose the *familiar* rather than the strange (for instance, in selecting examples and case studies) so that students can apply existing concepts and frames of reference, and build on them.

- Work with the *concrete* rather than the abstract, so that students' thoughts are not reliant solely on half-formed and loosely organized conceptualizations.

- Keep your treatment of the topic *simple*. Avoid side issues and cross-references until students have a base from which to comprehend them.

- Use *everyday language* as much as possible.

When teaching requires you to go to the difficult end of one of these dimensions, strive toward the easy end of the other three.

IN CONCLUSION

This chapter offers a first glimpse of distance teaching. If you are seriously involved, you will certainly need to read more. However, I must at least mention the following:

- *Assessment*. Spread it across the course as far as your budget will allow. Little and often keeps students motivated and moving in the right direction. It is easy to get a long way off track when studying in isolation.

- *Teaching through assignment marking.* This is a skilled activity. Comments on assignments provide the only personalized teaching that distance education students receive. If you employ others to mark assignments, they will need training.
- *Feedback systems.* Distance teachers never see the puzzlement in students' eyes. It is essential to have materials tried out during development by colleagues or, better still, by potential students, and to gather feedback systematically once a course is running. Otherwise you will waste a lot of time and money.
- *Keep it simple and direct.* If you follow only one rule, this is it.

Supplementary Reading

Distance teaching is a very broad subject. Where you start reading depends on what type of distance education you are concerned with and what aspect you are interested in. For an introduction to the basics of designing distance materials, you could try either of these:

Fred Lockwood, *The Design and Production of Self-Instructional Materials* (London: Kogan Page, 1998).

Derek Rowntree, *Preparing Materials for Open, Distance and Flexible Learning* (London: Kogan Page, 1993).

If you are particularly interested in online education, try these:

Greg Kearsley, *On-line Education: Learning and Teaching in Cyberspace* (Belmont, CA: Wadsworth Thomson Learning, 2000).

Rena M. Palloff and Keith Pratt, *Building Learning Communities in Cyberspace: Effective Strategies for the Online Classroom* (San Francisco: Jossey-Bass, 1999).

If you want a broader view of distance education, try these:

Desmond Keegan, *Foundations of Distance Education*, 3rd ed. (London: Routledge, 1996).

Otto Peters, *Learning and Teaching in Distance Education: Analyses and Interpretations from an International Perspective* (London: Kogan Page, 1998).

You can follow up the theme of framing and teaching narrative in A. Northedge, "Organising Excursions into Specialist Discourse Communities: A Sociocultural Account of University Teaching," in G. Wells and G. Claxton (eds.), *Learning for Life in the 21st Century: Sociocultural Perspectives on the Future of Education* (Oxford: Blackwell, 2001).

Teaching for Higher-
Level Goals

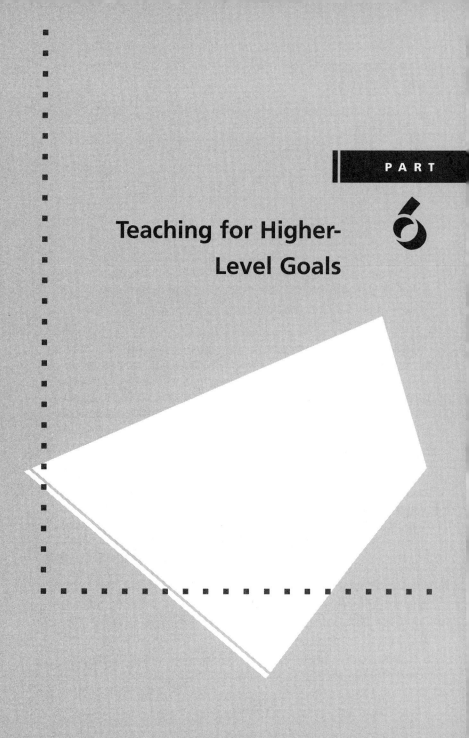

23 Teaching Students How to Learn

■ ■ ■ ■ ■ ■ ■ ■ ■ ■ ■ ■ ■ ■ ■ ■ ■

For many years, the study of student learning was divorced from the study of teaching. Good teaching practices were assumed to be universals that did not depend on individual differences among students or on teaching students to think and learn. Recent developments in educational and cognitive psychology have changed our views of the teaching and learning process, and provide both conceptual and practical information about the ways that students learn and how instructors can use this information to inform their teaching practices. We now know that it is the interaction of good instructional practices with students' strategic use of learning strategies and skills, motivational processes and self-regulation that results in positive learning outcomes (Weinstein et al., 2000). However, many college students do not know what to do to learn the content in all the different content domain areas that they study in college. All instructors have some implicit or explicit conceptions or theories about what it means to learn and think in their own discipline. Helping stu-

This chapter was written by Claire Ellen Weinstein of the University of Texas at Austin, Debra K. Meyer of Elmhurst College, Jenefer Husman of the University of Alabama, Gretchen Van Mater Stone of Shenandoah University, and Wilbert J. McKeachie of the University of Michigan.

dents become aware of these conceptions is an important aspect of teaching. As students learn subject matter they also need to learn something about the skills involved in learning that subject matter. For example, students need to know how to reason through problems in engineering, how to read math texts, and how to identify important information about a piece of literature. Therefore, it is important that you use effective instructional practices for presenting content information, as well as effective instructional practices for fostering the development and elaboration of both general learning strategies (such as previewing a textbook chapter) and content-specific learning strategies (such as how to learn mathematical formulas).

THE IMPORTANCE OF GOALS AND SELF-REFLECTION

How can you help students to become more effective learners? We know that strategic learners need to be able to set and use meaningful goals to help them learn and to help them generate and maintain their motivation for studying (Schunk & Ertmer, 1999). As we saw in the chapter "Motivation in the College Classroom," we can help students become clearer about their goals by encouraging them to set useful goals for our classes. Unfortunately, many students are not clear about their educational goals in general or their goals for specific courses. Not every course will hold the same interest value for every student, but usually there are at least some aspects of the course that can be perceived as useful for each person. Providing your students with opportunities to identify how the material presented in your courses might be useful to them as they strive to reach their own educational, personal, social, or occupational goals can enhance motivation and cognitive effort (Husman et al., 2000). Even a brief class discussion about upcoming topics and how these topics might relate to present or future interests of the students can help. Asking students to write a brief paragraph or two about a topic and why it might be relevant to them now or in the future is another way to establish perceived relevance.

It is important to remember that we cannot give students goals—they must own their goals. However, with goal ownership comes responsibility. Students need to learn how to negotiate goals and how to respond to goal achievement and failure. In teaching students multiple learning strategies, you should stress the need to balance goals (for example, adjusting goals for grades with goals for learning; Hagen & Weinstein, 1995). Students also should learn how to implement strategies that will help them negotiate emotional responses to achieving or not achieving their goals (Boekaerts et al., 2000; Schutz & Davis, 2000). It is also important to assist students in establishing process rather than product goals. Even simply reminding students that the goal of the exercises or projects you assign to them is to gain mastery in the content of the lessons will support effective self-evaluation. Students are more likely to evaluate their success on the pieces of a project if they have goals for each of those pieces (Schunk & Ertmer, 1999).

In the following sections, we address several ways of learning how to learn in the college classroom through the instructor's role in increasing students' self-awareness, teaching domain-specific strategies, connecting new ideas with existing knowledge, modeling and teaching learning strategies, and providing feedback on these learning strategies.

INCREASING STUDENTS' SELF-AWARENESS

Students who are aware of their learning goals tend to reflect on what it takes to learn. Thinking about thinking, or knowing about knowing, has come to be known as *metacognition* (Flavell, 1979; Pintrich et al., 2000; Zimmerman, 1995). Metacognitive processes include knowledge about oneself as a learner, knowledge about academic tasks, and knowledge about strategies to use in order to accomplish academic tasks. Awareness about oneself as a learner helps students to allocate their personal resources or the resources that are available in their academic institution, such as group study sessions, tutoring programs, and learning centers. If students do not anticipate needing help with a potentially difficult course, or if they do not monitor their own comprehension closely, it is unlikely that they will take advantage of available resources. It will also be difficult for them to judge the personal resources they will need, such as extra study time or more opportunities for review and consolidation of the material before a test (Entwistle, 1992; Winne, 1996). Increasing student self-awareness is imperative for effective strategy instruction. If students attribute their successes or failures to luck, an easy test, or innate ability, then there is no need for effort, time management, or learning strategies (for a review, see Pintrich & Schunk, 1996). Therefore, college instructors should provide opportunities for students to reflect on the general characteristics of their approaches to learning and on the specific actions toward academic tasks. You may want to survey students to promote self-awareness of strategies by asking questions on the first major assignment or test, such as

1. How many hours do you spend a week studying for this course?

2. Are you up to date on course assignments and readings?

3. How do you take notes or study while reading the text?

4. How do you take notes in class? Do you review your notes? When? How?

Self-reflection is important for self-regulation, which Zimmerman (1989) defines as "the degree that [students] are metacognitively, motivationally, and behaviorally active participants in their own learning" (p. 4). As college faculty, we should increase student self-awareness of learning strategies and teach them when and how to use strategies (Svinicki et al., 1995; Weinstein et al., 2000).

USING EXISTING KNOWLEDGE TO LEARN NEW THINGS

College professors have long known that teaching an introductory course is often more difficult than teaching an advanced course in the same area. Although many explanations for this finding have been offered, most of them involve the students' lack of prior knowledge. It is all but impossible to think or solve problems in an area without relevant knowledge. In addition, thinking about relevant knowledge also strengthens new learning by generating meaningful relations to new information. For example, thinking about the economic causes of World War I can help a student understand the economic causes of the second world war. Strategic learners understand the role of relevant prior knowledge and can use this knowledge to learn new things (Alexander & Judy, 1988). We tend to use prior knowledge in one of two main ways: to create direct relations and to create analogical relations. When we create direct relations, we directly relate our prior knowledge to what we are trying to learn. For example, comparing and contrasting the causes of the two world wars involve direct relations. However, there are times when we do not have directly applicable prior knowledge, but we do have knowledge in an area that is somehow similar and may help us to understand the new information, ideas, or skills we are trying to learn. For example, we use analogies to help us relate familiar and new things that share some key characteristics but are very different in other ways. Using a post office to explain aspects of computer storage, referring to social disagreements as a way to explain conflicts in organizations, and using the structure of a bird to explain design elements of an airplane are all ways we use analogies to help students build meaning for new concepts that may at first seem totally unfamiliar.

TEACHING DOMAIN-SPECIFIC AND COURSE-SPECIFIC STRATEGIES

College faculty teach students not only content about history, biology, or psychology but also modes of thought and strategies for learning (Donald, 1995). Different instructional means may result in students' having the same knowledge but not the same broader understanding needed for different applications using this new knowledge. Comparisons of college teaching methods typically find no significant differences in tests of knowledge. There are, however, differences between teaching methods in retention, application, and transfer (Donald, 1995).

Greeno (1991) suggests that general ways of thinking about the material need to be taught along with content because they are prerequisites to understanding content. Students who have no general modes of thinking for understanding science may be as lost in a biological science course as a student attempting to use conventional English narrative structures to understand it. Thus instructors have to consider ways of thinking not only as results of instruction but also as prerequisites for instruction. In addition, you must find ways of helping students transition from existing knowledge structures in their minds to more accurate or advanced knowledge structures.

In addition to thinking about how to provide students with instruction concerning the ways of thinking within their domains, you should also provide direct instruction concerning strategic approaches to the tasks specific to their content area. You can influence your students' strategic learning by helping them understand the nature and requirements of academic tasks in the course. As we assign a variety of academic tasks throughout the course, we should define clearly how each assignment relates to course learning goals, so that students can approach them strategically. There are two levels at which we should address strategies: the domain of the course (say, how to think and write like a psychologist) and the course-specific materials and pedagogy (how lectures and labs are organized, how collaborative problem solving is structured). Many college students approach all their courses in the same the way; we must explicitly teach learning strategies that are domain specific to our courses. For example, different disciplines have different discourse structures, different forms of argument, and different ways of approaching and solving problems. The domain differences between our course and our students' other courses should be clearly established. To be self-regulated, students must learn strategies that are appropriate for the domain (Alexander, 1995; Boekaerts, 1995). College faculty have found that cognitive modeling, thinking out loud, and demonstrating the use of texts in a self-regulated manner are ways to provide opportunities for students to learn about domain-specific strategies (Coppola, 1995). Most students cannot write like a scientist unless they are taught scientific writing. Domain-specific approaches to learning are especially critical in introductory courses. Therefore, you should consider activities such as

1. Previewing the textbook and its text structure.
2. Providing anonymous examples of student work to illustrate both do's and don'ts.
3. Giving sample items from previous tests as practice.
4. Being clear about terminology that has domain-specific meaning.

In addition to learning strategies that are applicable to the domain of the course, students must learn strategies that are effective with the instructor's methodological and material choices. When modeling the use of the course textbook as a domain-specific strategy, the instructor also can explicitly outline how the text complements or supplements the lecture or lab materials. As we introduce students to new approaches (for instance, problem-based learning or writing-across-the-curriculum techniques), it is important to also introduce them to the skills needed to successfully participate in our methods and enhance their confidence in applying these skills (Bridges & Hallinger, 1996). Therefore, faculty should help students approach their courses strategically by outlining their individual instructional approaches and materials. For example,

1. As you deliver your first lecture, take notes on the overhead to emphasize the important points.
2. Before you begin a specific pedagogical approach, such as the case study method, take time to explain the method and the skills necessary to use it successfully.

We must remember that faculty can be models of self-regulated learning (Pintrich & Greeno, 1994). Therefore, we should strive to model discipline-specific thinking processes and course-specific strategies for learning in our classrooms. If an instructor models self-regulation and provides feedback and guidance concerning the students' self-regulation, the instructor can have a significant affect on the students' self-regulation (Schunk & Zimmerman, 1998).

We have said that strategic learners can take much of the responsibility for helping themselves study effectively and reach their learning goals. For these students, a core component of strategic learning is their repertoire of cognitive learning strategies (Weinstein & Mayer, 1986; Weinstein et al., 2000). Cognitive learning strategies are goal-directed approaches and methods of thought that help students to build bridges between what they already know or have experienced and what they are trying to learn. These strategies are used to help build meaning in such a way that new information becomes part of an organized knowledge base that can be accessed in the future for recall, application, or problem solving. Research has shown that one of the hallmarks of expertise in an area is an organized knowledge base and a set of strategies for acquiring and integrating new knowledge (Chi et al., 1988).

The simplest forms of learning strategies involve repetition or review, such as reading over a difficult section of text or repeating an equation or rule. A bit more complexity is added when we try to paraphrase or summarize in our own words the material we are studying. Other strategies focus on organizing the information we are trying to learn by creating some type of scheme for the material. For example, creating an outline of the main events and characters in a story, making a timeline for historical occurrences, classifying scientific phenomena, and separating foreign vocabulary into parts of speech are all organizational strategies. Some learning strategies involve elaborating on or analyzing what we are trying to learn to make it more meaningful and memorable. Using analogies to access relevant prior knowledge, comparing and contrasting the explanations offered by two competing scientific theories, and thinking about the implications of a policy proposal are examples of elaboration strategies.

We can have a tremendous impact helping students to develop a useful repertoire of learning strategies. One of the most powerful ways of teaching these strategies is modeling. By using different types of strategies in our teaching, we can expose students to a wide variety of strategies in different content areas. However, it is not enough to simply use strategies in our teaching. It is also necessary to teach students how to do this on their own when they are studying. For example, after paraphrasing a discussion in class, point out what you did and why you did it. Briefly explain to the students what paraphrasing is and why it helps us to learn. You also could explain that it helps us to identify areas that we might not understand. If we have trouble paraphrasing something we are studying, it probably means we have not yet really learned it.

Finally, you should provide students with opportunities over time to practice and reflect on their uses of different learning strategies. As Pintrich, Wolters, and Baxter (2000) noted, modeling the ways to learn strategically in our courses is necessary, but not sufficient. We must structure opportunities for students to practice using these strategies. We also need to ask students not only *what* they think, but *how* they think, and *if* this was the most effective process for them. Guided practice with feedback is a powerful way to teach students how to learn because it provides students with opportunities to practice strategies and evaluate them.

Testing practices also influence students' use of learning strategies. Rote memory questions such as "According to the author, the shortage of teachers depends on three factors. Which three?" produce surface-level processing, whereas deep-level processing can be induced by questions such as "Explain the meaning of the following quotation: 'Too many poor teachers will drive good ones out of the market.'" According to Pressley and McCormick (1995), one of the most powerful ways to influence the degree to which students use deep rather than surface strategies is through test demands. Students are more willing to learn to use deep processing strategies when it is evident to them that these types of strategies help them to meet the demands of the test.

METHODS FOR CHECKING UNDERSTANDING

Strategic learners must be skillful self-regulators who periodically check on the usefulness of their learning methods by monitoring their progress toward learning goals and subgoals (Zimmerman, 1998). Without checking actively on their progress, many students may think that they understand when, in fact, they do not. Often students do not realize there are holes in their understanding until they receive their grade on a test. This is because the test is the first time they were asked to check their new knowledge in a way that would identify gaps or misunderstandings. Strategic learners know that the time to check your understanding is way before taking a test or other formal assessment measure. Checking understanding and looking for gaps in knowledge integration should be an ongoing activity present in every studying and learning context.

Checking our understanding can be as simple as trying to paraphrase or apply what we have been trying to learn. In fact, many homework or project assignments are designed to help students identify gaps in their knowledge or areas of misunderstanding so that they can be corrected. Getting past these problems helps students to deepen their understanding of a topic. Many of the learning strategies we discussed earlier also can be used to test understanding. For example, trying to paraphrase in our own words what we are reading in a textbook is a good way to help build meaning, but it also helps us to identify gaps or errors in our understanding. If we try to apply our knowledge and have difficulty using it, or if we try to explain it to someone else and can't do it, we will also know that we have some comprehension problems. Monitoring our comprehension is an important part of strategic learning that fosters self-regulation. Only when we know we have a problem in our understanding or a gap in our knowledge can we do something about it.

A very useful method for checking on understanding and helping to teach a variety of learning strategies is the use of cooperative learning. Cooperative learning is a method that builds on peer tutoring. We have long known that in many traditional tutoring situations, it is the tutor, and not the student receiving the tutoring, who benefits the most. While processing the content for presentation, the tutor is consolidating and integrating his or her own content knowledge. At the same time, the tutor is learning a great deal about how to learn. The tutor needs to diagnose the tutee's learning problem, or knowledge gap, in order to help overcome it. Refer to the chapter on active learning for a more complete discussion of the benefits of cooperative learning within "learning cells."

KNOWING HOW TO LEARN IS NOT ENOUGH— STUDENTS MUST ALSO WANT TO LEARN

Strategic learners know a lot about learning and the types of strategies that will help them meet their learning goals. However, knowing what to do is not enough. Knowing how to do it is still not enough. Students must want to learn if they are to use the knowledge, strategies, and skills we have addressed so far. It is the interaction of what Scott Paris and his colleagues have called "skill and will" that results in self-regulated learning (Hofer et al., 1998; Paris et al., 1983; Pintrich & De Groot, 1990). Many students know much more about effective study practices than they use. Just like the overweight person who is an expert in weight loss techniques, knowledge is not always sufficient for action. We all have many different potential goals and actions competing for our attention and resources at any point in time. Which goals we select and how much effort we put toward the goals we have selected are at least partially determined by our motivations. Strategic learners know how to learn, but they also want to be effective learners. It is the interaction of skill and will that gives direction to their actions and helps them to persist at tasks, even in the face of obstacles.

One way to enhance students' perceptions of their competence is by giving performance feedback that focuses on strategic effort and skill development. Simply telling students that they did well doesn't really focus on their role in the performance. Telling a student, "This is great! I can really see the effort you put into this," says a lot more. Talking directly about students' strategic efforts and the skills they are developing helps them to focus on their role in the learning process. Remember, a key component of strategic learning is a belief that you can play an active role. If students do not believe they can make a difference, they will not use many of the effective strategies we have been discussing. Many students listen to strategy instruction and believe the strategies are very useful—but not for them!

Our task is to help students understand that they can take more responsibility for their own learning. Remember that motivation results from a number of interacting factors (Murphy & Alexander, 2000; Pintrich & De Groot, 1990). As we discussed under goal setting, establishing the potential usefulness of new learning helps to generate interest and direction for students' learning activities. The chapter "Motivation in the College Classroom" includes a more complete discussion of the effects of motivation on learning.

PUTTING IT ALL TOGETHER—EXECUTIVE CONTROL PROCESSES IN STRATEGIC LEARNING

We have discussed both skill and will as important components of strategic learning. A third essential component is the use of executive control processes. These control processes are used to manage the learning process from the beginning (setting the learning goal) to the end result. Strategic learners use these processes to (1) organize and manage their own approach to reaching a learning goal; (2) keep themselves on target and warn themselves if they are not making sufficient progress toward meeting the goal in a timely and effective manner; and (3) build up a repertoire of effective strategies they can call on in the future to complete similar tasks, thereby increasing their learning efficiency and productivity (Paris & Paris, 2001; Weinstein, 1988). When students are facing new and unfamiliar tasks, they must do a lot of planning to help identify potentially effective methods to achieve their goals for task performance. Unfortunately, many students simply adopt a trial-and-error approach to learning or try to adapt to the current task other familiar strategies they have used for different tasks. Students do not realize that this approach is often neither effective nor efficient. The time invested in generating, following, monitoring, and perhaps modifying a plan is a good investment for reaching learning goals now and in the future. As we develop expertise, we do not need to dwell on developing a plan for each task we face. Generating and evaluating plans for reaching learning goals helps build up an effective repertoire that we can call on in the future when similar learning needs arise.

Several instructional approaches emphasize how college instructors can help students generate, maintain, and evaluate their learning (self-regulate their learning within college coursework). For example, Zimmerman and Paulson (1995) reported a four-phase sequence to teach self-monitoring skills. Such skills are essential for checking understanding and assessing the effectiveness of strategies. When self-monitoring is successful, the student not only learns more but also develops better strategies. In addition, students' successes increase their self-efficacy in the course and their motivation to learn. As college instructors, we must be careful not to overemphasize one stage of learning (for instance, planning over implementation). Thus another important aspect of learning is the use of volitional strategies. For example, Trawick and Corno (1995) have outlined a volitional training plan that includes specific instructional activities, modeling, role playing, record keeping, and instructor and peer feedback. They emphasize that faculty need to teach volitional skills as well as cognitive and motivational strategies. Finally, in addition to learning how to learn course content and learning how to control motivation and volition, Boekaerts (1995; Boekaerts & Niemivirta, 2000) emphasize that students must also learn "emotion control," the management of emotions and levels of arousal while learning.

College faculty can help facilitate self-regulated learning by encouraging students to share examples of successful approaches to learning with each other. Guided discussions about what is and isn't working helps students refine their own methods and get ideas for other potential approaches. They also focus students' attention on the importance of not simply working hard, but also working strategically to meet their goals. Discussions of self-regulated learning should emphasize the need to change strategies in different contexts and for different purposes. Working strategically should be addressed as a challenging endeavor, cognitively, motivationally, and affectively. The students' successes in meeting these challenges are among the intrinsic rewards of learning and teaching.

IN CONCLUSION

Teaching strategic learning is more than an investment in your students' future learning; it also is an investment in the present. Strategic learners are better able to take advantage of your instruction and their studying activities. The time you invest will come back to you in enhanced student understanding and performance, as well as increased motivation. It is also important to remember that all of us have goals for what we hope the students in our classes will learn. In today's rapidly changing world, the ability to acquire or use knowledge and skills is more important than compiling a static knowledge base. There is an old Talmudic expression that loosely translates as "If you give people a fish, you have fed them for a day, but if you teach them how to fish, you have fed them for a lifetime!" As college instructors our task is to provide edible fish (content knowledge), but our task is also to teach our students how to fish (learning how to become strategic learners in our field).

Supplementary Readings

P. R. Pintrich, D. R. Brown, and C. E. Weinstein, *Student Motivation, Cognition, and Learning: Essays in Honor of Wilbert J. McKeachie* (Hillsdale, NJ: Lawrence Erlbaum, 1994).

M. Pressley and C. B. McCormick, *Cognition, Teaching and Assessment* (New York: HarperCollins, 1995).

C. E. Weinstein and B. L. McCombs, *Strategic Learning: The Merging of Skill, Will and Self-Regulation in Academic Environments* (Mahwah, NJ: Lawrence Erlbaum, in press).

CHAPTER

24 Teaching Thinking

■ ■ ■ ■ ■ ■ ■ ■ ■ ■ ■ ■ ■ ■ ■ ■ ■

Everyone agrees that students learn in college, but whether they learn to think has been controversial.

In the last few decades this controversy has diminished to some degree. Employers, parents, and taxpayers alike expressed disappointment in, and distress about, the performance of college graduates, which produced some pressures for college teachers to pay closer attention to the learner and how learning occurs. This shift of focus is sometimes referred to as change from *content-centered instruction* to *learner-centered teaching* (Barr & Tagg, 1995).

Content-centered teachers tend to define their primary objective as sharing important facts and concepts with students, with limited attention to the process of learning itself and the thinking that learning requires. Many content-centered teachers believe that merely providing exposure to the ideas of the discipline will cause students' thinking to evolve naturally over time. Some believe that the capacity to think is innate and that, therefore, spending valuable class time promoting changes in thinking seems unnecessary or even misguided.

This chapter was written by Jane S. Halonen and Felicia Brown-Anderson of James Madison University and Wilbert J. McKeachie of the University of Michigan.

284

In contrast, learner-centered teaching elevates the process of learning by requiring students to grapple with ideas. Teachers with this pedagogical philosophy accept and relish their responsibility for fostering changes in how students think by emphasizing active learning strategies. Cognitive scientists report that underlying brain structures change to support enduring learning when students think about the course material in more meaningful ways (Leamnson, 2000). Knowledge about how memory functions bolsters the viewpoint that students can improve their thinking skills through well-designed college courses.

Improving thinking is sometimes couched in terms of improving critical thinking and problem-solving skills (Halpern, 1996). The frequency with which college and university mission statements now include improved thinking skills suggests how seriously higher education is responding to this shift in paradigm about the role of thinking in students' academic development.

Any given course provides the opportunity for an instructor to teach students how to think better. Typically, the course will reflect hallmarks of its discipline. Each course in sequence can build the thinking skills practiced within the discipline as the student develops to professional levels. However, it can be daunting, or at least inefficient, to attempt improvements in students' thinking without adopting a systematic approach to the task. As a result, a variety of critical thinking and problem-solving models have emerged as frameworks to encourage the development of thinking.

SETTING GOALS FOR THINKING

Benjamin Bloom and his colleagues (1956) collaborated on the development of a popular framework to improve an instructor's ability to teach thinking, regardless of the discipline. Bloom's taxonomy became a foundation for teaching across all levels. The original work suggested that thinking skills could be subdivided and sequenced in terms of sophistication. Some skills represent *lower-order* thinking, including knowledge, comprehension, and application. The *higher-order* skills required greater complexity and effort, including analysis, synthesis, and evaluation. Bloom and his colleagues suggested that a thoughtful course design that relied on the taxonomy for guidance could clarify assignment expectations and enhance student performance. The taxonomy became a widely used tool for teachers developing test questions and promoting more complex thinking skills.

Recently, Anderson, Krathwohl, and colleagues (2001) revised Bloom's taxonomy to improve its pedagogical utility and accuracy. Anderson's team recognized that "knowledge" was not really a process, as originally proposed in the taxonomy, but the context in which thinking takes place. They differentiated the various kinds of knowledge (factual, conceptual, procedural, and metacognitive) that learning encompasses. They changed the first level of the taxonomy from "knowledge" to "remember." Throughout the revised taxonomy, Anderson and his colleagues developed more outcome-oriented language to assist teachers in developing workable objectives and learning activities. For example, they changed "evaluation" to "evaluate" to stress the action by using appropriate verbs rather than nouns. (See Figure 24.1 for other examples.) As in the original taxonomy, Anderson's team retained the hierarchical design in which each skill level builds on the prior level, but they reorganized the sequence of higher-order skills. In Anderson's revision, "create" (formerly "synthesis") assumes the status of the most complex thinking skill, followed by "evaluate," reversing their original relationship in Bloom's sequence.

Unfortunately, the constraints of testing formats used with large classes often prompt teachers to limit themselves to lower-order objectives. Multiple-choice tests tend to emphasize remembering and understanding. Skilled item writers can use multiple-choice tests to tap higher-order objectives; however, these items are much more difficult to create. Familiarity with Bloom's taxonomy or Anderson's revision can help produce a more systematic approach to teaching thinking skills. Beginning courses in a discipline will emphasize lower-level thinking skills but should not be devoid of higher-order challenges. As students progress in their majors, they should face more complex thinking demands. Research papers, structured class discussions, and original presentations can facilitate the development of higher levels of thinking when instructors frame their directions properly. Students can analyze and evaluate concepts, incorporating

FIGURE 24.1 **Anderson, Krathwohl, and Colleagues' (2001) Revision of Bloom's Taxonomy**

The revision retains the hierarchical nature of thinking skills, but offers a new sequence in the hierarchy and emphasizes action verbs to promote more effective design of test questions and assignments.

Higher-Order Skills	**Create** Reorganize elements into a new pattern, structure, or purpose (*generate, plan, produce*) **Evaluate** Come to a conclusion about something based on standards/criteria (*checking, critiquing, judging*) **Analyze** Subdivide content into meaningful parts and relate the parts (*differentiating, organizing, attributing*) **Apply** Use procedures to solve problems or complete tasks (*execute, implement*) **Understand** Construct new meaning by mixing new material with existing ideas (*interpret, exemplify, classify, summarize, infer, compare, explain*)
Lower-Order Skills	**Remember** Retrieve pertinent facts from long-term memory (*recognize, recall*)

Source: Anderson, L. W., & Krathwohl, D. R. (Eds.). (2001). *A taxonomy of learning, teaching, and assessment: A revision of Bloom's taxonomy of educational objectives.* New York: Longman.

them into a coherent viewpoint, which should improve their ability to benefit from what they have learned and to generalize their learning to new situations. Emphasizing higher-order skills will enhance students' cognitive complexity (cf. Perry, 1970). Advanced courses that only develop and test lower levels of thinking simply shortchange students by limiting their conceptual development and thinking practices.

IMPROVING THINKING QUALITY

What are some strategies that will promote better-quality thinking in your students' performance?

1. Integrate course content with opportunities to practice thinking. Experts suggest that the factual knowledge attained through course experience rapidly deteriorates unless the ideas can be meaningfully encoded or practiced with some regularity until the knowledge becomes secure in memory (Eriksen, 1983). Instructors can easily get caught up in the press of time to cover content in textbooks that are likely to be impossible to cover completely. Instead, give yourself permission to focus on developing thinking skills along with selected course content. Provide ample opportunities to practice thinking in class, particularly if you plan to test students on the quality of their thinking.

2. Establish a classroom climate that facilitates thinking. Take time to think yourself before answering a question, and explain how you derive an answer to model thinking skills. Build in reflection, thinking, and discussion time to reinforce the importance of those activities. Furthermore, the syllabus should reflect your commitment to helping students expand their thinking skills to prepare them properly for challenges beyond the course.

3. Be explicit about what kind of thinking you are asking students to do. The more cognitive clues that you can provide to help them translate your directions, the more satisfying their performance will be. Basing your instructions on Bloom's taxonomy, Anderson's revision, or a similar model, and sharing the model with the students, can help them be conversant in differentiating

thinking skills. Providing criteria that specify how to achieve grade levels linked to specific thinking achievements can motivate best performance as well as help students articulate their achievements (Mentkowski & Associates, 2000).

4. Give accurate feedback to distinguish good from poor-quality thinking. Less effective thinking can be shaped more easily when students understand how their contributions may be deficient. Acknowledge something of value in a student's answer when you can. Encourage off-target contributions, but gently point out that more could be said or other directions could be taken and ask the class to collaborate to improve the response. When good thinking occurs pronounce it sound, explain your rationale, and congratulate the thinker, whether the contribution occurs in class discussion, small groups, or writing assignments.

5. Reframe the value of asking questions. Asking questions can be an uninviting or unnerving prospect, especially for beginning students. Asking questions can be misinterpreted. Students sometimes equate asking questions in class with ignorance. On the other hand, peers can ostracize students who are good at asking questions because they can be perceived as attempting to curry favor with the instructor. The instructor must neutralize negative attitudes and redefine asking questions as not just honorable but a primary goal of the course and the entire college experience.

6. Consider the impact of learning styles on thinking and expression. Students differ in how quickly or well they can respond to probe questions. Many students can respond quickly and accurately to lower-order thinking challenges but balk at more sophisticated challenges. Some students simply require more reflection time before they can confidently express their conclusions. Design challenges that will invite a full range of responses, from simple to complex, and involve diverse learning styles.

IN CONCLUSION

Learning thinking skills is not easy, but students will not make progress without specific training. Along with specific discipline-based strategies that sharpen their thinking skills, students need to develop habits of reflection—of thinking about their experience, their successes and failures, their plans and purposes, their choices, and their consequences.

Teaching thinking skills also is not easy. Teachers need to commit to the importance of building thinking into course design, to provide plenty of practice opportunities, and to offer developmental feedback to achieve their desired outcomes.

Supplementary Reading

John Dewey's classic *How We Think* (Boston: Houghton Mifflin, 1998), written over a half-century ago, underlies much of the work since his time and is still fresh and helpful today.

David Levy's book *Tools of Critical Thinking* (Boston: Allyn and Bacon, 1997) deals with many of the biases and errors in everyday thinking and includes excellent exercises to help students become better thinkers.

One aspect of good thinking is reflection. See Jean MacGregor (ed.), Student Self-Evaluation: Fostering Reflective Thinking [Special issue], *New Directions for Teaching and Learning*, 1993, 56.

Also helpful in teaching thinking are the following:

D. F. Halpern and associates, *Changing College Classrooms: New Teaching and Learning Strategies for an Increasingly Complex World* (San Francisco: Jossey-Bass, 1994).

E. Langer, *The Power of Mindful Learning* (Reading, MA: Addison-Wesley, 1997).

M. Mentkowski and associates, *Learning That Lasts: Integrating Learning, Development, and Performance in College and Beyond* (San Francisco: Jossey-Bass, 2000).

R. J. Sternberg and E. L. Grigorenko, *Teaching for Successful Intelligence* (Arlington Heights, IL: Skylight Professional Development, 2000).

Teaching Values: 25
Should We? Can We?*

As you may suspect, this chapter would not be in this book if the answer to either question in its title were "no." So, after answering "yes," I will try to engage you in thinking with me about the more difficult questions: What should we teach? And how should we teach?

Valuing is as natural as thinking or breathing. We automatically make value judgments about our experiences. "This was good, that was bad; this is beautiful, that's ugly." You have already made judgments about the value of this book. Our students are continually valuing. It would be strange if their college experiences had no impact on that valuing process. And we as teachers are continually guided in our behavior by our values. I write on this topic because of my own basic values. They

---

* In thinking about our role in teaching values, I owe much to Brewster Smith, both for his writing about psychology and values and for my interactions with him through the years. We served together for many years on the Board of Directors of the American Psychological Association, and I always admired the consistency with which he exemplified his own values in his behavior and comments on various controversial issues. We haven't always agreed, but I think we both tried to represent our values when issues came before us.

influence this choice of topic; they strongly influence what I'm going to write; and they influenced me in thinking that it was important to get you to think with me about our role in teaching values. And because my major point is that we ought to be more open in our discussion of values, I should begin by giving you a brief statement of my own values—the perspective from which this chapter is written.

I'm a strongly religious person, a humanist active in my local American Baptist church. I believe strongly that love and respect for other human beings is not a *relative* value—simply a current norm taught in our society—but rather a universal value that should guide the behavior of all human beings at all times. As a Baptist I have a passionate commitment to talking with people about theology, philosophy of religion, ethics, and values issues. I believe that no one has the ultimate answer to the question human beings have wrestled with since the beginning of human self-consciousness—What is Good? Each of us must make a commitment to the best we can conceive of, to give our insights to fellow human beings, and to welcome their thoughts in order that we may come closer to ultimate truth.

SHOULD WE?

That, of course, implies that I think we *should* teach values. In fact, I argue that we can't avoid teaching values. Value neutrality, so-called value-free teaching, is simply advocacy by default. It's using our influence covertly, rather than openly. Our choices of content, our choices of teaching methods, our very ways of conducting classes reveal our values and influence our students' reactions.

My own subject matter, psychology, is particularly value laden. Concepts such as "mental health," "adjustment," "maturity," "personality integration," and "effective leadership" all involve value terms that we sometimes teach to our students as if they were scientific constructs developed in an empirical way on the basis of research without any value implications. The practice of psychology and the research that psychologists have done have clear implications for political and ethical behavior.

I was a mathematics major as an undergraduate, and even in this purest of disciplines there were values. Some proofs were more beautiful than others; the examples and illustrations intended to maintain our interest carried certain implicit values. So, even though some disciplines probably face value questions less directly than others, we teachers cannot escape values. We can't avoid teaching values.

"But," you say, "isn't it a misuse of our position if we indoctrinate students with our values?" True. Probably our avoidance of explicit attention to values results from our concern about the evil of indoctrination. But there are two aspects to my answer.

The *first* is that I would have no compunction about indoctrination with respect to such values as honesty and respect for other individuals as human beings. We cannot teach our students well if they plagiarize papers, fake laboratory results, or cheat on examinations. We cannot carry out effective classroom discussions without an atmosphere of respect for others' feelings or a sense of shared humanity. In a multicultural society like ours there is a special need for thinking seriously about values—how we differ and what we share. Certainly we want our students to value learning.

The *second* is that we can help students to become more sensitive to values issues, to recognize value implications, to understand others' values, without indoctrination. Even with respect to fundamental values (such as honesty), student discussion, exploration, and debate about their implications are more useful than simple advocacy. Open consideration of the complexity of value issues is probably less subversive than disregarding values altogether.

CAN WE?

This leaves us with this chapter's second question: Can we? Do we have an impact? There is research evidence that we do. Students do change during their college years. There have been a number of studies of college graduates versus noncollege graduates (with reasonable controls for socioeconomic status and other factors) that show differences. In general these are supported by longitudinal studies showing similar differences between student values at the beginning of their college years as compared with their values toward the end of their senior year (Pascarella & Terenzini, 1991).

Among the sometimes modest *average* changes, there are great *individual* changes, as well as changes of particular groups according to the curricula chosen, social groupings, or other elements of the college culture. So students change; the issue for us is: Does our teaching make a difference?

Certainly teaching is one element of the culture that supports or opposes other elements of the culture, some of which may be pulling in different directions. The social culture, the fraternity/sorority culture, the athletic culture, the bar and tavern culture, the administrative, institutional culture—even the culture of religious groups—these and others are also influencing the students.

Here again we have some research evidence. Teaching can make a difference. A number of studies, in fact, have found changes in values and attitudes in individual courses in which different teaching methods were compared. In general, courses with more emphasis on discussion or active learning methods have more influence than those in which students are passive (McKeachie et al., 1990). Thus we can answer the question—Can we?—affirmatively. The questions now become: What should we be teaching? How should we teach values?

WHAT VALUES SHOULD WE TEACH?

Those who say we should be taking a neutral stance on values typically are restricting their definition of values to sociopolitical ones. Very few would dispute the fact that we are concerned about honesty, respect for others, and rationality. A major goal of education presumably is to increase students' skills in critical, rational thinking. We want students to value rational thought, but not at the exclusion of other ways of knowing and thinking. In considering problems in society or in their everyday lives, our graduates will, I hope, look for evidence rather than react on the basis of unreasoning prejudice; they will be aware of the implications of their values but not let their values close their minds. Particularly in social science courses we ask our students to ask "What is the evidence?" before jumping to conclusions. Even those who point out that "rationality" has sometimes been defined in ways that confirm power relationships present rational arguments and evidence for their position. Our greater sensitivity to the issues raised by feminist and other critics is itself a tribute to rationality.

In psychology courses we expect our students to learn respect for individuality and freedom of choice, particularly as this involves treatment of human beings in research studies. We train our graduate students not to exploit their status or power over students or clients for participation in research or for sexual or other activities that are outside the bounds of the normal college course requirements.

The big question in teaching is what to do about controversial social and political values. Here it seems to me that we are not privileged to demand acceptance of our own values, as I think we are privileged to do with respect to requiring academic honesty. But this does not imply avoiding values issues. Too often we communicate—by the way we handle touchy material—that you don't rock the boat by taking a position.

In avoiding controversial issues we communicate the notion that it may be all right to talk about these things in dormitories or in other places, but not in educational settings where rational arguments and the complexities of the issue are more likely to be salient.

The apple of temptation for us as teachers is that we may too easily accept affirmation of values that we share, letting students get away with simply stating a position with which we agree, without asking for rational support, as we might for a position that conflicts with our own.

On the other side, however, is the problem of dealing with those with whom we disagree. There is the danger that we will yield to the temptation of demolishing the student with the force of our logic, but arguing can also be a way of showing respect. Remember that the power you have in your role as teacher may make it difficult for the student to muster a strong defense. Take it easy until students trust you enough to argue without fear of retribution. It is all too easy to intentionally, or unintentionally, coerce students into overt agreement.

Perry (1970, 1981) has described the development of Harvard students as progressing from the dualistic belief that things are either true or false, good or evil, through a stage of relativism in which they feel all beliefs are equally valid, to a stage of commitment to values and beliefs that are recognized to be incomplete and imperfect but are open to correction and further development. We may not all reach Perry's highest stage, or we may reach it in some areas but not in others, but Perry suggests that as teachers and members of the community of learners, we have the responsibility not only to model commitment and open-mindedness but also to share our own doubts and uncertainties. He says:

> We need to teach dialectically—that is, to introduce our students, as our greatest teachers have introduced us, not only to the orderly certainties of our subject matter, but to its unresolved dilemmas. This is an art that requires timing, learned only by paying close attention to students' ways of making meaning. (Perry, 1981, p. 109)

We need to teach students to begin to become aware of the complexities of their positions, of the fact that there are always costs and gains—tradeoffs between competing values. Just as teachers in music are not satisfied when their students simply like a particular symphony or a particular kind of music, but insist that the students develop a disciplined appreciation of the complexity underlying their preferences, so, too, in other disciplines we need to help students value and understand the pros and cons, the arguments and evidence that are involved in critical judgments and decisions. In the social sciences we need to communicate that liking people or liking certain kinds of people or institutions and their values is not enough. Our ethical judgments in human affairs need to have at least as much complexity in their analysis and exposition as we would give to analyzing the strengths and weaknesses of our favorite baseball team or our judgments of restaurants.

My major concern is not that we teach values such as honesty, which we agree are essential to the academic enterprise, but that we be open and explicit in helping our students to become *sensitive* to values issues. Whichever side they come out on, they should be aware that large numbers of things that we take for granted in this world involve serious moral and ethical values. Much of the evil that I see is not just the result of lack of values but rather a lack of sensitivity to value implications of actions or policies that are more or less taken for granted or are accepted as part of one's role in an institution—governmental, business, or academic.

In college I hope that students will develop firm enough commitments and have enough practice in considering values issues that in most situations they automatically act in accordance with their values. But I also hope that they will be more likely and able to think about values implications in the many areas in which values are not salient or where values are in conflict.

The Dutch psychologist Jan Elshout (1987) suggests that there are three levels of problems. I believe that his metaphor can be extended to values issues and decision making as well.

Elshout says that the first zone is one in which no thinking is needed. The problem solver can solve the problem automatically on the basis of previous knowledge and expertise. Similarly, there are situations in which we don't have to think about values issues because we automatically do the right thing. (This is not to imply that such values are immune from examination!)

But there is a second, problematic zone where the solution is not obvious, and the problem solver has to think about alternative ways of approaching the problem because there is no obvious solution. Nonetheless, the problem solver tackles the problem because he or she has skills and strategies that may lead to a solution. Similarly, there are ethical issues that we recognize as ethical problems and can resolve with appropriate consideration of the pros and cons.

Elshout then suggests that there is a top zone where the situation is so complicated, so remote from our experience, that we don't know what approach to use and our usual strategies of problem solving are no longer likely to be very effective. So, too, in ethics there are problems that we fail to recognize, or if recognized, simply avoid thinking about.

In the area of ethics and values we hope that as teachers we can expand the area in which humane values are carried out as the normal pattern of behavior; we hope to increase our students' ability to consider and weigh conflicting values in the middle zone, to consult others when in doubt, and we also hope to cut down the big area where our students avoid considering values because the whole area seems so complicated that they don't want to think.

HOW CAN WE TEACH VALUES?

We exemplify and communicate our values in what we teach and in the way we teach. Teaching values does not mean neglecting knowledge. Knowledge is a powerful sword to protect students from biased, emotional appeals.

Probably every teacher, whether in the arts, the sciences, or the professions, tries to teach students that it is not enough simply to respond to material or performance as good or bad, but rather to be able to back up one's judgment with evidence that is reasonable in terms of the standards of that discipline. We communicate that value by our comments on papers, our reactions to student comments or performance, and ultimately by our grades. So we have a group of values that we accept and either explicitly or implicitly communicate to our students through our behavior as teachers.

Our values also affect our course planning. We begin with the goals we take for the course. Who should determine those goals? Is this something to be determined by the university, by the department, by the instructor, or should students be involved? Personally, I have faith that in a situation in which students and faculty members participate jointly, our decisions will come out with reasonable values, reasonable content, and reasonable coverage—all the things that we worry about when we're thinking about how to set up a course. A cooperative approach exemplifies the value of respect for others. Asking students to write or discuss their goals for the course involves thinking about values. Asking them at the end of the course to think about what goals they have achieved and how these are related to their long-term goals sensitizes students to values issues.

Modeling Values

We demonstrate our values and those of our discipline in almost every class. Yesterday I spent a good part of the class period having students introduce one another. I indicated that this represented the value to me of knowing students as individuals rather than as faces in a crowd. Even in classes of 500 I have used seating charts so that I could call students by name.

Perhaps most important is the model of ethical behavior we provide (see the chapter on ethics). Clearly, sarcasm, favoritism, and failure to respect diversity of students' cultures, values, and attitudes represent a negative model. But avoiding unethical behavior is not enough. How do we handle legitimate requests for exceptions from a policy printed in our syllabus? Do we weigh individual needs or are we rule-bound? How do we handle students with handicaps or learning disabilities? When a student comment is wrong or inappropriate, do we make it clear that we are criticizing the idea and not the person?

What about the ethical decisions we face in preparing and conducting the course? Do we give proper credit to the sources we use? Are our assignments and learning assessments dictated by student learning or by our own need to save time? Are we conscientious about preparation and attendance at class? Are we ethical in our use of licensed software? Each of the ethical situations discussed in the chapter on ethics is an opportunity for you to model your values.

Service Learning

Although current students are not as idealistic as some earlier generations, idealism isn't dead among students. The annual nationwide surveys of American college freshmen carried out by UCLA Higher Education Research Institute show that goals such as helping other people and developing a philosophy of life, which had been dropping in relation to more materialistic goals, are now resurgent. In fact, 81 percent of 2000–2001 freshmen reported that they do volunteer services. The Institute reports a rising interest in spirituality and the meaning of life among both faculty and students (Astin & Astin, 1999). Unfortunately, interest in political affairs hit an all-time low in the 2000–2001 cohort—28 percent versus 60 percent in 1966.

Evaluations of our University of Michigan service courses, Project Outreach and Project Community, suggest that these courses have had some success in affecting student values. Such courses tend to confirm and reinforce altruistic values and probably help make students' altruistic impulses become more realistic in the face of the complexities of helping other people.

Dealing with Alternative Views

One major values issue in teaching is whether to present a single view or multiple positions in areas where theories differ. Certainly our students prefer that we tell them the "truth." And I suppose that if you really believe strongly that a particular position is true, you should teach that position. But I don't think that relieves you of the obligation to let students know that there is a competing theory.

As teachers and scholars we must hold to the faith that even though there is little, if any, unchanging absolute "truth," the positions we hold to be closer to truth than the alternatives can be supported by evidence and reason. Our task is to help students develop the habits of thinking that are used in our disciplines, to determine what is more or less valid.

We don't develop these habits of thinking by avoiding areas where there are conflicting theories or values. Be up front about the differences. Use the two-column method described in the chapter "Facilitating Discussion" or set up a debate, perhaps asking participants to take the side opposite their own.

A classic values clarification exercise is to place the signs "Strongly Agree," "Agree," "Disagree," and "Strongly Disagree" on the four walls of the classroom. Read a controversial statement and ask students to stand by the wall that represents their position. Ask students to defend their positions and to move to another wall if their opinion changes during the discussion. At the end of the discussion you might have students write a minute paper on what they learned.

In the social sciences we can use cross-cultural research that indicates to our students that there are different ways of viewing the world and differing value positions on a number of things that we take for granted.

What Kinds of Teaching Methods Should We Use?*

There is some relevant research evidence here. One of the classic studies was done by Stern and Cope (1956; also Stern, 1962) at Syracuse some years ago. They selected authoritarian students with stereotyped conceptions of race, minorities, and others different from themselves. These students were assigned to a special discussion section. Their achievement in this homogeneous section proved to be superior to that of similar students in conventional sections of the course.

What did the teacher do with these students who were unusually difficult to teach? At the beginning of the term the instructor of the homogeneous section was distressed by the students' lack of responsiveness and negativism, but he adopted a strategy of frequently taking a devil's advocate position, in which he would present strong positions that would arouse the students so much that they simply had to respond. The ensuing debate resulted in changes that didn't occur in the classes where similar students were able to sit back and not participate. The students in the experimental class not only performed better academically but also became less ethnocentric and authoritarian than similar students in the conventional classes. This finding fits with research comparing discussions versus lectures, suggesting that more attitude change occurs in discussion sections.

The results of the studies of discussion methods, cooperative learning, and experiential learning fit with our theories of change. If we want students to change, they have to have a chance to express their ideas and values in words or actions and see how they work. They need reactions not only from teachers but also from peers and others who share or oppose their positions. They

---

* Both the chapter "Facilitating Discussion" and the following chapter have suggestions for handling controversial topics.

need to trust the teacher's good will and good sense. They need to feel that the class is a community in which each will be accepted despite differing views.

Cooperative peer learning can contribute to building community and often has a positive effect on attitudes and values. Cooperation is itself an important value in our culture, and success in learning how to work cooperatively with other students on a project or other learning experience is likely to have a positive impact on students' value for cooperation as well as on building the kinds of support and trust necessary for frank discussion of values issues.

We know that students remember the content of our courses better if they elaborate the content by relating it to other knowledge—if they question, explain, or summarize. Such elaboration is important in the values area as well. And it's important that the discussion and experiences be in places where there is mutual respect and support. Values are not likely to be changed much simply by passively listening and observing a lecturer. Change is more likely in situations in which the teacher and the students reflect, listen, and learn from one another.

THE TEACHER AS A PERSON

Teaching does not end at the classroom door. Wilson et al. (1975) found that professors who were perceived by students and colleagues as having significant impact on student development demanded high standards of performance and interacted a great deal with students both in and *out of* the classroom. When students see that you are willing to sacrifice time from your own endeavors in order to help them, you communicate your values.

The teaching methods one uses may be less important than aspects of teaching that cut across methods. The degree to which students feel we know them as individuals and care about their learning, the extent to which they feel they know us as individuals (not simply as experts or authorities), the openness we have to questions and opposing points of view, our willingness to risk change in ourselves—these have much to do with the students' willingness to open their values to examination and change. Parker Palmer (1998) says, "Good teaching comes from the identity and integrity of the teacher. . . . The connections made by good teachers are held not in their methods but in their hearts" (pp. 10–11).

IN CONCLUSION

We develop values by observing and modeling ourselves after others and testing out our values in thought and words and action. Teachers are significant models, and teacher behavior is important, both as it models values and as teachers create situations in which the expression of values becomes salient.

The process of value development and value change is very much like the process of scientific theory development or of self-development in general. We have experiences; we develop ways of trying to think about those experiences to make sense of them; we test our theories (in this case our values) by consciously thinking about them, by studying what others have said or done, by talking to other people, and by behaving and seeing what happens. My basic faith is that everyone has within himself or herself the capacity to discriminate good from evil and to act to achieve the good. William James said, "The significance of religious belief is not in affirmation, but in its consequences for behavior." And so it is with values in general.

St. Augustine wrote, "Hope has two lovely daughters, anger and courage. Anger at the way things are, and courage to see that they need not remain as they are." Let us have hope.

Supplementary Reading

A thoughtful discussion of these as well as ethical issues in teaching may be found in:

W. L. Humphreys, "Values in Teaching and the Teaching of Values," *Teaching-Learning Issues No. 58* (Knoxville: Learning Research Center, The University of Tennessee, 1986).

Self-reflective learning involves much consideration of values. See Jean MacGregor (ed.), *Student Self-Evaluation: Fostering Reflective Learning* [Special issue], *New Directions for Teaching and Learning*, 1993, 56.

Joseph Lowman has a helpful discussion of how to handle controversial issues in his book *Mastering the Techniques of Teaching* (San Francisco: Jossey-Bass, 1984).

Lawrence Kohlberg's book *Essays on Moral Development* (San Francisco: Harper & Row, 1981) is a good resource for thinking about moral development.

Parker Palmer provides a thought-provoking resource for teaching values in *The Courage to Teach: Exploring the Inner Landscape of a Teacher's Life* (San Francisco: Jossey-Bass, 1993).

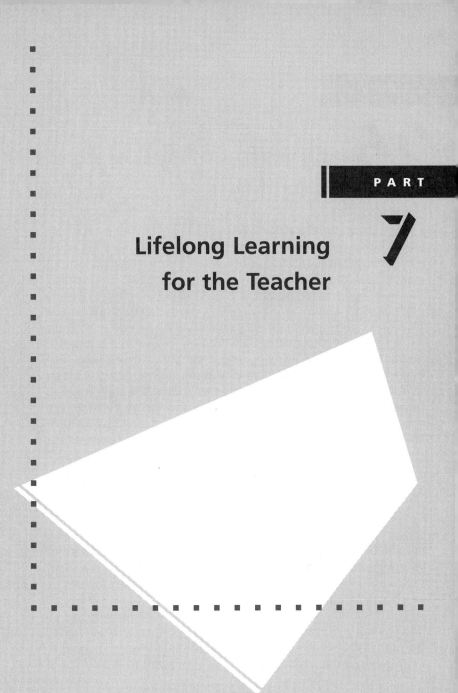

Lifelong Learning
for the Teacher

CHAPTER

26 Ethics in College Teaching

Imagine you're teaching a course at the introductory level, one that is required of all students who want to proceed on to major in your department. And let's suppose that you are approached by a student after the first exam, someone whose performance was much below standard. And that person offers you a considerable sum of money if you'll change a grade on the exam so the student can pass. What is the ethical thing to do in this situation?

Now suppose that it's the same situation, but instead of offering you money, the student pleads for an opportunity to retake the exam because of extenuating circumstances during the first test administration. Now what is the ethical choice?

Now it's the same situation, but this time you are the one who notices that a student who's been working hard in your class and whom you expected to do very well has instead failed the exam miserably. How does this situation compare with the others from an ethical standpoint?

The first of these scenarios seems fairly straightforward, a definite violation of ethics if you were to accept the money to change the grade. The second example is not as straightforward; to what extent should the student be allowed an opportunity that is not

This chapter was written by Marilla Svinicki of the University of Texas at Austin.

available to all the other students? Does providing that opportunity constitute unethical behavior? Or is it just unfair? Or is there a difference? And in the third instance, to what extent should your assessment of a student's abilities counter actual performance? Where do you draw the line in helping students? The most difficult questions that teachers face often have nothing to do with the content of the course or the way it is presented. They focus instead on the ethical issues of teaching, how we relate to our students, our institution, our discipline, and society at large. What are our responsibilities to each constituency and what do we do when they conflict? Unfortunately there are no easy answers to these questions. I raise them here as food for thought because you *will* face them sometime in your teaching career.

This chapter addresses the issue of ethics in teaching. What do we mean by "ethics in teaching"? In recent years, more and more is being written about the topic as the teaching mission of the university comes under increasing scrutiny (Cahn, 1994; Fisch, 1996; Lewis, 1997; Matthews, 1991; Strike, 1988). It seems only proper that those who currently teach and those who aspire to a faculty career be introduced to the concept.

What is an ethical question in teaching? Ethical questions are sometimes defined in terms of right and wrong (Strike, 1988); in terms of cultural norms such as honesty, promise keeping, and so on (Smith, 1996); or as "general guidelines, ideals, or expectations that need to be taken into account, along with other relevant conditions and circumstances, in the design and analysis of teaching" (Murray et al., 1996, p. 57).

In general, *ethical standards are intended to guide us in carrying out the responsibilities we have to the different groups with whom we interact.* Ethics violations can occur when we are tempted to act contrary to those standards. Ethical dilemmas occur when multiple responsibilities conflict or have more than one right answer (Strike, 1988). It is often surprising to consider all the different things that can cause ethical problems for instructors. They range from the obvious bribe attempt previously described to failure to present all legitimate sides of an issue adequately, to accepting remuneration for extra tutoring for a class with which one is already connected.

In a 1991 research study of psychologists teaching at academic institutions, Tabachnick, Keith-Spiegel, and Pope report reactions to various ethical questions involved in teaching at the college level. Respondents were asked to report how frequently they engaged in a wide range of various activities and the extent to which those activities were ethical or unethical. The activities included things as drastic as sexual harassment and more mundane activities such as teaching materials that the instructor had not yet fully mastered.

The behavior *most often* engaged in was teaching when not adequately prepared, although it was not a consistent pattern for most people. The authors attribute this more to busy workloads and rapid advances in the field than to the shirking of responsibilities. The rarest of behaviors were those related to sexual harassment. Whether this is an accurate reflection of behavior or a reluctance to report such behavior is impossible to tell. Also rare were actual sexual encounters with students.

Perhaps the most interesting sources of ethical conflicts for this group were a result of the conflicting roles of mentor/sponsor and evaluator. For example, over two-thirds believed that allowing a student's likability to influence a grade was unethical, but over two-thirds reported doing it at some point anyway. The same sort of dilemma is seen when instructors interact socially with students. On the one hand, the interaction with faculty is reported as vital to student growth by Pascarella and Terenzini (1991); on the other, it raises the possibility of conflict.

In a more recent study (Braxton & Bayer, 1999), a national sample of faculty in higher education was asked to rate the acceptability of a range of violations of teaching standards, such as "The instructor insists that the student take one particular perspective on course content" or "The instructor does not introduce new teaching methods or procedures." The researchers identified 126 different behaviors that a teacher might engage in and asked the participants to rate how strong a sanction each behavior should bring. The authors then identified two levels of sanctions that they felt were present in the data. The most serious sanctions were for those norms they labeled as inviolable. These included seven clusters: condescending negativism, inattentive planning, moral turpitude, particularistic grading, personal disregard, uncommunicated course details, and uncooperative cynicism.

The second set of clusters was labeled "admonitory norms," behaviors that, though inappropriate, didn't evoke as strong a reaction from the participants. These included advisement negligence, authoritarian classrooms, inadequate communication, inadequate course design, inconvenience avoidance, insufficient syllabus, teaching secrecy, and undermining colleagues. When these clusters were compared across institutional types and disciplines, only two were identified by all groups of faculty as inappropriate: moral turpitude and authoritarian classrooms. Demographic characteristics of the respondents did not make a difference in what they felt was inappropriate behavior. The final conclusion by the authors was that there were four values that seemed to undergird the judgments of the participants: respect for students as individuals, equal consideration for all students, an obligation to prepare for teaching, and an obligation to participate in the governance and life of the institution. If you find these results intriguing, you might want to respond to the original survey yourself and compare your responses with those of the national sample. The survey, College Teaching Behaviors Inventory, can be found in Braxton and Bayer's 1999 book reporting their findings.

Values like these are becoming more and more common in discussions about teaching in higher education (Markie, 1994; Carr, 2000). In fact, the American Association of University Professors has provided a statement of professional ethics dealing with the responsibilities of faculty members which highlights what they consider to be the special responsibilities of one in an academic position (AAUP, 1987). A similar set of principles was developed by the Society for Teaching and Learning in Higher Education (STLHE) and distributed to faculty in Canadian institutions (Murray et al., 1996). Perhaps these standards can help highlight what a faculty member should consider in making personal choices.

RESPONSIBILITIES TO STUDENTS

Both the AAUP guidelines and the STLHE guidelines recognize that one of a faculty member's first responsibilities is to the students. The specifics that follow illustrate the broad range of impact that faculty can have on student lives.

To Encourage the Free Pursuit of Learning

The primary purpose of teaching is to encourage learning; therefore the first ethical responsibility an instructor has is to that goal. All that we do to prepare and conduct well-designed instruction is part of that responsibility. The ethical instructor knows the content to be learned, the students who will do the learning, and the methods that could be used to foster the learning. The STLHE guidelines state this explicitly in their first and second principles: content competence and pedagogical competence (Murray et al., 1996). In a discussion of the ethics of teaching psychology, Matthews (1991) interprets the American Psychological Association's professional standards as they apply to teaching and cites the issues of responsibility and competence as two key contributors to encouraging learning. In her interpretation, faculty members are responsible for remaining current and presenting accurate and balanced views of the field, an idea also related to the concept of scholarly behavior discussed later in this chapter.

There are many ways an instructor might violate these standards. Here are two examples:

- Most obvious is to fail in our duties in class preparation. One can't always be in top form, but just as we expect students to come to class prepared, we must make the same effort. This is one of the most commonly occurring violations reported by the sample (Tabachnick et al., 1991) and was identified as a key admonitory norm by Braxton and Bayer (1999).

- A second, less obvious way is failing to remain current both in the content area and in instructional methods that foster learning. Although it is unlikely that faculty would not be current in the content, it is very likely that faculty will not have kept up with research into better instructional methods.

A second part of this responsibility is to protect and encourage the autonomy of our students so that eventually they no longer need our constant guidance. The STLHE guidelines list this as the fourth of their eight principles: "to contribute to the intellectual development of the student" (Murray et al., 1996). If students are to develop into thinking individuals, we must structure our interactions with them in such a way as to both model and support independent thinking, even when this means they might end up disagreeing with us.

To Demonstrate Respect for Students

Ethical instructors also respect the "otherness of students" (Churchill, 1982); that is, the individual and independent nature of the students and the fact that students are at different stages of their lives than are the instructors. For example, instructors need to be aware of the special needs of their students, whether those be cultural, physical, or based on background (Matthews, 1991). This also means respecting students' goals, their choices, and their value as individuals (Strike, 1988), another key value listed by Braxton and Bayer (1999).

The most obvious venue for this particular principle is in the interactions we have with students in and out of class. During class, the way we respond to students' questions and comments should convey the idea that everyone's participation is welcome and respected. How we respond to a student's question affects more than just the student who asked it. And outside of class, the way we greet students who come to office hours or see us in the halls speaks volumes about the level of respect we have for them. We show respect by being available when we say we will be, by keeping promised appointments, by being willing to listen to students' concerns, by giving as much thought and preparation to our interactions with undergraduates as we do to those with graduate students and colleagues.

An example of a not-so-obvious need to respect students as individuals is discussed in an article by Grauerholz and Copenhaver (1994) about the use of experiential teaching methods, especially those that involve a great deal of self-disclosure on the part of students. The choice of instructional strategies such as journaling and small-group problem sharing may violate your students' rights and be harmful as well as unethical, unless done with a great deal of care and concern for the students' well-being. To guard against the possibility of harm, here are some suggestions on how to structure the experience. For example, you should carefully choose strategies and make their purpose clear to your students. It might also be appropriate to allow alternative ways of satisfying the learning requirement for those who do not feel comfortable with these methods. Use of such teaching methods raises the issue of trust because when students trust an instructor, they are more willing to engage in self-examination. Making self-examination safe for students is reason enough to be sure that one's relationship with students is one of trust and respect.

Similar issues of trust arise during the discussion of sensitive topics, such as race, sexual preference, and religion. When faced with a potentially sensitive situation, you can

- Provide early disclosure of the potentially sensitive nature of the topics.

- Make sure that students understand what is being presented as fact and what as opinion.

- Offer extra time outside of class to those students who need to discuss the topics and their reactions to them (Koocher & Keith-Spiegel, 1998).

In my own case, I have advised faculty to draw up a set of "rules of engagement" for sensitive topics which could spark heated debate in class. These rules would specify how these debates would be conducted and would include such things as cooling-down activities, the obligation to be able to state the other person's position before attacking it, the avoidance of personalizing arguments, and so on. If such guidelines are provided early in the course, students can feel more comfortable when sensitive topics are raised.

This does not mean that the topics will be avoided, because that would be a violation of the first of our guidelines: open inquiry. One can see how this conflict would raise ethical dilemmas for teachers, especially in disciplines where sensitive topics are the norm rather than the exception.

To Respect Confidentiality

The issue of self-disclosure leads to another large component of respect: the belief that students have a right to privacy in their dealings with us. Not only does this principle have the weight of ethics behind it, in many cases it also carries the weight of law. Here, however, we are speaking of less egregious violations of privacy, such as discussing a single student's situation with someone who does not have a legitimate interest in that student's case. Practices such as leaving student papers out so that they can be retrieved at the students' convenience might be a violation of this principle because that means students have access to their peers' work (Murray et al., 1996). At my institution, the posting of grades in a public place in any way that would allow an individual's grade to be identified by others is prohibited.

To Model the Best Scholarly and Ethical Standards

A teacher, whether by accident or by design, is more to students than a content expert. The teacher is a model of all that it means to be a scholar, a thinking person. We teach not only what we know but also what we are. Part of the ethics of teaching is to realize this responsibility and to become the best models we can be, which requires some serious self-reflection on our personal standards of scholarship and living. Clark Kerr (1994), in a discussion of ethics in the academic culture, supports this struggle when he says that we are obliged to present a variety of perspectives, our own as well as others, so that the facts can be judged for themselves. This does not imply that you must always take a dispassionate stance; but even, or perhaps especially, when you feel strongly about an issue, it is necessary to demonstrate by your actions that intelligent people can disagree and still remain rational. Giving students the ability to differentiate emotion from reason is an especially important responsibility of instructors, according to Hanson (1996). As she says, "Teachers who can nimbly convey the strengths of a position they in fact oppose, who can clearly display the weaknesses in a position they in fact embrace, are *modeling* a critical engagement from which students may learn their most important lessons" (p. 35).

To Foster Honest Academic Conduct and to Ensure Fair Evaluation

Perhaps the most obvious ethical problems arise in the area of evaluation of student learning, a point echoed in both the AAUP guidelines and those from the STLHE. Instructors are the arbiters of entrance into the profession and are therefore responsible for seeing to it that standards are upheld. However, we are also responsible for guaranteeing that all are given a fair chance of demonstrating their abilities. When we allow academic dishonesty to go unheeded, we violate the rights of all the students who are abiding by the rules. If we fail to establish an evaluation system that accurately assesses the students' progress, we are abdicating our responsibilities to both the students and the profession.

The most important type of fairness for students is interactional fairness (how individuals are treated), followed by procedural fairness (the degree to which there is impartiality in how grades 'are determined and performance evaluated), and finally outcome fairness (the degree to which grades and other outcomes reflect performance) (Rodabaugh, 1996).

The conflicts most often occur when this standard of fairness is pitted against the first responsibility of respecting the individual and fostering independence. The examples that opened this chapter speak to this issue. How important is it that all students be evaluated in the same way? Are we being fairer if we maintain standards and vary conditions of evaluation or if we use individual standards according to the special situation of each student? Which factors are legitimate considerations? There is no agreement on these issues. The best we can do is to continue to discuss and deliberate, alone and in groups, because the conditions under which we operate today will not be the same as those in the future.

To Avoid Exploitation, Harassment, or Discrimination

One of the variables that should be at the forefront of our thinking about the ethics of teaching is the great power discrepancy between teacher and students. Whether we like it or not, whether we seek it or not, by virtue of our position alone, we are invested with a great deal of power over the lives of our students. To make matters worse, many students invest us with even more power than we are entitled to. For this reason, both the AAUP and the STLHE guidelines list one or more principles concerning harassment, exploitation, and discrimination.

Abuse of this power is at the base of many of the ethical traps that lie strewn across our paths as teachers. The very special nature of the relationship between teacher and student is all too easy to abuse (Smith, 1996). The most blatant examples of unethical behavior, those most frequently mentioned in written codes of ethics, deal with exploitation or harassment of various types: sexual, racial, religious, even intellectual. The most egregious of these (and possibly the most debated) is sexual harassment in the form of improper relationships between instructors and students. Braxton and Bayer (1999) list this as the one inviolable norm that retained its importance regardless of type of institution surveyed or discipline represented by the respondent. It could be held forth as the most important norm they identified. The area of the proper relationships between teachers and students is particularly difficult for graduate students, who are both teachers and students; because of their age they occupy a place between their own students and their own professors. Thus they can be either harasser or harassed. Intimate relationships between teachers and students are generally considered inappropriate at least. The best decision for an instructor or a student is to keep the relationship on a professional level as long as the power imbalance exists.

But there are plenty of other forms of exploitation that occur in academia. For example, requiring students to engage in class activities that are unrelated to the educational purposes of the course but that serve our personal ends is an abuse of power. Making derogatory comments about population subgroups is an obvious example of harassment.

Another area of ethical problems involves receiving special considerations or benefits as a result of being in a position of authority. For example, is it a violation of ethics to adopt a less-than-adequate book simply because of an incentive made available by the publisher? How legitimate is it to accept an invitation to a party or other event as the guest of a student in your class? Does it matter if that student is no longer in your class? Does it matter if the event is somehow connected with the student's academic program; for example, a dinner honoring that student's work? We must be aware that by our position alone we will sometimes be put in a compromised situation in all innocence on our part or the student's.

RESPONSIBILITIES TO COLLEAGUES, THE INSTITUTION, AND THE DISCIPLINE

The AAUP and STLHE guidelines go beyond those focused just on our role as teacher; they deal with all aspects of faculty life, including relations with colleagues and responsibilities to the institution for which we work and to the discipline we represent. Taken as a whole, however, the same ideas apply. The standards cluster around the issues of promoting and defending free and honest inquiry, showing respect for others, meeting institutional and professional responsibilities, and continuing to grow as scholars throughout professional life.

Ethical failures in this area include falsification of research results, failure to give due credit to the work of colleagues or students, unwillingness to participate in institutional governance, and unfair or unfounded evaluation of colleagues. More difficult choices might be continuing to teach in a situation that does not meet the needs of the students, such as overcrowded or understaffed classes; ignoring the inadequate teaching of colleagues; taking on so much outside work that work with the students suffers; or refusing to teach a sufficient number of "service" courses to help students graduate in a timely manner (Hogan & Kimmel, 1992; Keith-Spiegel et al., 1996; Kerr, 1994; Matthews, 1991; Tabachnick et al., 1991).

MAKING ETHICAL CHOICES

The array of possibilities for ethical decisions seems endless. How, then, can we avoid stumbling somewhere along the line? Although there are no easy answers, there may be some ways of thinking about our actions as professional that will maximize the possibility of acting ethically. Some very interesting strategies are suggested by several authors in a book on ethical dimensions of teaching edited by Fisch (1996), and the reader is pointed in that direction.

Here, however, I draw the following principles for evaluating one's actions from two sources, the first five from Brown and Krager (1985) and the last from Schön (1983).

1. *Autonomy.* Am I acting in ways that respect freedom and treat others as autonomous?
2. *Nonmalfeasance.* Am I causing harm through either commission or omission?
3. *Beneficence.* Do my actions benefit the other person rather than myself?
4. *Justice.* Do I treat those for whom I am responsible equitably?
5. *Fidelity.* Do I uphold my part of any relationship?
6. *Acting consciously.* What are the assumptions on which I base my actions, and are they valid?

IN CONCLUSION

It is a great privilege to be a teacher. But all great privileges carry great responsibilities as well. Many of those responsibilities are subtle, thrust on us by the expectations of others rather than sought by us. Keeping these six principles in mind won't solve all the ethical dilemmas you face as a teacher, but they might give you a way to reflect on them alone and with other teachers. That reflection should never stop, because conscious reflection on values is perhaps the cornerstone of the ethics of teaching.

Supplementary Reading

American Association of University Professors, "Statement on Professional Ethics," *Academe*, 1987, 73(4), 49.

S. M. Cahn, *Saints and Scamps: Ethics in Academia*, 2nd ed. (Totowa, NJ: Rowman & Littlefield, 1994).

D. Carr, *Professionalism and Ethics in Teaching*, (New York: Routledge, 2000).

L. Fisch (ed.), Ethical Dimensions of College and University Teaching: Understanding and Honoring the Special Relationship Between Teachers and Students [Special issue], *New Directions for Teaching and Learning*, 1996, 66.

C. Kerr, "Knowledge Ethics and the New Academic Culture," *Change*, 1994, 26(1), 8–16.

M. Lewis, *Poisoning the Ivy: The Seven Deadly Sins and Other Vices of Higher Education in America* (Armonk, NY: M. E. Sharpe, 1997).

P. Markie, *A Professor's Duties: Ethical Issues in College Teaching* (Totowa, NJ: Rowman & Littlefield, 1994).

D. Schön, *The Reflective Practitioner* (San Francisco: Jossey-Bass, 1983).

Vitality and Growth Throughout Your Teaching Career

I have just completed my 55th year of teaching psychology at the University of Michigan. I am not as effective as I was 50 years ago because I don't know the students' culture well enough to build good bridges between the course content and what is in their heads. But I continue to be exhilarated going to class and to feel upbeat when I leave. And I continue to pick up new ideas to try out in next term's class. Teaching is still fun for me, and I am depressed that some faculty members (a minority) don't continue to develop and enjoy their teaching. What can be done to foster enjoyment and continued development?

Part of my answer lies in motivation research and theory. Human beings have survived as a species because we are learners. We enjoy learning; we become curious when we confront something more complex than we are accustomed to; we like to confront and master challenges; we take pleasure in becoming and feeling competent.

Human beings are also a social species. We are stimulated by interaction with other human beings; in times of stress, we rely on social support; we learn from one another. Recent primate research suggests that we are also naturally altruistic. We get pleasure from helping others.

Teaching is thus an ideal career. There is infinite complexity and challenge. Each class is different, each student is unique, there is always more to learn. New developments in our discipline, new research and theory about learning and teaching, new technology, and creative new ideas for teaching continually emerge. Our roles often shift as changes in curriculum (such as an emphasis on interdisciplinary team teaching) occur or as new technology presses us to develop new skills or to undertake new forms of distance education. There are never-ending opportunities to grow in competence and understanding.

And teaching is both an intellectual and a social activity. Each term, students come up with new questions, stimulate new insights. Classes offer ever-changing interpersonal dynamics. Getting to know and like each new group provides a continuing source of satisfaction and stimulation. And it is particularly rewarding when former students speak warmly of how we have made a difference in their lives.

The human interactions also offer challenges. There are always some students who seem to be uninterested, some who are confrontational, some who seldom appear. Trying to find out more about the reasons for their behavior, getting to know them better, finding their interests and trying to relate the course material to their interests and goals, involving them in teamwork with other students, demonstrating that you are committed to their learning—all of these may fail, but when something works, what satisfaction!

From the standpoint of motivation theory, it is thus clear that teaching offers great potential for continued vitality, growth, and satisfaction. But these do not come automatically. It is easier for some than for others. Enthusiasm for one's subject matter, an outgoing personality, a commitment to teaching well—these give one a big head start. But good teaching consists of learnable skills, and all your good qualities may go for naught if you teach at a level over the students' heads, are disorganized, evaluate student performance erratically, or lack the skills to implement your good intentions.

And those who are not naturally bubbling over with enthusiasm, outgoing, or even sure that they want to teach can still become effective teachers. In fact, developing as a teacher is a recursive activity. As you develop some skills and strategies that work, they generate positive reactions; this in turn increases your confidence and liking for your students; and that in turn generates more reflection and thinking about teaching as well as interest in developing additional skills, which continues the positive cycle.

HOW CAN YOU DEVELOP EFFECTIVE SKILLS AND STRATEGIES?

The easy answer is "Practice, practice, practice." Practice is important, but just as in sports or music, if one is practicing the wrong technique, one is not likely to improve. Psychologists would add to the "practice" maxim "Practice with feedback—knowledge of results." Moreover, there are additional complications.

1. What should one practice? If I have never heard or seen a particular method in use, such as team learning, I cannot practice it until I have read about it, heard about it, or seen it used. Thus the developing teacher needs to learn about possibly useful skills and strategies.

2. Methods of teaching differ in their difficulty. Which should I try first? As I indicated in the first few chapters of this book, there are a number of useful techniques that are easy to implement and are likely to work well the first time you try them. I advocate using such techniques as problem posting, minute papers, and the two-column method as techniques for stimulating attention and active learning early in the term, explaining their value for learning. These are low-risk, high-payoff, easy-to-use strategies that will help both you and the students build confidence that the class will be a useful learning experience. If you are lecturing or leading discussions, they can help activate student interest and attention. And using them gives you a chance to practice your lecturing or discussion skills in smaller segments.

3. How can I continue to perfect my skills? Here is where practice with feedback comes in. How can we get good feedback on what works and what doesn't?

Now let's examine in more detail how one can learn about what methods or strategies to use and how to get feedback.

LOOKING FOR NEW IDEAS, NEW METHODS, AND ALTERNATIVE STRATEGIES FOR HANDLING PROBLEMS

There are three possibilities: reading, hearing, and seeing.

Reading

I mention this first because you have been reading this book, which was written on the premise that most faculty members have learned how to learn from reading. At the end of each chapter are suggestions for other books or sources that can provide additional insights or suggestions. In addition to the more general resources to which we have referred, there are journals in each discipline dealing with teaching and education in that discipline. Subscribing to such a journal or to one of the newsletters or journals dealing with teaching, such as the *National Teaching and Learning Forum, The Teaching Professor, College Teaching, Change, New Directions for Teaching and Learning,* and *Innovative Higher Education,* will provide regular stimulation to think of new ideas.

Journals dealing with research on learning and teaching are also important sources. *Educational Psychologist, Journal of Higher Education, British Journal of Educational Psychology, Journal of Educational Research, Journal of Educational Psychology,* and similar journals in the United States and other countries can help you avoid falling for the latest fad as well as stimulate you to think about implications for your own teaching.

Hearing, Discussing

Peers are among the best sources of ideas. Talking about teaching with colleagues can be an invaluable source of ideas as well as provide emotional support when a class hasn't gone well. The colleagues need not be in one's own discipline. You will often get interesting ideas from teachers in other disciplines. I often give workshops on teaching for faculty members from a variety of fields. I am kept humble by the typical comment on feedback sheets: "The best thing about the workshop was getting acquainted with and getting ideas from faculty members in other fields who have similar interests and problems."

National and international conferences, such as the International Conference on Improving Learning and Teaching, as well as the disciplinary conventions, also have sessions that provide opportunities for learning.

Seeing, Experiencing

One of the best ways to learn a new skill is to see it performed. As you talk to your colleagues about teaching, ask if they would mind if you observed a class to see how they actually use a particular method and perform a particular skill. Faculty development centers frequently sponsor workshops in which you can see and experience particular methods of teaching or uses of technology. Videotapes demonstrating various methods of teaching are also available.

HOW CAN YOU GET AND USE FEEDBACK TO CONTINUE TO IMPROVE YOUR TEACHING?

Feedback from Student Performance

We haven't taught well if students haven't learned; so the ultimate test of our teaching is evidence of learning. Unfortunately, just as students blame the instructor if they fail to learn, we blame the students for not learning. "The students weren't willing to work." "The class wanted to be entertained rather than taught." "These students should never have been admitted to college. They are simply not prepared for college work."

But, as I have said previously, everyone can learn. Our task is to facilitate learning, and if our students are not learning we have not motivated them, presented material at an appropriate level, arranged activities that would promote effective learning, or taught the students how to learn more effectively.

All too often we pay attention to mistakes, poor papers, and items that were missed on examinations as the basis for assigning grades but fail to think about how we might have better taught the material that was missed. Asking a colleague to look over a few student papers will not only help determine whether your expectations were unreasonable but also result in suggestions for ways of presenting the particular area in which students are not performing well. In every discipline there are some concepts or skills that seem to be particularly difficult to teach. Often, experienced teachers have strategies for overcoming these difficulties. When I team-taught the beginning statistics course with an expert, I learned how to do a better job of teaching standard deviation, which had been difficult for me to get across to my students in the past.

Feedback from Peers

In the preceding paragraphs I have indicated the value of peer feedback on papers and in team teaching. But probably the most common form of feedback from peers is based on classroom visitation. As Centra (1975) demonstrated, classroom observation by peers is a very unreliable source of evidence for decisions about promotion or merit pay. If you know that an observer's judgment is going to affect your career, it is likely that you will either be so anxious that you will not perform at your normal level or that you will put on an especially good performance for the observer's benefit.

Even when the observer is not there to obtain evidence for our personnel files, we are likely to be concerned about what kind of impression we will make. Consequently, the choice of the observer and the nature of the observation are important considerations. Clearly we want an observer who will be helpful and whom we can trust. Bob Wilson at Berkeley found that retired faculty members were particularly helpful, not only because of their experience in teaching the discipline, but also because they were not involved in personnel decisions. Campbell Crockett, former dean at the University of Cincinnati, formed "helping pairs" among new teachers. Here the partners are in the same boat—both learning, presumably helping and being helped by each other—a symmetrical arrangement that reduced the threat.

The usefulness of peer observation depends partly on what you want to find out. If there is a particular aspect of your teaching that you are concerned about, be sure that the observer knows what to look for. Knowing what to look for is in fact a general principle applying to observations. Meeting with the observer to tell him or her before the observation what your goals are and what you are planning to do will increase the helpfulness of the observation. Centra (1993) gives some sample forms used for colleague observations, and you may work out your own observation form using items from these forms.

But the major usefulness of colleague observation comes from your discussion after the observation. Here you have a chance to question, probe for examples, and ask for suggestions.

Feedback from Faculty Development Specialists

Most colleges and universities now have faculty or staff members who are assigned the task of improving instruction. Often they are available to videotape or observe classes. Videotaping would seem on the face of it to be especially helpful. "To see oursels as others see us . . . would frae monie a blunder free us." There is certainly some truth in Robert Burns's familiar saying. Nonetheless, videotaping may not be the best feedback. Research on feedback from films half a century ago demonstrated that when we see our teaching on film (or videotape), we are so captured by our minor mannerisms and appearance that we are likely to miss the critical items of feedback. Only when the videotape is viewed with a consultant who calls our attention to the more important items is seeing the videotape likely to result in improvement.

One method used by many faculty developers is small-group instructional diagnosis (SGID), originated by D. Joseph Clark at the University of Washington. This combines observation with feedback from students.

Typically a consultant using SGID meets before the class with the instructor who desires feedback, to learn about the class and the instructor's goals and needs, as well as to establish the procedures. The instructor explains the procedure to the class, assuring the class that comments will be confidential and used only to help him or her learn how the course is going. After teaching for about half the class period, the instructor turns the class over to the observer and leaves the room. The observer then asks the students to form small groups to discuss their learning experiences in the group. Often the observer asks the groups to answer such questions as "What aspects of the class have helped you learn? What aspects have been unhelpful? What suggestions do you have?"

After about 10 minutes, a member previously designated as reporter gives each group's answers to the questions. The consultant summarizes the reports and asks for student comments. After the class, the consultant discusses the reports with the teacher and offers encouragement, suggestions if the instructor is unsure about what alternatives might help, and clarification if the instructor finds some comments confusing or contradictory. At the next class meeting, the instructor discusses the feedback, indicating what changes will be made or why certain things cannot be changed.

Feedback from Students

Probably the most familiar form of feedback from students is student ratings of teaching. Student ratings are now administered in almost all colleges and universities in the United States and are becoming common in other countries. However, their primary purpose is often to collect data for personnel evaluation, and this complicates and sometimes conflicts with their usefulness for improving teaching. One problem is that those who use student ratings for personnel purposes often feel (unjustifiably) that they need to use a standard form that can be used to compare teachers, across disciplines, in a variety of types of classes, in required as well as elective courses, in large and small classes, and in a variety of contexts. The result is that the questions on the form are so general that they may be irrelevant to a particular class and, even if relevant, are worded so generally that they offer little guidance for improvement. Moreover, they are typically given at the end of the semester, when it is too late to make much improvement for the class from which the feedback comes.

An additional barrier to the use of these forms for improvement is that faculty members are likely to be defensive about low ratings, rejecting the validity of the student responses. Among the common defenses are such responses as

- "Students aren't competent observers or respondents."
- "Students want easy courses. I set high standards."
- "Student ratings are determined primarily by the instructor's personality rather than by competence."

■ "Students may give low ratings now but will appreciate my
   teaching after they've been out of college a few years."

As you may suspect, each of these excuses is invalid. There has
been more research on student ratings than on any other topic—
something over 2,000 studies. Here's what the research says
about each of the aforementioned rationalizations.*

1. *The validity of student ratings.* Because we've said that you can't
be a good teacher unless students have learned, the question
becomes: Can students judge whether or not they are learning?
The answer is clearly "yes." In multisection courses, average ratings of the value of the course or of the teacher's effectiveness correlate significantly with average scores on achievement tests, both
final examinations and standardized tests. Moreover, they correlate with other course outcomes, such as motivation for further
learning or measures of attitude change. In addition, when an
instructor is teaching more than one section or more than one
course, student ratings correlate well with the instructor's own
judgments of which classes were taught most successfully.

2. *Hard versus easy courses.* Large national studies reveal that, on
the average, more difficult courses are given higher student ratings than easy courses. Very likely this is a curvilinear relationship. Although students prefer challenging courses, courses that
are so difficult that students cannot meet the challenge will
receive lower ratings (Marsh, 2001).

3. *Teacher personality.* There is little doubt that some personality
characteristics affect ratings. Enthusiastic, expressive, warm,
friendly teachers will in general receive higher ratings than teachers who are more reserved and distant from their students.
However, these personality characteristics are also related to student learning. This doesn't mean that you need to change your
personality to become effective, but if you don't have an outgoing, warm personality, you can still be effective and could become
even more effective by, for example, using more gestures and
learning student names.

---

* Probably the best reviews of this research may be found in Perry and Smart
(1997).

4. *I'll be appreciated later.* I often wish this were true when I get a negative comment (and there are always a few). But both the classic studies by Drucker and Remmers (1951) half a century ago and my more recent ones found that alumni ratings of faculty members correlate highly with those given 10 years or more before. So there are very likely some cases when there is delayed appreciation of what a teacher did, but it's the exception rather than the rule.

So, how can we use student ratings for continued growth in teaching effectiveness?

Keys to Improvement with Feedback from Students

1. *Get the feedback early enough to make a difference for the students who give it.* I typically collect feedback from students after the third or fourth week of the term. Others collect ratings about the middle of the term. In either case, the important thing is that you have a chance to adjust to this particular class. (Remember that each class is different. What works well in one class may not in the next.) As I mentioned with respect to SGID, I review the feedback with the class, indicating which suggestions I intend to implement, and I discuss differences of opinion among students. (Usually some students want more discussion, some want less, and all assume that everyone else feels as they do.) I also explain why I am not adopting some suggestions and give the reasons why I believe that what I have done, and will do, is important for their learning.

2. *Don't feel that you need to use the standard form.* If you want ratings, choose items that will be useful to you. The advantage of ratings is that you can cover a number of aspects of teaching relatively quickly. But open-ended questions are often equally or more useful. Usually I simply ask students to write on two questions:

- "What have you liked about the course so far?" or "What aspects of the course have been valuable for your learning so far?"

- "What suggestions do you have for improvement?"

Sometimes I use questions such as

- "What have you done that has helped you learn effectively in this course?"
- "What do you need to do to improve your learning in this course?"
- "What have you done to help other students in the course to learn?" (Helping other learners not only provides altruistic satisfaction but also aids one's own learning. And this is true for teachers as well.)
- "What has the teacher done that has helped you learn?"
- "What would you like the teacher to do that would facilitate your learning?"

If I am teaching a large multisection course, I sometimes ask each section to choose two representatives to meet with me to provide feedback. The representatives are given a few minutes at the end of their discussion section to talk with their classmates about suggestions, and then meet with me. Because they can say, "Some students say . . . ," they feel free to relay negative as well as positive reactions, and the face-to-face meeting gives me a chance to question more deeply as well as to get their suggestions about what to do.

Feedback need not be limited to midterm or end-of-term assessment. You can ask students for comments on a particular class session in the last five minutes of class.

3. *Supplement end-of-course ratings.* All faculty members in our college are required to collect student ratings at the end of the term. Five items are mandatory, and the rest of the items may be chosen by the department and instructor from a large list of possible items, including some open-ended items. I choose two types of items—those having to do with goals of education and those dealing with specific behaviors.

The items with respect to goals that I choose are usually something like

- "I became more interested in the subject matter of this course."

- "My intellectual curiosity has been stimulated by this course."
- "I am learning to think more clearly about the area of this course."

Behavioral items include

- "The instructor knew students' names."
- "The instructor gestures with hands and arms."
- "The instructor gives multiple examples."
- "The instructor points out practical applications."
- "The instructor encourages student questions and student comments."
- "The instructor signals transitions to a new topic."

Although faculty members often make some improvements as a result of feedback from student ratings, Murray (1983, 1997) has shown that improvement is much more likely to occur when behavioral items are used rather than more generic abstract items.

Whether or not there is a choice of items, I find it helpful to ask students to rate or comment on specific aspects of the course. Some of these change from term to term whereas some carry over if they have worked well. These include such aspects as the syllabus, the team research project, the textbook they used, videotapes, field trips, and journals.

Consultation

Whatever form of feedback you use, research clearly shows that you are more likely to improve if you discuss the feedback with someone. Your consultant can help you put ratings in perspective, pointing out the positives and reducing the sting of the negatives. (I and, I think, most of us tend to note and remember the negative comments more than the positives.) The consultant can also suggest strategies to try that may help deal with areas that seem to need improvement. A consultant can offer support and encouragement. All too often, poor student ratings lead to defensiveness, dislike for students, and poorer teaching rather than to improvement. In such cases, hope is important, and a consultant can help promote hope.

Classroom Assessment and Research

A little over a decade ago, Pat Cross and Tom Angelo compiled a set of 30 techniques to help faculty members monitor student learning. Five years later, they published a second edition of classroom assessment techniques, including 50 techniques (Angelo & Cross, 1993). Some of these, such as the minute paper and one-sentence summary, have been described earlier in this textbook. But you cannot fail to find among the 50 several that will help you get feedback on your students' learning, including directed paraphrasing, misconception check, pro and con grid, concept maps, course-related self-confidence surveys, and "what's the principle?"

Classroom Research (Cross & Steadman, 1996) is an example of the scholarship of teaching—systematically evaluating methods, approaches, or techniques that you are using in your teaching. In classroom research you may use some of the classroom assessment techniques to get evidence about the effectiveness of an innovation you are trying (or of something you have been doing for a long time). In addition, you may use regular classroom tests or other measures of achievement. You may even carry out an experiment comparing two alternative methods or the method you formerly used with one you would like to try.

Both classroom assessment techniques and classroom research not only provide useful data but also are motivating. They stimulate you to think about your teaching and what you expect students to gain from it. They enrich both your conceptual thinking about education and your repertoire of skills.

Self-Evaluation

Our emphasis on gathering data and getting consultation may have implied that improvement depends on external sources of feedback and help. But self-evaluation is also a potential resource for continued growth—perhaps the most important of all. In recent years, portfolio assessment has become a major element in evaluating teaching. Although portfolios have been used primarily in evaluation for personnel decisions, preparing and maintaining a portfolio can be an important aid to improvement even if it won't be used for promotion or salary purposes. The portfolio provides a stimulus to thinking about your teaching, about your goals and the evidence that will tell you how well you've achieved your goals—all this will contribute to your continued development.* Preparing a portfolio takes time, but all useful activities take time. If you feel that you don't have time for a portfolio, at least keep a journal in which you write regularly about your teaching, your students, and your classes.

IN CONCLUSION

The great thing about teaching is that there is always more to learn. The various sources of ideas and feedback that I have described help us to improve. As we improve, our students respond more positively, and their increased interest and enthusiasm sparks us to even more effort and enjoyment. Obviously, the course is not always onward and upward. There are moments of frustration and despair, but there are enough good times to help us through those that are not so good. And as we gain additional skill and assurance, our relations with students become more satisfying.

Most of this book has dealt with interactions in the classroom, but research has shown that those faculty members who have the most impact on students spend time with students outside the classroom. This is not only important for the students' development, it also contributes to one's continuing vitality as a teacher.

---

* As compared with earlier editions of *Teaching Tips,* this chapter has paid much less attention to evaluation for tenure or for post-tenure review. I have deliberately focused on improvement because I believe that a teacher who uses the methods discussed here for continual development will be well equipped for personnel evaluations.

Our interactions with students and faculty are critical to the development of a community of learners—teachers and students, learners all.

Over the years, I have visited hundreds of colleges and universities, both in this country and in others. What most impresses me is that, no matter how difficult the circumstances, there are always some vital, effective teachers. They come in no one personality, no one discipline, no one institution. Somehow teachers find a way to cope with adverse environments and are able to stimulate effective learning. They enjoy teaching despite unfavorable circumstances.

This chapter has discussed at length ways to grow. However much you are intrigued by new possibilities, it is important not to forget what you enjoy doing. My final advice is "HAVE FUN!"

As I look back at my discussion of basic human motives at the beginning of this chapter, I think once again, "What a marvelous career teaching provides for satisfying our fundamental human needs!"

In Robert Bolt's *A Man for All Seasons,* Sir Thomas More assures his protégé that, if he becomes a teacher, he will be an outstanding teacher. "But if I were," demurs the ambitious young man, "who would know it?" More replies, "You, your friends, your students, God. Not a bad audience that."*

Not a bad audience indeed!

Supplementary Reading

The many books recommended as supplementary reading in previous chapters are relevant to your life-long learning, but to save you the trouble of looking back, I will mention here once again several books that nicely cover the major areas of teaching:

J. Biggs, *Teaching for Quality Learning at University* (Buckingham, UK: SRHE and Open University Press, 1999).

B. G. Davis, *Tools for Teaching,* 2nd ed. (San Francisco: Jossey-Bass, 1993).

---

* For the reference to Sir Thomas More I am indebted to Nick Skinner, who used these words in concluding his address as recipient of the Canadian Psychological Association Award for Distinguished Contribution to Psychology in Education and Training (Skinner, 2001).

J. Lowman, *Mastering the Techniques of Teaching*, 2nd ed. (San Francisco: Jossey-Bass, 1995).

P. Ramsden, *Learning to Teach in Higher Education* (London and New York: Routledge, 1992).

W. A. Wright and associates, *Teaching Improvement Practices: Successful Strategies for Higher Education* (Bolton, MA: Anker, 1995).

Stephen Brookfield's *Becoming a Critically Reflective Teacher* (San Francisco: Jossey-Bass, 1995) will help you with one of the most important aspects of your development—reflecting on your experience—and fits nicely with your use of classroom assessment techniques.

I am probably biased, but I do think that *Student Motivation, Cognition, and Learning: Essays in Honor of Wilbert J. McKeachie*, edited by Paul Pintrich, Donald Brown, and Claire Ellen Weinstein (Hillsdale, NJ: Erlbaum, 1994), gives you an excellent introduction to a variety of research areas relevant to teaching.

A briefer useful resource is Janet G. Donald and Arthur M. Sullivan (eds.), *Using Research to Improve Teaching* [Special issue], *New Directions for Teaching and Learning*, 1985, *23*.

Three volumes are particularly helpful in the area of evaluation and assessment of teaching:

J. Centra, *Reflective Evaluation: Enhancing Teaching and Determining Faculty Effectiveness* (San Francisco: Jossey-Bass, 1993).

R. P. Perry and J. C. Smart (eds.), *Effective Teaching in Higher Education: Research and Practice* (New York: Agathon, 1997).

P. Seldin and associates, *Changing Practices in Evaluating Teaching* (Bolton, MA: Anker, 1999).

Finally, for a thoughtful, stimulating perspective differing from American cognitivist/constructivist approaches, read Ference Marton and Shirley Booth's *Learning and Awareness* (Mahwah, NJ: Erlbaum, 1997). Marton's phenomenographic research at Gothenburg, Sweden, has been enormously influential in thinking about learning and teaching in higher education.

REFERENCES

Adams, M. (1992). Cultural inclusion in the American college classroom. *New Directions for Teaching and Learning, 49,* 5–17.

Adelman, C. (1999). *The new college course map and transcript files: Changes in course-taking and achievement, 1972–1993* (2nd ed., pp. 198–204). Washington, DC: U.S. Department of Education.

Alexander, P. A. (1995). Superimposing a situation-specific and domain-specific perspective on an account of self-regulated learning. *Educational Psychologist, 30,* 189–193.

Alexander, P. A., & Judy, J. E. (1988). The interaction of domain-specific and strategic knowledge in academic performance. *Review of Educational Research, 58*(4), 375–404.

Alger, J., Chapa, J., Gudeman, R., Marin, P., Maruyama, G., Milem, J., Moreno, H., & Wilds, D. (2000). *Does diversity make a difference?* Washington, DC: American Council on Education and American Association of University Professors.

Allen, B. P., & Niss, J. F. (1990). A chill in the college classroom? *Phi Delta Kappan, 71,* 607–609.

Alverno College Faculty. (1994). *Student Assessment Learning at Alverno College.* Milwaukee, WI: Alverno Productions.

American Association of University Professors (AAUP). (1987). Statement on professional ethics. *Academe, 73*(4), 49.

American Council on Education and University of California at Los Angeles Higher Education Research Council. (1996). *The American freshman: National norms for fall 1996.* Washington, DC: American Council on Education.

Anderson, J. A., & Adams, M. (1992). Acknowledging the learning styles of diverse populations: Implications for instructional design. *New Directions for Teaching and Learning, 49,* 19–33.

Anderson, L. W., & Krathwohl, D. R. (Eds.). (2001). *A taxonomy for learning, teaching, and assessment: A revision of Bloom's taxonomy of educational objectives.* New York: Longman.

Andre, T. (1987). Questions and learning from reading. *Questioning Exchange, 1*(1), 47–86.

Angelo, T. A., & Cross, K. P. (1993). *Classroom assessment techniques: A handbook for college faculty* (2nd ed.). San Francisco: Jossey-Bass.

Annis, L. F. (1981). Effect of preference for assigned lecture notes on student achievement. *Journal of Educational Research, 74,* 179–181.

———. (1983a). The processes and effects of peer tutoring. *Human Learning, 2,* 39–47.

————. (1983b). *Study techniques.* Dubuque: Wm. C. Brown.

Arce, J., & Betancourt, R. (1997). Student-designed experiments in scientific lab instruction. *Journal of College Science Teaching, 27,* 114–118.

Asante, M. K. (1987). *The Afrocentric idea.* Philadelphia: Temple University Press.

————. (1988). *Afrocentricity.* Trenton, NJ: Africa World Press.

Association of American Colleges and Universities. (2000). *Americans see many benefits to diversity in higher education, finds first-ever national poll on topic* [Online]. Available: www.aacu-edu.org/Initiatives/ legacies.html

Astin, A. (1975). *Preventing students from dropping out.* San Francisco: Jossey-Bass.

Astin, A. W., & Astin, H. S. (1999). *Meaning and spirituality in the lives of college faculty: A study of values, authenticity, and stress.* Los Angeles: UCLA Higher Education Research Institute.

Bargh, J. A., & Schul, Y. (1980). On the cognitive benefits of teaching. *Journal of Educational Psychology, 72*(5), 593–604.

Barr, R. B., & Tagg, J. (1995). From teaching to learning—A new paradigm for undergraduate education. *Change, 27,* 12–25.

Baxter Magolda, M. B. (1992). *Knowing and reasoning in college: Gender-related patterns in students' intellectual development.* San Francisco: Jossey-Bass.

Beach, R., & Bridwell, L. (1984). Learning through writing: A rationale for writing across the curriculum. In A. Pellegrini & T. Yawkey (Eds.), *The development of oral and written language in social contexts.* Norwood, NJ: Ablex.

Belenky, M. F., Clinchy, B. M., Goldberger, N. R., & Tarule, J. M. (1986). *Women's ways of knowing: The development of self, voice, and mind.* New York: Basic Books.

Benjamin, L. (1991). Personalization and active learning in the large introductory psychology class. *Teaching of Psychology, 18*(2), 68–74.

Berge, Z. (2000). *Concerns of online teachers in higher education* [Online]. Available: http://www.emoderators.com/zberge/iste98.html

Berlyne, D. E. (1954a). An experimental study of human curiosity. *British Journal of Psychology, 45,* 256–265.

————. (1954b). A theory of human curiosity. *British Journal of Psychology, 45,* 180–181.

————. (1960). *Conflict, arousal, and curiosity.* New York: McGraw-Hill.

Bieron, J. F., & Dinan, F. J. (2000). Not your ordinary lab day. *Journal of College Science Teaching, 30*(1), 44–47.

Biggs, J. (1999). *Teaching for quality learning at university.* Philadelphia: Buckingham.

Blackwell, J. E. (1990). Operationalizing faculty diversity. *AAHE Bulletin, 42*(10), 8–9.

Bligh, D. (2000). *What's the use of lectures?* San Francisco: Jossey-Bass.

Bloom, B. S. (Ed.). (1956). *Taxonomy of educational objectives, handbook I: Cognitive domain.* New York: Longmans, Green.

Bloom, B. S., Englehart, M. D., Furst, E. J., & Krathwohl, D. R. (1956). *Taxonomy of educational objectives: Cognitive domain.* New York: McKay.

Boekaerts, M. (1995). Self-regulated learning: Bridging the gap between metacognitive and metamotivational theories. *Educational Psychologist, 30,* 195–200.

Boekaerts, M., & Niemivirta, M. (2000). Self-regulation in learning: Finding a balance between learning- and ego-protective goals. In M. Boekaerts, P. R. Pintrich, & M. Zeidner (Eds.), *Handbook of self-regulation* (pp. 417–450). San Diego: Academic Press.

Boekaerts, M., Pintrich, P. R., & Zeidner, M. (Eds.). (2000). *Handbook of self-regulation.* San Diego: Academic Press.

Bonk, C. J., & Cunningham, D. J. (1998). Searching for learner-centered, constructivist, and sociocultural components of collaborative educational learning tools. In C. J. Bonk & S. K. King (Eds.), *Electronic collaborators: Learner-centered technologies for literacy, apprenticeship, and discourse* (pp. 25–50). Mahwah, NJ: Erlbaum.

Border, L. B., & Chism, N. V. N. (Eds.). (1992). Teaching for diversity [Special issue]. *New Directions for Teaching and Learning, 49.*

Boss, J. (1994). The effect of community service on the moral development of college ethics students. *Journal of Moral Education, 23,* 183–198.

Bowser, B. P., Jones, T., & Young, G. A. (Eds.). (1995). *Toward the multicultural university.* Westport, CT: Praeger.

Boyer, E. (1990). *Scholarship reconsidered: Priorities of the professoriate.* Princeton, NJ: Carnegie Foundation for the Advancement of Teaching.

Brandell, M., & Hinck, S. (1997). Service learning: Connecting citizenship with the classroom. *NASSP Bulletin, 81,* 49–56.

Braxton, J. M., & Bayer, A. (1999). *Faculty misconduct in collegiate teaching.* Baltimore: Johns Hopkins Press.

Bridges, E. M., & Hallinger, P. (1996). Problem-based learning in leadership education. *New Directions for Teaching and Learning, 68,* 53–61.

Brown, G. (1978). *Lecturing and explaining.* London: Methuen.

Brown, G., & Atkins, M. (1988). *Effective teaching in higher education.* London: Methuen.

Brown, R. D., & Krager, L. (1985). Ethical issues in graduate education: Faculty and student responsibilities. *Journal of Higher Education, 56,* 403–418.

Brown, S., & Glassner, A. (Eds.). (1999). *Assessment matters in higher education: Choosing and using diverse approaches.* Buckingham, UK: Open University Press.

Cahn, S. (1994). *Saints and scamps: Ethics in academia.* Lanham, MA: Rowan and Littlefield Publishers, Inc.

Cambridge, B. (1996). Looking ahead. *AAHE Bulletin, 10–11.*

Campbell, R. (1999). Mouths, machines, and minds. *The Psychologist, 12,* 446–449.

Caron, M. D., Whitbourne, S. K., & Halgin, R. P. (1992). Fraudulent excuse making among college students. *Teaching of Psychology, 19*(2), 90–93.

Carr, D. (2000). *Professionalism and ethics in teaching.* New York: Routledge.

Center for Teaching and Learning. (1998). *Teaching for inclusion.* Chapel Hill, NC: University of North Carolina at Chapel Hill.

Centra, J. A. (1975). Colleagues as raters of classroom instruction. *Journal of Higher Education, 46,* 327–337.

————. (1993). *Reflective faculty evaluation: Enhancing teaching and determining faculty effectiveness.* San Francisco: Jossey-Bass.

Champagne, A. B., Klofper, L. E., & Anderson, J. H. (1980). Factors influencing the learning of classical mechanics. *American Journal of Physics, 48,* 1074–1079.

Chang, T. M., Crombag, H. F., van der Drift, K. D. J. M., & Moonen, J. M. (1983). *Distance learning: On the design of an open university.* Boston: Kluwer-Nijhoff.

Chesler, M. A. (1994). *Perceptions of faculty behavior by students of color.* Ann Arbor, MI: Center for Research on Learning and Teaching, University of Michigan [Online]. Available: http://www.crlt.umich.edu/occ7.html

Chi, M. T. H., Glaser, R., & Farr, M. J. (Eds.). (1988). *The nature of expertise.* Hillsdale, NJ: Erlbaum.

Chronicle of Higher Education. (September 1, 2000a). *The Chronicle of Higher Education 2000-01 almanac issue, 47*(1).

Chronicle of Higher Education. (June 2, 2000b). *College campuses will grow more diverse, report says, 46*(27), A51.

Churchill, L. R. (1982). The teaching of ethics and moral values in teaching. *Journal of Higher Education, 53*(3), 296–306.

Clark, R. E. (1994a). Media and method. *Educational Technology Research and Development, 42*(3), 7-10.

————. (1994b). Media will never influence learning. *Educational Technology, Research and Development, 42*(2), 21–29.

Cohen, P., Kulik, J., & Kulik, C.-L. (1982). Educational outcomes of tutoring: A meta-analysis of findings. *American Educational Research Journal, 19*(2), 237–248.

Collett, J., & Serrano, B. (1992). Stirring it up: The inclusive classroom. *New Directions for Teaching and Learning, 49,* 35–48.

Collins, A. (1977). Processes in acquiring knowledge. In R. C. Anderson, R. J. Spiro, & W. E. Montague (Eds.), *Schooling and the acquisition of knowledge* (pp. 339–363). Hillsdale, NJ: Erlbaum.

Collins, A., & Stevens, A. L. (1982). Goals and strategies of inquiry teaching. In R. Glaser (Ed.), *Advances in instructional psychology* (pp. 65–119). Hillsdale, NJ: Erlbaum.

Coppola, B. P. (1995). Progress in practice: Using concepts from motivation and self-regulated learning research to improve chemistry instruction. *New Directions for Teaching and Learning, 63,* 87–96.

————. (2000). Targeting entry points for ethics in chemistry teaching and learning. *Journal of Chemical Education, 77,* 1506–1511.

Coppola, B. P., Ege, S. N., & Lawton, R. G. (1997). The University of Michigan undergraduate chemistry curriculum: 2. Instructional strategies and assessment. *Journal of Chemical Education, 74,* 84–94.

Coppola, B. P., & Lawton, R. G. (1995). 'Who has the same substance that I have?' A blueprint for collaborative learning activities. *Journal of Chemical Education, 72,* 1120–1122.

Costin, F. (1972). Three-choice versus four-choice items: Implications for reliability and validity of objective achievement tests. *Educational and Psychological Measurement, 32,* 1035–1038.

Covington, M. V. (1999). Caring about learning: The nature and nurture of subject-matter appreciation. *Educational Psychologist, 34,* 127–136.

Creed, T. (1997). PowerPoint, No! Cyberspace, Yes. *National Teaching and Learning Forum, 6*(4), 5–7.

Cronbach, L. J., & Snow, R. E. (1977). *Aptitudes and instructional methods: A handbook for research on interaction.* New York: Irvington.

Cross, K. P., & Steadman, M. H. (1996). *Classroom research: Implementing the scholarship of teaching.* San Francisco: Jossey-Bass.

Darder, A. (1996). Creating the conditions for cultural democracy in the classroom. In C. Turner, M. Garcia, A. Nora, & L. Rendon (Eds.), *Racial and ethnic diversity in higher education* (pp. 134–149). New York: Simon & Schuster.

Day, R. S. (1980). Teaching from notes: Some cognitive consequences. *New Directions for Teaching and Learning, 2,* 95–112.

Deci, E., & Ryan, R. M. (1985). *Intrinsic motivation and self-determination in human behavior.* New York: Plenum.

Deutsch, M. (1949). An experimental study of the effects of cooperation and competition upon group processes. *Human Relations, 2,* 199–232.

Dewey, R. (1995, March). Finding the right introductory psychology textbook. *APS Observer,* 32–35.

Dillon, J. T. (1982). The effect of questions in education and other enterprises. *Journal of Curriculum Studies, 14,* 127–152.

Domin, D. S. (1999). A review of laboratory instruction styles. *Journal of Chemical Education, 76*, 543–547.

Donald, J. G. (1995). Disciplinary differences in knowledge validation. *New Directions for Teaching and Learning, 64*, 7–17.

Drucker, A. J., & Remmers, H. H. (1951). Do alumni and students differ in their attitudes toward instructors? *Journal of Educational Psychology, 42*, 129–143.

Duchastel, P. C., & Merrill, P. F. (1973). The effects of behavioral objectives on learning: A review of empirical studies. *Review of Educational Research, 43*, 53–69.

D'Ydewalle, G., Swerts, A., & de Corte, E. (1983). Study time and test performance as a function of test expectations. *Contemporary Educational Psychology, 8*(1), 55–67.

Eccles, J. S., Midgley, C., Wigfield, A., Buchanan, C. M., Reuman, D., Flanagan, C., & MacIver, D. (1993). Development during adolescence: The impact of stage-environment fit on young adolescents' experiences in schools and in families. *American Psychologist, 48*, 90–101.

Ehrmann, Stephen C. (1995, March/April). Asking the right questions: What does research tell us about technology and higher learning? *Change, 27*(2), 20–27.

Elshout, J. J. (1987). Problem solving and education. In E. DeCorte, H. Lodewijks, R. Permentier, & P. Span (Eds.), *Learning and instruction: European research in an international context* (Vol. 1). Oxford: Leuven University Press/Pergamon Press.

Entwistle, N. J. (1992). Student learning and study strategies. In B. R. Clark & G. Neave (Eds.), *Encyclopedia of higher education*. Oxford: Pergamon.

Eriksen, S. C. (1983). Private measures of good teaching. *Teaching of Psychology, 10*, 133–136.

Falk, D. (1995, Winter). Preflection. A strategy for enhancing reflection. *NSEE Quarterly, 13*.

Feldman, K. A., & Newcomb, T. M. (1969). *The impact of college on students* (Vol. 2). San Francisco: Jossey-Bass.

Ferguson, M. (1990). The role of faculty in increasing student retention. *College and University, 65*, 127–134.

Fisch, L. (Ed.). (1996). Ethical dimensions of college and university teaching: Understanding and honoring the special relationship between teachers and students [Special issue]. *New Directions for Teaching and Learning, 66*.

Flavell, J. H. (1979). Metacognition and cognitive mentoring: A new area of cognitive-developmental inquiry. *American Psychologist, 34*, 906–911.

Foos, P. W., & Fisher, R. P. (1988). Using tests as learning opportunities. *Journal of Educational Psychology, 88*(2), 179–183.

Friedman, E. G., Kolmar, W. K., Flint, C. B., & Rothenberg, P. (1996). *Creating an inclusive curriculum.* New York: Teachers College Press.

Gamson, W. A. (1966). *SIMSOC: A manual for participants.* Ann Arbor, MI: Campus Publishers.

Gay, G. (1995). Curriculum theory and multicultural education. In J. A. Banks & C. A. Banks (Eds.), *Handbook of research on multicultural education* (pp. 25–43). New York: Simon & Schuster Macmillan.

Gibbs, G. (1999). Using assessment strategically to change the way students learn. In S. Brown & A. Glassner (Eds.), *Assessment matters in higher education: Choosing and using diverse approaches* (pp. 41–54). Buckingham, UK: Society for Research in Higher Education/Open University Press.

Goldschmid, M. L. (1971). The learning cell: An instructional innovation. *Learning and Development, 2*(5), 1–6.

———. (1975, May). *When students teach students.* Paper presented at the International Conference on Improving University Teaching, Heidelberg, Germany.

Goldschmid, M. L., & Shore, B. M. (1974). The learning cell: A field test of an educational innovation. In W. A. Verreck (Ed.), *Methodological problems in research and development in higher education* (pp. 218–236). Amsterdam: Swets and Zeitlinger.

Grasha, A., & Yangarber-Kicks, N. (2000). Integrating teaching styles and learning styles with instructional technology. *College Teaching, 48*(1), 2–10.

Grauerholz, E., & Copenhaver, S. (1994). When the personal becomes problematic: The ethics of using experiential teaching methods. *Teaching Sociology, 22*(4), 319–327.

Greeno, J. G. (1991). Number sense as situated knowing in a conceptual domain. *Research in Mathematical Education, 22*, 170–218.

Gruber, H. E., & Weitman, M. (1960, April). *Cognitive processes in higher education: Curiosity and critical thinking.* Paper read at Western Psychological Association, San Jose, CA.

———. (1962, April). *Self-directed study: Experiments in higher education* (Report No. 19). Boulder: University of Colorado, Behavior Research Laboratory.

Gurin, P. (1999). Expert report of Patricia Gurin. In *The compelling need for diversity in higher education, Gratz et al. v. Bollinger, et al.* Ann Arbor, MI: University of Michigan [Online]. Available: http://www.umich.edu/~urel/admissions/legal/expert/gurintoc/html

Hagen, A. S., & Weinstein, C. E. (1995). Achievement goals, self-regulated learning, and the role of classroom context. *New Directions for Teaching and Learning, 63,* 43–56.

Haines, D. B., & McKeachie, W. J. (1967). Cooperative vs. competitive discussion methods in teaching introductory psychology. *Journal of Educational Psychology, 58,* 386–390.

Hall, R. M., & Sandler, B. R. (1982). *The classroom climate: A chilly one for women?* Project on the Status and Education of Women. Washington, DC: Association of American Colleges.

Halpern, D. F. (1996). *Thought and knowledge: An introduction to critical thinking.* Mahwah, NJ: Erlbaum.

Hannafin, M., Land, S., & Oliver, K. (1999). Open learning environments: Foundations, methods, and models. In C. M. Reigeluth (Ed.), *Instructional-design theories and models* (Vol. 2, pp. 115–140). Mahwah, NJ: Erlbaum.

Hanson, K. (1996). Between apathy and advocacy: Teaching and modeling ethical reflection. *New Directions for Teaching and Learning, 66,* 33–36.

Harasim, L. (1990). Online education: An environment for collaboration and intellectual amplification. In L. Harasim (Ed.), *Online education: Perspectives on a new environment* (pp. 39–64). New York: Praeger.

———. (1993). Networlds: Networks as a social space. In L. M. Harasim (Ed.), *Global networks* (pp. 15–34). Cambridge: MIT Press.

Harter, S. (1978). Effective motivation reconsidered: Toward a developmental model. *Human Development, 21,* 34–64.

Hartley, J., & Davies, I. K. (1978). Note-taking: A critical review. *Programmed Learning and Educational Technology, 15,* 207–224.

Hartman, F. R. (1961). Recognition learning under multiple channel presentation and testing conditions. *Audio-Visual Communication Review, 9,* 24–43.

Hartman, H. J. (1990). Factors affecting the tutoring process. *Journal of Developmental Education, 14*(2), 2–6.

Hartman, N. (1989). Syndicate based peer group learning: An alternative process. *South African Journal of Higher Education, 3,* 98–106.

Helton, P. (2000, Fall). Diversifying the curriculum: A study of faculty involvement. *Diversity Digest* [Online]. Available: http://www.inform.umd.edu/diversityweb/Digest/F00/research.html

Henderson, L., & Buising, C. (2000). A research-based molecular biology laboratory. *Journal of College Science Teaching, 30*(5), 322–327.

Hettich, P. (1990). Journal writing: Old fare or nouvelle cuisine? *Teaching of Psychology, 17,* 36–39.

Higginbotham, C., Pike, C. F., & Rice, J. K. (1998). Spectroscopy in sol-gel matrices: An open-ended laboratory experience for upper-level undergraduates. *Journal of Chemical Education, 75,* 461.

Hillocks, G. (1982). The interaction of instruction, teacher comment, and revision in teaching the composing process. *Research in Teaching of English, 16,* 261–278.

Hodgkinson, H. L. (1995). Demographic imperatives for the future. In B. P. Bowser, T. Jones, & G. A. Young (Eds.), *Toward the multicultural university* (pp. 3–19). Westport, CT: Praeger.

Hofer, B. (1997). *The development of personal epistemology: Dimensions, disciplinary differences, and instructional practices.* Unpublished doctoral thesis, University of Michigan.

Hofer, B. K., Yu, S. L., & Pintrich, P. R. (1998). Teaching college students to be self-regulated learners. In D. H. Schunk & B. J. Zimmerman (Eds.), *Self-regulated learning: From teaching to self-reflective practice* (pp. 57–85.) New York: Guilford.

Hofstede, G. (1986). Cultural differences in teaching and learning. *International Journal of Intercultural Relations, 10,* 301–320.

Hofstein, A., & Lunetta, V. N. (1982). The role of the laboratory in science teaching: Neglected aspects of research. *Review of Educational Research, 52*(2), 201–217.

Hogan, P., & Kimmel, A. (1992). Ethical teaching of psychology: One department's attempts at self-regulation. *Teaching of Psychology, 19*(4), 205–210.

Houston, J. P. (1983). Alternate test forms as a means of reducing multiple-choice answer copying in the classroom. *Journal of Educational Psychology, 75*(4), 572–575.

Hovland, C. I. (Ed.). (1957). *The order of presentation in persuasion.* New Haven, CT: Yale University Press.

Hurtado, S. (1997). How diversity affects teaching and learning. *Educational Record, 77*(4), 27–29.

Husman, J., Derryberry, P. W., & Crowson, H. M. (2000, August). *Instrumentality: An important motivational construct for education?* Poster presented at the annual meeting of the American Psychological Association, Washington, DC.

Irvine, J. J., & York, D. E. (1995). Learning styles and culturally diverse learners: A literature review. In J. A. Banks & C. A. Banks (Eds.), *Handbook of research on multicultural education* (pp. 484–497). New York: Simon & Schuster Macmillan.

Johnson, D. M. (1975). Increasing originality on essay examinations in psychology. *Teaching of Psychology, 2,* 99–102.

Johnson, D. W., & Johnson, R. T. (1975). *Learning together and alone:*

Cooperation, competition and individualization. Englewood Cliffs, NJ: Prentice-Hall.

Johnson, D. W., Maruyama, G., Johnson, R., Nelson, D., & Skon, L. (1981). The effects of cooperative, competitive, and individualistic goal structures on achievement: A meta-analysis. *Psychological Bulletin, 89,* 47–62.

Johnstone, D. B. (1992). *Learning productivity: A new imperative for American higher education* [Monograph]. State University of New York, Studies in Public Higher Education [Edited Version Online]. Available: http://192.52.179.128/program/nlii/articles/johnstone. html

Jonassen, D. H. (2000). *Computers as mindtools for schools: Engaging critical thinking.* Upper Saddle River, NJ: Merrill.

Jonassen, D. H., & Brabowski, B. L. (1993). *Individual differences, learning, and instruction.* Hillsdale, NJ: Erlbaum.

Jones, T., & Young, G. S. (1997). Classroom dynamics: Disclosing the hidden curriculum. In A. I. Morey & M. K. Kitano (Eds.), *Multicultural course transformation in higher education: A broader truth* (pp. 89–103). Needham Heights, MA: Allyn & Bacon.

Karenga, M. (1995). Afrocentricity and multicultural education: Concept, challenge, and contribution. In B. P. Bowser, T. Jones, & G. A. Young (Eds.), *Toward the multicultural university* (pp. 41–64). Westport, CT: Praeger.

Katz, D. (1950). *Gestalt psychology.* New York: Ronald Press.

Keith-Spiegel, P., Wittig, A., Perkins, D., Balogh, D. W., & Whitley, B. (1996). Intervening with colleagues. *New Directions for Teaching and Learning, 66,* 75–78.

Keller, F. S. (1968). Goodbye teacher, . . . *Journal of Applied Behavior Analysis, 10,* 165–167.

Kendrick, J. R. (1996). Outcomes of service learning in an introduction to sociology course. *Michigan Journal of Community Service Learning, 3,* 72–81.

Kerr, C. (1994). Knowledge ethics and the new academic culture. *Change, 26*(1), 8–16.

Kiewra, K. A. (1989). A review of notetaking: The encoding storage paradigm and beyond. *Educational Psychology Review, 1*(2), 147–172.

King, A. (1990). Enhancing peer interaction and learning in the classroom. *American Educational Research Journal, 27,* 664–687.

———. (1997). Ask to think—Tell why: A model of transactive peer tutoring for scaffolding higher-level complex learning. *Educational Psychologist, 32,* 221–235.

Kitano, M. K. (1997). What a course will look like after multicultural change. In A. I. Morey & M. K. Kitano (Eds.), *Multicultural course transformation in higher education: A broader truth* (pp. 18–34). Needham Heights, MA: Allyn & Bacon.

Kluger, A. N., & DeNisi, A. (1996). The effects of feedback intervention on performance: A historical review, a meta-analysis, and a preliminary feedback intervention theory. *Psychological Bulletin, 119,* 254–284.

Knoedler, A. S., & Shea, M. A. (1992). Conducting discussion in the diverse classroom. In D. H. Wulff & J. D. Nyguist (Eds.), *To improve the academy* (Vol. 11, pp. 123–135). Stillwater, OK: New Forums Press.

Koocher, G., & Keith-Spiegel, P. (1998). *Ethics in psychology: Professional standards and cases.* Mahwah, NJ: Erlbaum.

Kovac, J. (1999). Professional ethics in the college and university science curriculum. *Science & Education, 8,* 309–319.

Kozma, R. (1994). Will media influence learning? Reframing the debate. *Educational Technology, Research and Development, 42*(2), 7–19.

Krathwohl, D., Bloom, B. S., & Masia, B. (Eds.). (1964). *Taxonomy of educational objectives, handbook II: Affective domain.* New York: David McKay.

Kulik, J. A., Kulik, C.-L., & Bangert-Drowns, R. L. (1988). *Effectiveness of mastery learning programs: A meta-analysis.* Ann Arbor: University of Michigan, Center for Research on Learning and Teaching.

LaPree, G. (1977). Establishing criteria for grading student papers: Moving beyond mysticism. *Teaching and Learning, 3*(1).

Larson, C. O., et al. (1984). Verbal ability and cooperative learning: Transfer of effects. *Journal of Reading Behavior, 16,* 289–295.

Leamnson, R. (2000). Learning as biological brain change. *Change, 32,* 34–40.

Lehrer, R. (1993). Authors of knowledge: Patterns of hypermedia design. In S. P. Lajoie & S. J. Derry (Eds.), *Computers as cognitive tools* (pp. 197–227). Hillsdale, NJ: Erlbaum.

Leith, G. O. M. (1977). Implications of cognitive psychology for the improvement of teaching and learning in universities. In B. Massey (Ed.), *Proceedings of the Third International Conference, Improving University Teaching* (pp. 111–138). College Park: University of Maryland.

Lepper, M. R., & Hodell, M. (1989). Intrinsic motivation in the classroom. In C. Ames & R. Ames (Eds.), *Research on motivation in education* (Vol. 3, pp. 73–105). San Diego: Academic Press.

Lepper, M. R., & Malone, T. W. (1985). Intrinsic motivation and instructional effectiveness in computer-based education. In R. E. Snow & M. J. Farr (Eds.), *Aptitude, learning and instruction: III. Conative and affective process analyses.* Hillsdale, NJ: Erlbaum.

Lewis, M. (1997). *Poisoning the ivy: The seven deadly sins and other vices of higher education in America.* Armonk, NY: Sharpe.

Lidren, D. M., Meier, S. E., & Brigham, T. A. (1991). The effects of minimal and maximal peer tutoring systems on the academic performance of college students. *Psychological Record, 41,* 69–77.

Lifson, N., Rempel, P., & Johnson, J. A. (1956). A comparison between lecture and conference methods of teaching psychology. *Journal of Medical Education, 31,* 376–382.

Lin, Y-G., McKeachie, W. J., & Kim, Y. C. (in preparation). College Student Intrinsic and/or Extrinsic Motivation and Learning.

Lopez, G., & Chism, N. (1993). Classroom concerns of gay and lesbian students. *College Teaching, 41*(3), 97–103.

Lynch, E. W. (1997). Instructional strategies. In A. I. Morey & M. K. Kitano (Eds.), *Multicultural course transformation in higher education: A broader truth* (pp. 56–70). Needham Heights, MA: Allyn & Bacon.

Maier, N. R. F. (1952). *Principles of human relations.* New York: Wiley.

————. (1963). *Problem-solving discussions and conferences.* New York: McGraw-Hill.

Maier, N. R. F., & Maier, L. A. (1957). An experimental test of the effects of "developmental" vs. "free" discussion on the quality of group decisions. *Journal of Applied Psychology, 41,* 320–323.

Mann, R. D., et al. (1970). *The college classroom: Conflict, change, and learning.* New York: Wiley.

Marcinkiewicz, H. R., & Clariana, R. B. (1997). The performance effects of headings within multiple-choice tests. *British Journal of Educational Psychology, 67,* 111–117.

Markie, P. (1994). *A professor's duties: Ethical issues in college teaching.* Totowa, NJ: Rowman & Littlefield.

Markies, G. B., Howard, J., & King, D. C. (1993). Integrating community service and classroom instruction enhanced learning: Results from an experiment. *Educational Evaluation and Policy Analysis, 15,* 410–419.

Marsh, H. W. (2001). Distinguishing between good (useful) and bad workloads on students' evaluations of teaching. *American Educational Research Journal, 38,* 183–212.

Marton, F., & Säljö, R. (1976a). On qualitative differences in learning: I—Outcome and process. *British Journal of Educational Psychology, 46,* 4–11.

————. (1976b). On qualitative differences in learning: II—Outcome as a function of the learner's conception of the task. *British Journal of Educational Psychology, 46,* 115–127.

Matthews, J. (1991). The teaching of ethics and the ethics of teaching. *Teaching of Psychology, 18*(2), 80–85.

Matthews, R. S., Cooper, J. L., Davidson, N., & Hawkes, P. (1995).

Building bridges between cooperative and collaborative learning. *Change, 27*(4), 35–40.

Mazur, E. (1997). *Peer instruction: A user's manual.* Upper Saddle River, NJ: Prentice Hall.

McCabe, D. L., & Trevino, L. K. (1996). What we know about cheating in college: Longitudinal trends and recent developments. *Change, 28*(1), 29–33.

McClelland, D., Atkinson, J. W., Clark, R. A., & Lowell, E. L. (1953). *The achievement motive.* New York: Appleton-Century-Crofts.

McCluskey, H. Y. (1934). An experimental comparison of two methods of correcting the outcomes of examination. *School and Society, 40,* 566–568.

McKeachie, W. J. (1990). Learning, thinking, and Thorndike. *Educational Psychologist, 25*(2), 127–141.

McKeachie, W. J., Lin, Y-G., Forrin, B., & Teevan, R. (1960). Individualized teaching in elementary psychology. *Journal of Educational Psychology, 51,* 285–291.

McKeachie, W. J., Pintrich, P. R., & Lin, Y-G. (1985). Teaching learning strategies. *Educational Psychologist, 20*(3), 153–160.

McKeachie, W. J., Pintrich, P. R., Lin, Y-G., Smith, D. A. F., & Sharma, R. (1990). *Teaching and learning in the college classroom: A review of the research literature* (2nd ed.). Ann Arbor: NCRIPTAL, University of Michigan.

McKeachie, W. J., Pollie, D., & Speisman, J. (1955). Relieving anxiety in classroom examinations. *Journal of Abnormal and Social Psychology, 50,* 93–98.

McKinnon, M. (1999). PBL in Hong Kong. *PBL Insight, 2*(1), 1–6.

McNett, J. M., Harvey, C., Athanassiou, N., & Allard, J. (2000). Cognitive development in the management classroom: Bloom's taxonomy as a teaching tool. In T. B. Massey (Ed.), *Contributed papers: 25th International Conference on Improving Learning and Teaching.* Johann Wolfgang Goethe University, Frankfurt, Germany. College Park, MD: Improving Learning and Teaching.

Mentkowski, M., & Associates. (2000). *Learning that lasts.* San Francisco: Jossey-Bass.

Mentkowski, M., & Loacker, G. (1985, September). Assessing and validating the outcomes of college. *New Directions for Institutional Research,* 47–64.

Metzger, R. L., Boschee, P. F., Haugen, T., & Schnobrich, B. L. (1979). The classroom as learning context: Changing rooms affects performance. *Journal of Educational Psychology, 71*(4), 440–442.

Milem, J. F. (2001). The educational benefits of diversity: Evidence from multiple sectors. In M. J. Chang, D. Witt-Sandis, J. Jones, & K. Hakuta (Eds.), *Compelling interest: Examining the evidence on racial dynamics in higher education*. Palo Alto: Stanford University Press.

Milem, J. F., & Hakuta, K. (2000). The benefits of racial and ethnic diversity in higher education. In D. W. Wilds (Ed.), *Minorities in higher education, 1999–2000* (pp. 39–67). Washington, DC: American Council on Education.

Miller, H. (1998). Assessment with a purpose. *Innovation Journal 1998*, 35–37.

Miller, J. E., & Groccia, J. E. (1997). Are four heads better than one? A comparison of cooperative and traditional teaching formats in an introductory biology course. *Innovative Higher Education, 21*, 253–273.

Mills, P., Sweeney, W. V., Marino, R., & Clarkson, S. A. (2000). New approach to teaching introductory science: The gas module. *Journal of Chemical Education, 77*, 1161–1165.

Monaco, G. E. (1977). *Inferences as a function of test-expectancy in the classroom*. Kansas State University Psychology Series, KSU-HIPI Report 73–3.

Mueller, D. J., & Wasser, V. (1977). Implications of changing answers on objective test items. *Journal of Educational Measurement, 14*(1), 9–13.

Murphy, K. L., Drabier, R., & Epps, M. L. (1997). *Incorporating computer conferencing into university courses*. Fourth annual Distance Education Conference [Online]. Available: http://disted.tamu.edu/~kmurphy/dec97pap.htm

Murphy, P. K., & Alexander, P. A. (2000). A motivated exploration of motivation terminology. *Contemporary Educational Psychology, 25*, 3–53.

Murray, H. G. (1983). Low-inference classroom teaching behaviors and student ratings of college teaching effectiveness. *Journal of Educational Psychology, 75*, 138–149.

———. (1997). Effective teaching behaviors in the college classroom. In R. P. Perry & J. C. Smart (Eds.), *Effective teaching in higher education: Research and practice* (pp. 171–204). New York: Agathon.

Murray, H., Gillese, W., Lennon, M., Mercer, P., & Robinson, M. (1996). Ethical principles for college and university teaching. *New Directions for Teaching and Learning, 66*, 57–64.

Musil, C., Garcia, M., Hudgins, C., Nettles, M., Sedlacek, W., & Smith, D. (1999). *To form a more perfect union: Campus diversity initiatives*. Washington, DC: Association of American Colleges and Universities.

Myers-Lipton, S. (1994). *The effects of service-learning on students' attitudes toward civic responsibility, international understanding, and racial prejudice*. (Doctoral dissertation, University of Colorado).

———. (1996). Effect of a comprehensive service-learning program on college students' level of modern racism. *Michigan Journal of Community Service Learning, 3,* 44–54.

Naveh-Benjamin, M., & Lin, Y-G. (1991). *Assessing students' organization of concepts: A manual of measuring course-specific knowledge structures.* Ann Arbor: NCRIPTAL, University of Michigan.

Naveh-Benjamin, M., Lin, Y-G., & McKeachie, W. J. (1989). Development of cognitive structures in three academic disciplines and their relations to students' study skills, anxiety and motivation: Further use of the ordered-tree technique. *Journal of Higher Education Studies, 4,* 10–15.

Naveh-Benjamin, M., McKeachie, W. J., Lin, Y-G., & Tucker, D. G. (1986). Inferring students' cognitive structures and their development using the "ordered tree" technique. *Journal of Educational Psychology, 78,* 130–140.

Oppenheimer, T. (1997). The computer delusion. *The Atlantic Monthly, 280*(1), 45–62.

Paris, S. G., Lipson, M. Y., & Wixson, K. K. (1983). Becoming a strategic reader. *Contemporary Educational Psychology, 8,* 293–316.

Paris, S. G., & Paris, A. H. (2001). Classroom applications of research on self-regulated learning. *Educational Psychologist, 36,* 89–101.

Parsons, T. S. (1957). A comparison of instruction by kinescope, correspondence study, and customary classroom procedures. *Journal of Educational Psychology, 48,* 27–40.

Parsons, T. S., Ketcham, W. A., & Beach, L. R. (1958, August). *Effects of varying degrees of student interaction and student-teacher contact in college courses.* Paper presented at American Sociological Society, Seattle, WA.

Pascarella, E. T., & Terenzini, F. (1991). *How college affects students.* San Francisco: Jossey-Bass.

Patrick, H., Hicks, L., & Ryan, A. M. (1997). Relations of perceived social efficacy and social goal pursuit to self-efficacy for academic work. *Journal of Early Adolescence, 17*(2), 109–128.

Paul, J. B. (1932). The length of class periods. *Educational Research, 13,* 58–75.

Peckham, G., & Sutherland, L. (2000). The role of self-assessment in moderating students' expectations. *South African Journal of Higher Education, 14,* 75–78.

Peper, R. J., & Mayer, R. E. (1978). Note taking as a generative activity. *Journal of Educational Psychology, 70*(4), 514–522.

Perry, R. P., & Smart, J. C. (Eds.). (1997). *Effective teaching in higher education: Research and practice.* New York: Agathon.

Perry, W. G., Jr. (1970). *Forms of intellectual and ethical development in the college years: A scheme.* New York: Holt, Rinehart, and Winston.

———. (1981). Cognitive and ethical growth: The making of meaning. In

A. W. Chickering (Ed.), *The modern American college* (pp. 76–116). San Francisco: Jossey-Bass.

Pintrich, P. R., & De Groot, E. V. (1990). Motivational and self-regulated learning components of classroom academic performance. *Journal of Educational Psychology, 82,* 33–40.

Pintrich, P. R., & Garcia, T. (1991). Student goal orientation and self-regulation in the college classroom. In M. Maehr & P. R. Pintrich (Eds.), *Advances in motivation and achievement: Goals and self-regulatory processes* (Vol. 7, pp. 371–402). Greenwich, CT: JAI Press.

————. (1994). Self-regulated learning in college students: Knowledge, strategies, and motivation. In P. R. Pintrich, D. R. Brown, & C. E. Weinstein (Eds.), *Student motivation, cognition, and learning: Essays in honor of Wilbert J. McKeachie* (pp. 113–133). Hillsdale, NJ: Erlbaum.

Pintrich, P. R., & Schunk, D. H. (1996). *Motivation in education.* Englewood Cliffs, NJ: Prentice-Hall.

Pintrich, P. R., Smith, D. A. F., Garcia, T., & McKeachie, W. J. (1991). *A manual for the use of the Motivated Strategies for Learning Questionnaire (MSLQ).* Ann Arbor: National Center for Research to Improve Postsecondary Teaching and Learning, University of Michigan.

Pintrich, P. R., Wolters, C., & Baxter, G. (2000). Assessing metacognition and self-regulated learning. In G. Schraw & J. Impara (Eds.), *Issues in the measurement of metacognition* (pp. 43–97). Lincoln, NE: Buros Institute of Mental Measurements.

Prenger, S. M. (Ed.). (1999). *Teaching for inclusion: A resource book for UN faculty.* Lincoln, NE: Teaching and Learning Center, University of Nebraska.

Pressley, M., & McCormick, C. B. (1995). *Cognition, teaching and assessment.* New York: HarperCollins.

Pressley, M., et al. (1992). Encouraging mindful use of prior knowledge: Attempting to construct explanatory answers facilitates learning. *Educational Psychologist, 27*(1), 91–109.

Roberts, M. S., & Semb, G. B. (1990). Analysis of the number of student-set deadlines in a personalized psychology course. *Teaching of Psychology, 17,* 170–173.

Rodabaugh, R. (1996). Institutional commitment to fairness in teaching. *New Directions for Teaching and Learning, 66,* 37–46.

Rojewski, J. W., & Schell, J. W. (1994). Instructional considerations for college students with disabilities. In K. W. Prichard & R. M. Sawyer (Eds.), *Handbook of college teaching* (pp. 387–400). Westport, CT: Greenwood Press.

Ross, I. C. (1957). Role specialization in supervision. (Doctoral dissertation, Columbia University). *Dissertation Abstracts, 17,* 2701–2702.

Royer, P. N. (1977). Effects of specificity and position of written instructional objectives on learning from a lecture. *Journal of Educational Psychology, 69,* 40–45.

Ruhl, K. L., Hughes, C. A., & Schloss, P. J. (1987). Using the pause procedure to enhance lecture recall. *Teacher Education and Special Education, 10,* 14–18.

Russell, T. L. (1999). *No significant difference phenomenon.* North Carolina State University, Raleigh, NC.

Sadker, M., & Sadker, D. (1992). Ensuring equitable participation in college classes. *New Directions in Teaching and Learning, 49,* 49–56.

Sadler, D. R. (1987). Specifying and promulgating achievement standards. *Oxford Review of Education, 13*(2), 191–209.

Saunders, S., & Kardia, D. (1997). *Creating inclusive college classrooms.* Ann Arbor, MI: Center for Research on Learning and Teaching, University of Michigan [Online]. Available: http://www/crlt.umich.edu/F6.html

Sax, L. J., Astin, A. W., Korn, W. S., & Gilmartin, S. K. (1999). *The American college teacher: National norms for the 1998–1999 HERI Faculty Survey.* Los Angeles: Higher Education Research Institute, UCLA.

Schank, R., Berman, T. R., & Macpherson, K. A. (1999). Learning by doing. In C. M. Reigeluth (Ed.), *Instructional-design theories and models* (Vol. 2, pp. 141–160). Mahwah, NJ: Erlbaum.

Schoem, D., Frankel, L., Zúñiga, X., & Lewis, E. A. (Eds.) (1993). *Multicultural teaching in the university.* Westport, CT: Praeger.

Schomberg, S. F. (1986, April). *Involving high ability students in learning groups.* Paper presented at AERA in San Francisco.

Schön, D. (1983). *The reflective practitioner.* San Francisco: Jossey-Bass.

Schultz, P. A., & Weinstein, C. E. (1990). Using test feedback to facilitate the learning process. *Innovation Abstracts, 12*(22).

Schunk, D. H., & Ertmer, P. A. (1999). Self-regulatory processes during computer skill acquisition: Goal and self-evaluative influences. *Journal of Educational Psychology, 91,* 251–260.

Schunk, D. H., & Zimmerman, B. J. (1998). *Self-regulated learning: From teaching to self-reflective practice.* New York: Guilford.

Schutz, P. A., & Davis, H., A. (2000). Emotions and self-regulation during test taking. *Educational Psychologist, 35,* 243–356.

Shapiro, R. J., & Rohde, G. L. (2000, October). *Falling through the net: Toward digital inclusion.* Washington, DC: U.S. Department of Commerce [Online]. Available: http://www.esa.doc.gov/fttn00.htm

Siebert, A., Gilpin, B., Karr, M., & Ritter, B. (2000). *The adult student's guide to survival and success* (4th ed.). Portland, OR: Practical Psychology Press.

Silverman, R., Welty, W. M., & Lyon, S. (1994). *Educational psychology cases for teacher problem solving*. New York: McGraw-Hill.

Skinner, N. F. (2001). A course, a course, my kingdom for a course: Reflections of an unrepentant teacher. *Canadian Psychology, 42*, 49–60.

Sleeter, C. E. (1991). *Empowerment through multicultural education*. Albany, NY: State University of New York Press.

Smith, D. (1996). The ethics of teaching. *New Directions for Teaching and Learning, 66*, 5–14.

Smith, D. G., Gerbick, G. L., Figueroa, M. A., Watkins, G. H., Levitan, T., Moore, L. C., Merchant, P. A., Beliak, H. D., & Figueroa, B. (1997). *Diversity works: The emerging picture of how students benefit.* Washington, DC: Association of American Colleges and Universities.

Snow, R. E., & Peterson, P. L. (1980). Recognizing differences in student attitudes. *New Directions for Teaching and Learning, 2*.

Solomon, D., Rosenberg, L., & Bezdek, W. E. (1964). Teacher behavior and student learning. *Journal of Educational Psychology, 55*, 23–30.

Springer, L., Palmer, B., Terenzini, P., Pascarella, E., & Nora, A. (1996). Attitudes towards campus diversity. *Review of Higher Education, 20*(1), 53–68.

Stanton, H. (1992). *The University Teacher, 13*(1).

Stark, J. S., & Lattuca, L. R. (1997). *Shaping the college curriculum: Academic plans in action*. Boston: Allyn & Bacon.

Stern, G. G. (1962). Environments for learning. In N. Sanford (Ed.), *The American college*. New York: Wiley.

Stern, G. G., & Cope, A. H. (1956, September). *Differences in educability between steropaths, non-steropaths and rationals*. Paper presented at the American Psychological Association meeting, Chicago.

Strage, A. A. (2000). Service learning: Enhancing student learning outcomes in a college-level lecture course. *Michigan Journal of Community Service Learning, 7*, 5–13.

Strike, K. (1988). The ethics of teaching. *Phi Delta Kappan, 70*(2), 156–158.

Sturgis, H. W. (1959). The relationship of the teacher's knowledge of the student's background to the effectiveness of teaching: A study of the extent to which the effectiveness of teaching is related to the teacher's knowledge of the student's background. (Doctoral dissertation, New York University). *Dissertation Abstracts, 19*(11).

Sutman, F. X., Schmuckler, J. S., Hilosky, A., Priestley, W. J., Priestley, H., & White, M. (1998, April). *Evaluating the use of the inquiry matrix*. Paper presented at the annual conference of the National Association for Research in Science Teaching, San Diego [Online]. Available: www.narst.org/conference/98conference/sutman.pdf

Sutton, S. E. (1993). Seeing the whole of the moon. In D. Schoem, L.

Frankel, X. Zúñiga, & E. A. Lewis (Eds.), *Multicultural teaching in the university* (pp. 161–171). Westport, CT: Praeger.

Svinicki, M. D., Hagen, A. S., & Meyer, D. K. (1995). Research on learning: A means to enhance instructional methods. In R. Menges & M. Weimer (Eds.), *Better teaching and learning in college: Toward more scholarly practice* (pp. 257–296). San Francisco: Jossey-Bass.

Sweeting, L. (1999). Ethics in science for undergraduate students. *Journal of Chemical Education, 76,* 369–372.

Tabachnick, B., Keith-Spiegel, P., & Pope, K. (1991). Ethics of teaching: Beliefs and behaviors of psychologists as educators. *American Psychologist, 46*(5), 506–515.

Thistlethwaite, D. L. (1960). *College press and changes in study plans of talented students.* Evanston, IL: National Merit Scholarship Corporation.

Toombs, W., & Tierney, W. (1992). *Meeting the mandate: Renewing the college and department curriculum.* Washington, DC: Association for the Study of Higher Education. (ASHE-ERIC Higher Education Report No. 91–6).

Toppino, T. C., & Brochin, H. A. (1989). Learning from tests: The case of true-false examinations. *Journal of Educational Research, 83,* 119–124.

Travers, R. M. W. (1950a). Appraisal of the teaching of the college faculty. *Journal of Higher Education, 21,* 41–42.

———. (1950b). *How to make achievement tests.* New York: Odyssey Press.

Trawick, L., & Corno, L. (1995). Expanding the volitional resources of urban community college students. *New Directions for Teaching and Learning, 63,* 57–70.

Trujillo, C. M. (1986). A comparative examination of classroom interactions between professors and minority and non-minority college students. *American Educational Research Journal, 23,* 629–642.

Twigg, C. A. (1992). Improving productivity in higher education: The need for a paradigm shift. *Cause/Effect, 15*(2), 39–45.

Upcraft, M. L. (1996). Teaching and today's college students. In R. Menges, M. Weimer, & Associates (Eds.), *Teaching on solid ground: Using scholarship to improve practice* (pp. 21–41). San Francisco: Jossey-Bass.

Van Overwalle, F., Segebarth, K., & Goldchstein, M. (1989). Improving performance of freshmen through attributional testimonies from fellow students. *British Journal of Educational Psychology, 59,* 75–85.

Veenstra, M. V. J., & Elshout, J. J. (1995). Differential effects of instructional support on learning in simulation environments. *Instructional Science, 22,* 363–383.

Wager, E. D., & McCombs, B. L. (1995). Learner-centered psychological principles in practice: Designs for distance education. *Educational Technology, 35*(2), 32–35.

Wakely, J. H., Marr, J. N., Plath, D. W., & Wilkins, D. M. (1960, March). *Lecturing and test performance in introductory psychology.* Paper presented at Michigan Academy, Ann Arbor.

Wales, C. E., & Nardi, A. (1982, November). *Teaching decisionmaking with guided design* (Idea paper no. 9). Kansas State University, Center for Faculty Evaluation and Development.

Warren, R. (1954). A comparison of two plans of study in engineering physics. (Doctoral dissertation, Purdue University). *Dissertation Abstracts, 14,* 1648–1649.

Weaver, R. L., II, & Cotrell, H. W. (1985). Mental aerobics: The half-sheet response. *Innovative Higher Education, 10,* 23–31.

Webb, N. J., & Grib, T. F. (1967, October). *Teaching process as a learning experience: The experimental use of student-led groups* (Final Report, HE-000–882). Washington, DC: Department of Health, Education and Welfare.

Weiner, B. (1986). *An attributional theory of motivation and emotion.* New York: Springer-Verlag.

Weinstein, C. E. (1988). Executive control processes in learning: Why knowing about how to learn is not enough. *Journal of College Reading and Learning, 21,* 48–56.

Weinstein, C. E., Husman, J., & Dierking, D. R. (2000). Self-regulation interventions with a focus on learning strategies. In M. Boekaerts, P. Pintrich, & M. Zeidner (Eds.), *Handbook of self-regulation.* San Diego: Academic Press.

Weinstein, C. E., & Mayer, R. E. (1986). The teaching of learning strategies. In M. Wittrock (Ed.), *Handbook of research on teaching* (pp. 315–327). New York: Macmillan.

Weinstein, G., & Obear, K. (1992). Bias issues in the classroom: Encounters with the teaching self. *New Directions for Teaching and Learning, 52,* 39–50.

Wilhite, S. C. (1983). Prepassage questions: The influence of structural importance. *Journal of Educational Psychology, 75*(2), 234–244.

Williams, K. (2000, February). Internet access in U.S. public schools and classrooms: 1994–99 (NCES 2000-086). *Education Statistics Quarterly: Elementary and Secondary Education.* Washington, DC: U.S. Department of Education, Office of Educational Research and Improvement, National Center for Education Statistics [Online]. Available: http://nces.ed.gov/pubs2000/qrtlyspring/4elem/q4-8.html

Wilson, R. C. (1986). Improving faculty teaching: Effective use of student evaluations and consultation. *Journal of Higher Education, 57,* 196–211.

Wilson, T. D., & Linville, P. W. (1982). Improving the academic performance of college freshmen: Attribution therapy revisited. *Journal of Personality and Social Psychology, 42,* 367–376.

Winne, P. (1996). A metacognitive view of individual differences in self-regulated learning. *Learning and Individual Differences, 8,* 327–353.

Witkin, H. A, & Moore, C. A. (1975). *Field-dependent and field-independent cognitive styles and their educational implications.* Princeton, NJ: Educational Testing Service.

Wlodkowski, R., & Ginsberg, M. (1995). *Diversity and motivation: Culturally responsive teaching.* San Francisco: Jossey-Bass.

Zimbardo, P. G., & Newton, J. W. (1975). *Instructor's resource book to accompany psychology and life.* Glenview, IL: Scott, Foresman.

Zimmerman, B. J. (1989). Models of self-regulated learning and academic achievement. In B. J. Zimmerman & D. H. Schunk (Eds.), *Self-regulated learning and academic achievement: Theory, research, and practice* (pp. 1–25). New York: Springer-Verlag.

———. (1995). Self-regulation involves more than metacognition: A social cognitive perspective. *Educational Psychologist, 30*(4), 217–222.

———. (1998). Developing self-fulfilling cycles of academic regulation: An analysis of exemplary instructional models. In D. H. Schunk & B. J. Zimmerman (Eds.), *Self-regulated learning: From teaching to self-reflective practice* (pp. 1–19.) New York: Guilford.

Zimmerman, B. J., & Paulson, A. S. (1995). Self-monitoring during collegiate studying: An invaluable tool for academic self-regulation. *New Directions for Teaching and Learning, 63,* 13–28.

Stanton, H., 152
Stark, J. S., 18
Steadman, M. H., 331
Stereotypes, 137–139
Stern, G. G., 301
Strategic learning, 270–283
Stress, tests and, 74
Strike, K., 307
Struggling students, 156
Student dyads, 190–191
Student ratings, 326–330, 329–330
Students
    age diversity among, 130
    autobiographies of, 42–43
    checking understanding of,
        278–279
    desire of to learn, 279–280
    inappropriate relationships
        with, 3–4
    maintaining involvement of,
        228–230
    new teaching methods and, 4
    nonparticipants, 41–44
    problem, 148–160
    psychological problems among,
        164–165
    respect for, 311–312
    self-awareness of, 272–273
    teacher responsibilities toward,
        309–315
    technology skills of, 210–213
    test grievances of, 89–90
    textbook selection by, 14–15
    using existing knowledge of,
        273–274
    valuing differences in, 128–147
    what they want from grades,
        104–105
Study skills, 162–163, 280
    for reading, 184–185
Sturgis, H. W., 35–36
Suicide, counseling to prevent, 165
Summaries
    in distance education, 265
    in lectures, 60–61
    of lectures, 61
    in peer learning, 193

Surface approach, 65
Sutherland, L., 71n
Sutman, F. X., 242–243
Sutton, S. E., 129
Sweeting, L., 242
Syllabus
    completing, 19
    drafting, 15–17
    excuses and, 157
    expectations in, 154
    information in, 16–17
    introducing in first classes,
        24–25
Syndicates, 191–192

Taxonomy of Educational Objectives,
    11, 71–72
Teachers
    learning from tests for, 87
    as people, 302–303
    self-regulation of, 276
    skills and strategy development
        for, 321
    technology skills of, 209–210
    vitality and growth of, 319–334
    what they want from grades,
        105
Teaching
    with cases, 199–200
    cultural limitations on, 3–4
    domain- and course-specific
        strategies, 274–278
    effects of technology on, 218,
        220–221
    ethics in, 306–318
    how to learn, 270–283
    how to think, 284–290
    inclusive, 132
    individualized, 165–167
    one-on-one, 255–256
    peer learning and, 188–189
    research vs., 5
    with technology, 206–218
    values, 291–304
Teaching assistants, 99, 126
    training and supervising, 233